# CLINT EASTWOOD

## INTERVIEWS

CONVERSATIONS WITH FILMMAKERS SERIES
PETER BRUNETTE, GENERAL EDITOR

http://www.upress.state.ms.us

Copyright © 1999 by University Press of Mississippi
All rights reserved
Manufactured in the United States of America

02  01  00  99        4  3  2  1

The paper in this book meets the guidelines for permanence and durability of
the Committee on Production Guidelines for Book Longevity of the Council
on Library Resources.

Insert photographs courtesy of Museum of Modern Art, Film Stills Archives

Library of Congress Cataloging-in-Publication Data

Eastwood, Clint, 1930–
    Clint Eastwood : interviews / edited by Robert E. Kapsis and
Kathie Coblentz.
        p.      cm. — (Conversations with filmmakers series)
    Includes index.
    ISBN 1-57806-069-9 (cloth : alk. paper). — ISBN 1-57806-070-2
(paper : alk. paper)
        1. Eastwood, Clint, 1930–      .  2. Motion picture actors and
actresses—United States—Interviews.   3. Motion picture producers
and directors—United States—Biography.   I. Kapsis, Robert E.
II. Coblentz, Kathie.   III. Title.   IV. Series.
PN2287.E37A5    1999
791.43'028'092—dc21
    [B]                                                98-43474
                                                        CIP

British Library Cataloging-in-Publication data available

# CONTENTS

# INTRODUCTION

For three decades, Clint Eastwood has appeared almost exclusively in films that he produced or co-produced himself, frequently under his own direction. Though he remains better known to many as a film star than as a filmmaker, he is in fact among the more prolific active directors. His most recent project, *True Crime,* is his twenty-second feature as director since 1971. It also marks the nineteenth time he has directed himself in a leading role, a figure very few contemporary actor-directors approach. Along the way, Eastwood the director has achieved wide recognition for a film style that is coolly classical and yet adamantly personal. A Hollywood insider, he retains an outsider's perspective through his refusal to heed cultural and aesthetic trends in film production. "I trust in my instinct and I make the films I believe in," he told Michael Henry in 1984.

As a star, Eastwood is often recalled chiefly for two early roles: the "Man With No Name" of three European-made Westerns, and "Dirty" Harry Callahan, the uncompromising cop who spoke softly and carried a big gun in five movies. All but one of these were directed by others, though not without a certain amount of input from Eastwood, as several interviews in this volume document. But on his own as a director, Eastwood has created a more varied body of work. Notably, his films have examined the artist's life (*Honkytonk Man,* 1982; *Bird,* 1988; *White Hunter, Black Heart,* 1990); called into question the ethos of masculinity and his own star image (*The Gauntlet,* 1977; *Bronco Billy,* 1980; *Tightrope,* 1984; *Heartbreak Ridge,* 1986; *Unforgiven,* 1992); and explored the Western, the most traditional American film genre, as an eloquent medium of personal expression (*High Plains Drifter,* 1973; *The Outlaw Josey Wales,* 1976; *Pale Rider,* 1985; *Unforgiven,* 1992).

As a producer-director, Eastwood has succeeded in maintaining a rare degree of independence within the Hollywood system. His star status and his long-standing reputation as an economical and efficient filmmaker are guarantees for the studio distributing his works that the project can be completely entrusted to the director because little financial risk is involved. Frank Wells, the former president of Warner Bros., told Peter Biskind in 1993, "You'd make the deal and not see him again until the preview—of an under-budget movie. We always did what he wanted to do." Still going strong in his fifth decade in films, Eastwood seems likely to keep selecting his projects on the basis of the only criterion he has cited repeatedly to interviewers: the story is something he himself would want to see on screen.

"So I directed this picture and I'm editing it myself and I think it's damn good."

Eastwood's 1971 comment to Rex Reed about his first directorial effort, *Play Misty for Me,* shows a singular amount of self-confidence for a first-time director. By then, however, he had seventeen years in the film industry behind him. Chosen as a participant in Universal's talent program in 1954, as a twenty-four-year-old aspiring actor, he began with a stint as a bit player on the big screen, but his first big break came in television four years later, when he was offered the second lead in the new Western series *Rawhide.* Over its long run he gained recognizability and an invaluable stock of experience in acting for the camera and observing how films are made. It was on location for *Rawhide's* endless cattle drive, as he states in several of these interviews, that his first directorial ambitions surfaced, only to be thwarted by the show's producers.

*Rawhide* led to his real breakthrough, in 1964, when an unknown director named Sergio Leone was looking for a convincing cowboy to star in a low-budget Western-style remake of Kurosawa's *Yojimbo,* to be shot in Rome and Spain. None of the candidates he approached would work for the paltry fistful of dollars he could offer, but one of them recommended *Rawhide's* clean-cut young trailhand, and Eastwood decided to take a chance on the odd project. *Per un pugno di dollari* (*A Fistful of Dollars*), released later that year, became an unexpected hit across Europe and founded a new genre, the "spaghetti Western."

The rest, one might say, is history—except that the historical record is blurred by the discrepancy between the star's and the director's accounts of their respective contributions to the appearance and nature of the taciturn, mysterious and preternaturally skillful gunslinger Eastwood played in *Fistful* and its two successors, *For a Few Dollars More* and *The Good, the Bad and the Ugly.* (For Eastwood's version, see the interview with Christopher Frayling in this volume.) It seems beyond dispute that Eastwood, against Leone's initial protests, cut back drastically on the exposition supplied in the original script, depriving the character of a background and his deeds of a ready explanation—like many of the protagonists of his subsequent films. Eastwood is fond of relating this anecdote to interviewers. For Tim Cahill he put it like this: "I kept telling Sergio, 'In a real A picture, you let the audience think along with the movie; in a B picture, you explain everything.'"

Leone's openness to his star's suggestions meant that their three films together gave Eastwood his first real experience in collaborating in the filmmaking process, although, as he complained to Stuart Kaminsky, the director "would never give me any credit for the style of a film I'd been in with him." More importantly at the time, they made Eastwood an international star, with the power such status entailed. At home, however, since a rights dispute with *Yojimbo*'s distributors was holding up the U.S. release of *Fistful,* he was still an unknown quantity, a minor TV cowboy who had yet to star in a domestically released feature film.

*Fistful* finally opened in the U.S. to generally mordant reviews but enthusiastic audiences in early 1967, followed within a year by its two equally crowd-pleasing successors. Still, it is startling to find Eastwood, shortly after the release of *Fistful,* dictating to United Artists the terms under which he would make his first domestic starring appearance for the company, which was distributing the Leone films. He proposed the project (the modest but thematically challenging Western *Hang 'em High*), imposed his choice of director (Ted Post), and proceeded to collaborate with Post on script revisions during the shoot. In order to serve as de facto co-producer in this fashion, he had established his own production company, which he christened Malpaso. For now, it was a corporate convenience for his deals with studios, but by 1970 it would have become the independent filmmaking concern he has employed ever since to assure that the ultimate control of virtually all of his projects resides with him, whether or not he chooses to direct them.

*Hang 'em High* was a huge hit, and Eastwood's singular career was underway. His initial strategy was to alternate fairly low-profile, low-budget productions (in which, through Malpaso, he retained some share of control over script, director, and casting) with the kind of big-budget project (where he worked solely as an actor) that could garner him sufficient prestige, as well as money, to ensure that he could function independently in the industry. To begin with, there were three films directed by Don Siegel: *Coogan's Bluff, Two Mules for Sister Sara,* and *The Beguiled.*

Eastwood's encounter with the veteran action director Siegel, with whom he would shoot five films in all, was a career milestone. Before they met, neither man had known the other's work, but they quickly found they were on the same filmmaking wavelength. Eastwood told Patrick McGilligan, "[Siegel]'s a very lean kind of director—he usually knows what he wants and goes in and shoots what he has intended to shoot, and doesn't protect himself like a lot of guys." Siegel's way of making movies, in fact, neatly accorded with Eastwood's own views on directing, often expressed in similar terms: know what you want, shoot fast, and move on as soon as you have it. Siegel, moreover, was open to suggestions from his star; as he would tell Stuart Kaminsky, "I found Clint very knowledgeable about making pictures, very good at knowing what to do with the camera.... He started to come up with ideas for camera set-ups.... And even if I decided not to use them they invariably gave me another idea." Eastwood affirmed to Kaminsky, "Don ... kind of breeds an atmosphere of participation."

This was the opposite of the atmosphere Eastwood encountered on the three other productions he was employed on in those years: *Where Eagles Dare, Paint Your Wagon,* and *Kelly's Heroes.* The waste of time, resources, and money on these shoots infuriated him, and he was frustrated by having little or no input into the finished films beyond his own performance. He was now more determined than ever to take charge of his career through Malpaso. Though he would not formally take a producing credit until *Firefox* (1982), *Kelly's Heroes* became the last film he would work on without the participation of his production company, except for 1993's *In the Line of Fire.* From this point on he was, in effect, his own producer, and in 1970 he would take the firmest step towards total career control by becoming his own director as well. Don Siegel signed his Director's Guild card.

However, after *Play Misty for Me* was completed, Eastwood persuaded Siegel to direct him in their fourth film together, one that would prove a different kind of career milestone. *Dirty Harry* was released shortly after *Misty* in late 1971. In a politically polarized era, it touched a sore spot with many critics because of its blatant anti-Miranda/Escobedo stance and its sympathetic portrayal of the eponymous rogue cop, who exercised brutality towards the presumed guilty, contempt for bureaucratic constraint, and total disregard for the letter of the law in his quest to safeguard the innocent. Some called its tendency "fascist." Audiences, however, loved the movie, which became Eastwood's highest grossing film to that date and spawned four sequels. The consequences for his future were twofold: as a performer, he was exalted into the ranks of the superstar in terms of international drawing power, but for most of the decade and beyond he would be considered politically *persona non grata* by many influential critics and other cultural arbiters.

Eastwood has often responded brusquely to the political charges against the film, dismissing them as groundless or misdirected; the filmmakers were not making a political statement but simply "telling a story." If pressed, he defended Harry as a before-his-time champion of victim's rights, at a time when advocates of the cause of the rights of the accused dominated the public debate. In several interviews, he characterized Harry's adherence to a "higher morality" as, in fact, "the opposite of fascism." Later, he sometimes dismissed such attacks as merely characteristic of the rhetoric of their era. But by 1994, when he had directed another film (*A Perfect World*) in which a relentless cop shoots a kidnapper without remorse and against his superior's orders—but now with his sympathies clearly against the cop, and his actor's persona embodied in the superior—he was willing to concede (in an interview not included here, in *Positif,* March 1994) that "*Dirty Harry* provided simple solutions to horribly complicated problems."

*Dirty Harry* was Eastwood's first film for Warner Bros., marking the beginning of what would become an informal near-exclusive relationship, to the mutual benefit of the studio (most of Eastwood's pictures would be profitable, some hugely so) and the producer-director-star (who would be granted an almost entirely free hand in selecting, producing, and promoting his projects). Eastwood also benefited from Warners' willingness to assist him in his ambition to become better respected as a filmmaker, as they helped him attain prestigious media exposure and supported his international promotional tours and his entries in film festivals. In return, many observers thought they noticed a pattern in Malpaso releases: for every "personal," "small" film with little commercial potential that Eastwood directed, he would direct or star in a project more clearly aimed at a mass audience and high grosses. Eastwood denies that this is a "conscious process," however, asserting that he never tries to guess the potential audience for a film. He told *Cahiers du cinéma* in 1992, "If you're constantly thinking about what the audience's reaction is going to be, you stop thinking in terms of how the film should look" — and even in his "commercial" vehicles it is not difficult to locate his personal themes and stylistic markers.

Malpaso remains a small and orderly operation, optimally suited to turning out the reasonably priced and efficiently produced features Eastwood has always preferred. Such vehicles are best suited to his spontaneous and instinctual approach to cinematic storytelling; moreover, they give him an edge in the industry by making his financial successes all the more profitable and his occasional failures more bearable. The company's small scale also tends to make it possible for the control of the entire operation to rest conveniently in one man's hands, and there has seldom been any doubt that that man is Eastwood.

Judging from remarks he made at the time of *Misty*'s release, Eastwood did not realize how fundamentally the fact that he had become a director would affect his subsequent career. As late as 1976, he told McGilligan, "I don't intend to direct every picture I make. In fact, I'd like to lay off a bit, directing. It's a terribly mind-fatiguing job to be both actor and director." Though he did continue to alternate films he directed with films he only appeared in, from *Misty* on he would show an increasing reluctance to work with directors over whom he could not exercise some measure of control, such as his long-time Malpaso associates James Fargo and Buddy Van Horn. Indeed, he has shown an increasing reluctance to submit to the direction of anyone else at all. In the seventies, after *Misty,* he directed five films and appeared in seven others; in the eighties, he directed eight films (and one television program) and appeared in only three others; in the nineties so far, he has directed eight films and only once submitted to another's direction.

On two occasions, when a director proved incapable of realizing a film as Eastwood envisioned it, that director was made to feel the consequences. In 1975, shortly after shooting began on *The Outlaw Josey Wales*, Eastwood dismissed the screenwriter-director Philip Kaufman and took over as director himself. The Directors Guild reacted by promulgating a rule (the "Eastwood rule") forbidding the replacement of a DGA member engaged for a film by anyone working in any capacity on the same film. Eastwood told

David Thomson, "I just had a line on it and loved the project and didn't want it to be done the way he was going to interpret it. And he didn't want to do it the way I wanted to do it." *Josey Wales,* done Eastwood's way, became a film he cites to this day as among his favorites of those he has directed, and many critics would come to see it as a turning point in his work.

The case of *Tightrope* is more complicated. In 1983, as a condition of acquiring Richard Tuggle's screenplay, Eastwood agreed to let Tuggle shoot the film as his directorial debut. But Tuggle (unlike Michael Cimino, who debuted as a director for Eastwood under similar circumstances with 1974's *Thunderbolt and Lightfoot*) reportedly came to the set the first day uncertain of what he wanted and unprepared for the technical demands of shooting the film—both cardinal sins to the ever-focused and efficient Eastwood. Because of the DGA's "Eastwood rule," Eastwood was prevented from formally dismissing him and assuming control as director. Tuggle received the directorial credit, and Eastwood has never expressly disavowed it. When Michael Henry asked him why he hadn't directed the film himself, he replied, "Richard Tuggle was anxious to direct it. He had written the script, which was excellent. . . . Why not let him direct it?" But the actual circumstances were soon hinted at in print, although the full story was not told until the appearance of Richard Schickel's 1996 biography, *Clint Eastwood*: "A compromise was worked out. The writer would stay on, contribute what he could in a collaborative way and receive directorial credit, while [Eastwood], literally, called most of the shots." *Tightrope* was received favorably by a number of prestigious reviewers who had previously been inclined to scorn Eastwood's output.

Though Eastwood insists on maintaining the ultimate control over his projects, many who have worked with him describe him as a benevolent chief who exercises this control in a cooperative spirit; Peter Biskind's profile in *Premiere* includes several such testimonies. Eastwood achieves the results he seeks by choosing collaborators he can trust to work freely within the parameters of his vision, and by keeping his ideas about a film supple enough to incorporate creative suggestions from all the participants. This applies both to actors, who have often praised the calm and the lack of pressure on his sets, and to his crew, many of whom have stayed with him for years or even decades. He dislikes the word "auteur," frequently affirming that he is part of an ensemble within which he likens

his role to that of "the leading force," or the "lieutenant to the platoon."
Most directors in Hollywood today, no matter how slight the artistic value
of the project, insist on a "possessory credit" of the sort that used to be reserved for filmmakers of the stature of a Hitchcock: "A Director X film," or
"A Film by Director Y." Eastwood's films never begin with his own name,
but with the name of his production company: "A Malpaso Company Film,"
"A Malpaso Production."

Eastwood's popularity as a film star has often overshadowed his directorial achievements, particularly in the popular press, where interviewers
have tended to concentrate on his on-screen persona. As for the serious
critics, many would long dismiss him as the "politically incorrect" co-cre-
ator of the "Dirty Harry" series. Since the late seventies, when he had a
half-dozen films as director behind him, he has courted the approval of
those who could boost his reputation as a filmmaker, expounding on his
body of work in interviews with cinema journals and film trade publications, several of which we have included here: *Film Comment, Millimeter,
American Film, American Cinemeditor, Daily Variety, Film & Video.* In these
sessions he frequently points out such often-overlooked features of his
films as their consistent employment of strong female characters, or he
notes how his macho image has been subject to scrutiny in many roles he
has played, like *Tightrope*'s sexually troubled cop, or *Bronco Billy*'s hero,
who endures a voluntary and unavenged humiliation for the sake of loyalty to a member of his troupe. Such statements are reflected in the works
of critics who were in the vanguard of the reevaluation of Eastwood's reputation, beginning in the early eighties.[1]

In 1980, Eastwood took *Bronco Billy* to the American cinema festival in
Deauville, France, his first appearance at a European film festival. Since
then he has regularly included European publicity tours in the promotional strategy for his most prestigious films. European critics have often
been quicker than their American counterparts to recognize artistic merit
in filmmakers who probe genre boundaries and express a personal aesthetic in movies directed at a popular audience. In Eastwood's case, the
effect was pronounced. In 1985, Paris's Cinémathèque française honored
him with a four-week retrospective; the first homage paid him in New York

---

1. For further discussion, see Robert Kapsis, "Clint Eastwood's Politics of Reputation,"
*Society* 30, no. 30/6 (September/October 1993): 70.

by the Museum of Modern Art had been a far briefer 1980 tribute. Interviews with him abound in European film journals and the popular press. France's venerable *Cahiers du cinéma* has published three over the years, and its archrival, *Positif* has published seven.

The European acclaim was augmented when three of Eastwood's films, *Pale Rider, Bird,* and *White Hunter, Black Heart,* competed at the Cannes Film Festival, and in 1992, his Oscar-winning *Unforgiven* was received perhaps even more enthusiastically in Europe than in the U.S.; no fewer than nine European magazines featured the film as a cover story. Eastwood's most recent directorial efforts have unquestionably met with more widespread critical approval abroad than at home, notably in France. In December 1992, Camille Nevers of *Cahiers du cinéma* flatly called Eastwood "at present, the greatest American filmmaker" — a judgment Serge Toubiana of *Cahiers* repeated in September 1995, regarding *The Bridges of Madison County.* In March 1998, in the Paris daily *Le Monde,* Jean-Michel Frodon called Eastwood's 1997 *Midnight in the Garden of Good and Evil,* which was widely disliked in the U.S., "his richest, most complex, and most courageous work."

Eastwood has been appreciative. In his 1992 *Cahiers* interview, he said, "Actually, the Europeans encouraged me much more from my first film as director, *Play Misty For Me,* than the Americans, who had a hard time convincing themselves I could be a director because they already had a hard time recognizing me as an actor."

In all, we have selected three interviews from British sources and seven from France and Germany for inclusion here. Among them are a key interview in *Positif* in which Eastwood relates the philosophy of the John Huston-like character he plays in *White Hunter, Black Heart* to his own ideas about filmmaking, and one from the time of *Bird'*s screening at Cannes (published here in full for the first time), in which he talks to the editor-publisher of Cologne's maverick film journal *Steadycam* about his film, his love of jazz, and his career. Standing for dozens of interviews with the general European press are two from *Le Monde* and one from *Le Nouvel observateur.* In one of these, Eastwood gives a novel answer to an often-repeated question: why did he wait eight years after acquiring the screenplay for *Unforgiven* before shooting the film? His habitual reply (the one the interviewer has already heard) was that he wanted to "age into" the role of William Munny. Here, he says: "It demanded a lot of preparation. I wanted to do it right."

*Bird,* Eastwood's portrait of the tormented jazz genius Charlie Parker, and his crepuscular "last Western" *Unforgiven* are the two films many consider his finest works as a director. They were also the occasions for his most interesting and revelatory interviews (*American Film, Steadycam, Cahiers, Le Monde*). They were both plainly films that engaged him deeply, thematically and aesthetically; he has often stated he believes jazz and the Western to be the two most truly American art forms. In the case of *Unforgiven,* he also took the occasion to respond to one of the lingering criticisms of his films, namely that they indulged in "mindless" or merely cathartic violence, and to reflect on what he termed the "moral implications of violence" and its role in American society—though his remarks were usually prefaced by a statement to the effect that he was not "doing penance" for his earlier on-screen mayhem.

As an interview subject, Eastwood has occasionally reminded his interviewers of his silent and indomitable film characters. David Thomson reported, "You don't have to be too imaginative to see the rock against which some of your questions break. It is startling and intimidating when an actor has so little need of your love, and not much softened if he still wants your respect." He evidently prefers to maintain close control of his interview sessions, and he sometimes seems to be answering another, more comfortable question, rather than the one the interviewer has asked. He may deflect questions he considers inappropriate, for instance on aspects of his private life, with silence or curt replies. In a recent televised interview (not included here) he impaled the hapless interviewer with his trademark stare when an "off-limits" topic was broached. He can be equally recalcitrant about perceived shifts in his political views. But most interviewers have reported him relaxed and quite willing to talk about a variety of topics. Those who have concentrated on his work as a filmmaker and questioned him knowledgeably have usually been rewarded with knowledgeable and detailed replies concerning the technical means he employs to achieve the results he seeks and the philosophical and stylistic precepts that guide his practical course.

Through the interviews collected here, it is possible to outline some of the elements of Eastwood's filmmaking philosophy, what Pascal Mérigeau calls the "Eastwood touch":

*On the director's role:* "You have to have the picture there in your mind before you make it. And if you don't, you're not a director, you're a guesser." (Gentry 1980)

*On the importance of the story:* "I try to concentrate above all on the story, because it's there that it's all tied up. . . . Then I try to see how the image can best agree with the story, what form I want the story to appear in, with what emotions, what sonorities." (Jousse and Nevers 1992)

*On spontaneity:* "Sometimes the imperfection of things is what makes them real. . . . So I tell everybody to just rehearse quietly, and I'll have the camera running. You get some marvelous little pieces because everybody's just doing it, they're not just sitting there thinking about acting in front of the camera. They're doing it for real." (Hentoff 1989)

*On the role of the audience:* "They must participate in every shot, in everything. I give them what I think is necessary to know, to progress through the story, but I don't lay out so much that it insults their intelligence. I try to give a certain amount to their imagination." (Thompson and Hunter 1976–77)

*On lighting:* "Every film must be lit in accordance with the subject, the optical expression of the film must reproduce what you think about it as a director." (Pavlovic 1988)

*On how easy it all is:* "I believe that when you're making a film, you've got everything in mind, in an almost subliminal way, and that all you have to do is make all that become reality on screen." (Mérigeau 1998)

Eastwood has been in the public eye for more than forty years, and the volume of material available on him is overwhelming. It was difficult to select from among the dozens of interviews we considered worthy for inclusion here. If we have finally included mostly interviews from film periodicals and the film trade press, it is because this is where we found the most extensive and interesting material on Eastwood *as a director.* We regret there was no room for several of the profiles in the popular press in which, especially in his first decade as a director, Eastwood made sure interviewers realized the extent of his involvement in the production of those of his films that were directed by others. For Judy Fayard's *Life* cover story (July 23, 1971), he granted the interview on a night he was actually directing himself in a scene in Siegel's *Dirty Harry.* Fayard watched him "climbing on and off a crane, fistfighting in a stunt scene six stories above the ground, and crawling on a window ledge on his hands and knees" for several hours until the 5:30 A.M. wrap. She reports that the sound man observed, "He'll make a hell of a good director. . . He knows the technical end, and he sets things up with the crew. He gets in with the guys right away."

For Chris Hodenfield's July 1979 *Look* profile, Eastwood saw to it that part of the interview was conducted in the sound laboratory where he was supervising the final mix for Siegel's *Escape from Alcatraz* (Siegel was in England working on another film). Hodenfield was duly impressed: "On the screen flickered the same 10-minute reel of film, over and over, until every gurgle and clank sounded just right. . . . Eastwood missed nothing. . . . Clint Eastwood has by now directed six pictures. And he meddles freely. . . . Eastwood even follows the final cut of a film right into the processing laboratory, so he can sit with the man who times the development. Eastwood likes the print a little dark, so he makes sure."

Eastwood summed up his commitment to filmmaking in an article for *Action,* the magazine of the Directors Guild (March/April 1973), which concluded, "I love acting and intend to continue doing it. But I must admit that the satisfaction of directing goes deeper than any other facet of film making. . . . But I suppose my involvement goes even deeper than acting or directing. I love every aspect of the creation of a motion picture, and I guess I'm committed to it for life." As we write, Eastwood has completed more than thirty films as producer, director, or star—most often all three—since that declaration was published. Like the character he played in *The Bridges of Madison County* (1995), he might well reply, when asked whether he loves his work, "Yeah—I'm obsessed by it, really."

There is inevitably some repetition in this anthology. Eastwood's views on directing have changed little over the years, and it is natural to find him repeating the same thoughts and anecdotes about specific films and specific aspects of filmmaking. As with all books in the *Conversations with Filmmakers* series, the interviews are presented unedited (typographical errors and a few other obvious errors of fact have been corrected), and in chronological order.

The editors would like to express their gratitude to all those who granted us their permission to make this material available, and also to those who granted permission to use interviews that we had to omit for reasons of space. In addition, we would like to thank the colleagues and friends who assisted us, notably Amy Stoller, for her unflagging professionalism and versatility, and Stephan Müller, for his aid in researching Eastwood's European reception. We also thank Peter Brunette, general editor of the Conversations with Filmmakers series, for offering us this project, and editor-in-chief Seetha Srinivasan of the University Press of

Mississippi, her colleague Elizabeth Young, and our editor Anne Stascavage, for their guidance and support. Finally, special thanks are due to Mary Lea Bandy of the Museum of Modern Art for her kind help on this book.

Translator's note: For the seven pieces translated from French and German (published here in English for the first time) we were unable to obtain copies or transcripts of the original interviews, which were conducted in English or through interpreters. It is inevitable that some distortion has occurred in the process of translating the material back into English, and we apologize for it. In preparing the translations, I have tried to stay close to the printed texts, while maintaining a colloquial tone consistent with the other interviews in the volume.

# CHRONOLOGY

Dates in parentheses following film titles are U.S. release dates unless otherwise noted. If a director is not named following the title or mentioned in the immediate context, the film was directed by Eastwood. Most biographical details are taken from Richard Schickel's *Clint Eastwood* (1996).

1930    Clinton Eastwood Jr., oldest child of Clinton Eastwood Sr., a bond salesman, and Ruth Runner Eastwood, is born on 31 May in San Francisco. He will have one sibling, a sister, Jeanne.

1930–40    The Eastwood family moves numerous times around California as Clinton Sr. takes what jobs he can find during the Depression.

1940–45    The Eastwoods settle in Piedmont, California, where Clinton Sr. works as a jewelry salesman, then, during the war, in a shipyard. Ruth Eastwood is also employed, working for IBM.

Attends Havens Elementary School, Piedmont Junior High School, and, briefly, Piedmont High School, before transferring to Oakland Technical High School.

1945–48    Works after school and during summer vacations at several jobs, including a summer working for the California State Forestry service, cutting timber and fighting fires.

1946    Attends a "Jazz at the Philharmonic" concert in Oakland and hears Charlie Parker for the first time. Begins playing jazz piano informally at the Omar Club in Oakland.

1948         Graduates from Oakland Technical High School; his parents have
             moved to Seattle, where Clinton Sr. will rise to an executive posi-
             tion with the Container Corporation of America.

1948–51      Works at a number of jobs in the Pacific Northwest: as a lifeguard,
             as a lumberjack and in a pulp mill for Weyerhaeuser, tending a
             blast furnace for Bethlehem Steel, in the parts department of
             Boeing Aircraft.

1951         Applies for admission to Seattle University, where he intends to
             major in music. Before hearing from the university, he is drafted
             into the army and stationed at Fort Ord on the Monterey
             Peninsula.

             Returning from a weekend furlough in Seattle, he is nearly lost at
             sea when the two-man plane he has hitched a ride in goes down,
             and he must swim the three miles to shore.

1951–53      Army service at Fort Ord. Works as a swimming instructor and as
             a projectionist for training films.

1953         Discharged from the army; meets Maggie Johnson, a graduating
             Berkeley student; marries her in Los Angeles, 19 December.

             Attends Los Angeles City College on the GI Bill (fall).

             Begins taking drama classes at the college and elsewhere; his
             teachers include the Michael Chekhov disciple George Shdanoff.

1954         After a screen test, he is offered a contract in Universal-
             International Studios' talent program, beginning on 1 May.

             Maggie Eastwood works in an export firm and as a swimsuit
             model.

1954–55      Assigned minor roles in seven Universal films, beginning with
             *Revenge of the Creature* (Jack Arnold, 1955). As part of the program,
             he receives extensive training in acting, diction, singing, danc-
             ing, riding, etc.

1955         Leaves Universal's employ, effective 25 October.

1956–58      Small parts in three more films and the second lead in the film
             he calls the "lousiest Western ever made," *Ambush at Cimarron
             Pass* (Jodie Copelan, 1958); occasional television work; digs swim-
             ming pools to supplement his income.

1958     Selected as second lead on the new Western series *Rawhide*. Films the first nine episodes, then the project is suspended for lack of sponsor interest.

December: *Rawhide* announced as a replacement series on CBS.

1959–66     Appears in most of the 217 episodes of *Rawhide* that air between 9 January 1959 and 4 January 1966.

The Eastwoods settle in Carmel-by-the-Sea, near Fort Ord.

1964     Stars in Western with working title *The Magnificent Stranger* for Sergio Leone in Almería (Spain) and Rome's Cinecittà. Released in Italy later that year as *Per un pugno di dollari* (*A Fistful of Dollars*), the film unexpectedly becomes a hit across Europe.

Birth of daughter Kimber Tunis (17 June), now Kimber Eastwood (with Roxanne Tunis, a stuntwoman on *Rawhide*)

1965–66     Stars in two more "spaghetti Westerns" for Leone: *For a Few Dollars More* (Italy, 1965; U.S., 1967) and *The Good, the Bad and the Ugly* (Italy, 1966; U.S., 1968).

1966     Directed by Vittorio de Sica in the final segment of an anthology film, *The Witches* (1967; not commercially released in the U.S.).

United Artists, which supplied backing for the third Leone film, acquires US rights to all three.

1967     *A Fistful of Dollars* opens in the US (Los Angeles, 18 January), followed by its two successors in July 1967 and January 1968.

Establishes his own production company, Malpaso, to share in the production of his first U.S. starring vehicle, the Western *Hang 'em High* (Ted Post, 1968), shot for UA in New Mexico and on a MGM studio set (late summer).

Signs three-picture deal with Universal, later extended (films made through 1975 are Malpaso productions for Universal unless otherwise noted).

First collaboration with Don Siegel, the cop drama *Coogan's Bluff* (1968), shot chiefly in New York City and the Mojave desert (November–December).

1968  January–May: In Austria and London for MGM's World War II thriller *Where Eagles Dare* (Brian G. Hutton, 1969).

Birth of son Kyle (19 May).

Summer–fall: In Oregon for Paramount's Western-themed musical *Paint Your Wagon* (Joshua Logan, 1969).

Release of his first two U.S.-made starring vehicles (August and October). Both are hits.

1969–70  Collaboration with Don Siegel continues with the Western *Two Mules for Sister Sara* (1970) and the Civil War drama *The Beguiled* (1971), shot respectively in Mexico in 1969 and in part near Baton Rouge, Louisiana in 1970.

1969  Shoots MGM's World War II adventure *Kelly's Heroes* (Brian G. Hutton, 1970) in Yugoslavia (summer-late fall); the last film he will work on in which his production company is not involved, except for 1993's *In the Line of Fire*.

1970  Death of Clinton Eastwood Sr.

Shoots his first film as director in Carmel and vicinity, *Play Misty For Me*, the story of a disc jockey (Eastwood) who is stalked by a crazed female fan.

1971  Shoots the controversial cop picture *Dirty Harry* in San Francisco for Don Siegel and Warner Bros., beginning what will become a near-exclusive relationship with Warners.

*Play Misty For Me* opens to mixed reviews; a modest success (November).

Begins shooting the Western *Joe Kidd* (John Sturges, 1972) in the High Sierras and Arizona.

*Dirty Harry* is released (December); despite some sharply negative critical reaction owing to its perceived political message, it is Eastwood's biggest audience success to date.

1972–75  Directs four more films; stars in two others: the first "Harry" sequel *Magnum Force* (Ted Post, 1973; Warners) and Michael Cimino's debut feature, the caper/buddy drama *Thunderbolt and Lightfoot* (1974; UA).

1972    Birth of daughter Alison (22 May).

Shoots his first Western as director, *High Plains Drifter* (1973), at Mono Lake, California.

Named to the National Council for the Arts (August).

Directs William Holden in the romance *Breezy* (1973).

1973    Named Quigley Publications Number One Box-Office Star for the first of five times (1973–74, 1984–85, 1994).

1974    Directs himself and does his own mountain climbing stuntwork in the espionage yarn *The Eiger Sanction* (1975), shot in Monument Valley and on the Eiger in the Swiss Alps.

1975    Dissatisfied with Universal's promotion of his films, Eastwood moves Malpaso's headquarters to the Warners lot in Burbank. (Subsequent films are Warners releases unless otherwise noted.)

Shoots the epic Western *The Outlaw Josey Wales* in Arizona, Utah and California; replaces director Philip Kaufman after a week, taking over as director himself. The Directors Guild reacts by promulgating the "Eastwood rule," forbidding the replacement of a DGA member engaged for a film by anyone working in any capacity on the same film.

Begins a professional and personal relationship with Sondra Locke, whom he will cast in a leading role in six films.

1976    *The Outlaw Josey Wales* released to mixed reviews, including some of his best to date (August).

*The Enforcer* (James Fargo), the second "Dirty Harry" sequel, partners Harry with a woman detective (Tyne Daly).

1977    Directs himself and Locke in the cop movie/romantic comedy *The Gauntlet*; shot in Nevada and Arizona for a Christmas release.

1978    *Film Comment* runs a cover story on "Clint Eastwood, Auteur."

Most popular film to date, the orangutan buddy picture *Every Which Way But Loose* (James Fargo), shot in the San Fernando Valley and elsewhere in the West for Christmas release.

Last collaboration with Siegel, *Escape from Alcatraz* (1979), shot for Paramount on the prison island in San Francisco Bay.

1979       Separation from his wife, Maggie, is announced.

Shoots *Bronco Billy* (1980), a Capraesque comedy, in the Boise, Idaho area.

First career survey in a French film magazine (*La Revue du cinéma*).

1980–84   Alternates "commercial" with "personal" projects: the *Every Which Way* sequel *Any Which Way You Can* (Buddy Van Horn, 1980), the cold war thriller *Firefox* (1982; the first film on which Eastwood is credited as producer), the picaresque Depression-era saga *Honkytonk Man* (1982), the penultimate "Dirty Harry" *Sudden Impact* (1983), the troubled cop/serial killer story *Tightrope* (1984), the "hard-boiled" spoof *City Heat* (Richard Benjamin, 1984; with Burt Reynolds); the gold-rush era Western *Pale Rider* (1985). Directs all but two of these, although Richard Tuggle receives directorial credit on *Tightrope* because Eastwood is forbidden by the DGA's "Eastwood rule" from replacing him as director.

1980       At Deauville (French festival of American film) with *Bronco Billy*, September.

Retrospective and tribute at New York's Museum of Modern Art (MOMA), December.

1981       Shoots *Firefox* in Vienna, the Austrian Alps and Los Angeles.

1982       Shoots *Honkytonk Man,* his most "personal" project from this period, in central California; on release (December) it "fails to find an audience" but attracts favorable critical attention, particularly in Europe.

1983       *Sudden Impact,* the only "Dirty Harry" film Eastwood directed, shot for December release; will become the highest-grossing of the series.

Shoots *Tightrope* in New Orleans; composes a musical theme for the soundtrack, a practice he will continue in several subsequent films.

Options David Webb Peoples's Western screenplay, *The Cut-Whore Killings* (written in 1976), concluding the purchase in 1985.

1984  Divorce from Maggie becomes final.

Shoots his third Western as director, *Pale Rider,* in Idaho.

*Tightrope* opens the Montreal Film Festival (16 August); on U.S. release, it is reviewed favorably by a number of upscale critics.

1985  Retrospectives at the Paris Cinémathèque française, Germany's Filmmuseum and Britain's National Film Theatre.

January: European tour (Paris, Munich, London) in connection with *Tightrope*'s European release and the retrospectives; made a Chevalier de l'ordre des arts et lettres in France; delivers Guardian Lecture in London (13 January).

May: First appearance at Cannes Film Festival with *Pale Rider.*

Malpaso produces Sondra Locke's debut film as director, *Ratboy* (1986).

Directs episode of Steven Spielberg's television series *Amazing Stories* (*Vanessa in the Garden,* a ghost story starring Harvey Keitel and Locke), his only television work, aside from documentaries and interviews, since *Rawhide.*

1986–88 Runs for and is elected Mayor of Carmel; serves a single two-year term.

1986  Directs *Heartbreak Ridge* for December release; Eastwood stars as an aging Marine sergeant facing separation from the Corps.

1987  Following extensive research to acquire original musical materials, begins shooting the Charlie Parker biopic *Bird.*

1988  Cecil B. DeMille Lifetime Achievement Award at the Golden Globes (January).

Completes principal photography on *Bird* (January).

Executive producer for *Thelonious Monk: Straight No Chaser* (Charlotte Zwerin), a documentary on the jazz pianist.

The last "Dirty Harry" film, *The Dead Pool* (Buddy Van Horn), is hastily shot for a July release.

May: Second Cannes appearance for *Bird*: Forest Whitaker named Best Actor for his portrayal of the title role; the film wins a Technical Grand Prize.

Private premiere of *Bird* at MOMA (14 September), marking the establishment of the Clint Eastwood Cinema Collection at MOMA and the announcement by the Wesleyan University Cinema Archives of its acquisition of Eastwood's papers.

*Bird* shown at the New York Film Festival (26 September); receives generally good reviews, but on release will play to small audiences.

Shoots the skip-tracer comedy-adventure *Pink Cadillac* (Buddy Van Horn, 1989) in the area of Reno, Nevada.

1989    *Bird* wins Eastwood a Golden Globe as Best Director (January).

Breaks with Sondra Locke.

Shoots *White Hunter, Black Heart,* in which he plays a John Huston-like film director, in London and Africa.

1989–90    Two "popular" films, *Pink Cadillac* and the cop drama *The Rookie* (shot in Los Angeles, 1990), fare poorly at the box office.

1990    May: Third Cannes appearance for *White Hunter, Black Heart,* which opens in September in the U.S. to mixed reviews and scanty audiences.

1991    Produces, directs, stars in, and composes the principal musical theme for *The Cut-Whore Killings,* which he has retitled *Unforgiven,* shot in remote areas of Alberta and in Sonora, California (September–November).

1992    Completes post-production work on *Unforgiven.*

*Unforgiven* released to the best reviews ever for an Eastwood film and excellent box office (7 August); rejected as a competition entry in the Venice film festival, it is shown in Deauville (September); European tour to promote it.

Stars in the thriller *In the Line of Fire* (Wolfgang Petersen, 1993) for Castle Rock and Columbia; accorded director approval, he selects the German Petersen.

*Unforgiven* wins numerous year-end critics' awards.

1993    January: *Unforgiven* wins Eastwood his second Best Director Golden Globe.

March: *Unforgiven* wins the Directors Guild of America award for Outstanding Directorial Achievement in Motion Pictures.

29 March: *Unforgiven,* nominated for nine Oscars, wins four, including Directing and Best Picture. Re-released for the Oscar buildup, the film's gross receipts surpass one hundred million.

Meets Dina Ruiz, anchorperson for a Salinas, California TV station, when she interviews him in connection with the Oscars.

Directs and plays a supporting role in the prison escape/road movie *A Perfect World,* shot in Texas, starring Kevin Costner and an eight-year-old boy (April–July).

Birth of daughter Francesca Ruth Fisher Eastwood (7 August) (with his companion Frances Fisher, who appeared in *Pink Cadillac* and *Unforgiven*).

Tribute to Eastwood at MOMA (27 October); retrospective of his films (October–December).

*In the Line of Fire* (July) a hit; *A Perfect World* (November) is more successful with critics than audiences in the U.S., but will do very well abroad.

1994    Produces *The Stars Fell on Henrietta* (James Keach, 1995), filmed in Texas, starring Frances Fisher.

May: President of the jury at the Cannes Film Festival. Made a Commandeur de l'ordre des arts et lettres.

June: Agrees to direct the mid-life romance *The Bridges of Madison County* (based on the bestseller by Robert James Waller) when the last of several directors attached to the project, Bruce Beresford, resigns. Engages Meryl Streep to play opposite himself; shooting begins in September in Madison County, Iowa.

1995    Receives the Irving G. Thalberg Memorial Award for his body of work as a producer at the Oscar ceremony, 27 March.

*The Bridges of Madison County* opens in the U.S. to generally favorable reviews and respectable box office (June).

*Bridges* is shown at Deauville (September), followed by a European promotional tour.

1996    American Film Institute Lifetime Achievement Award (29 February).

Marries Dina Ruiz (31 March).

Film Society of Lincoln Center tribute (6 May).

Shoots the political thriller *Absolute Power* for Castle Rock and Columbia, partly on location in Washington and Baltimore; Eastwood stars as a gentleman thief who witnesses a murder.

A tribute to his love of jazz and his championing of it in his films: "Eastwood After Hours" at Carnegie Hall (17 October).

Birth of daughter Morgan (12 December).

1997    February: *Absolute Power* released to mixed reviews; May: *Absolute Power* the closing-night feature at Cannes (out of competition).

Shoots *Midnight in the Garden of Good and Evil,* based on John Berendt's bestseller and starring Kevin Spacey and John Cusack, in Savannah, Georgia (May–June); upon its release in November, reviews are split between resoundingly negative and firmly laudatory.

1998    In France to receive honorary César (28 February); *Midnight* is a critical success in Europe, particularly France.

Awarded Lifetime Achievement Award in Motion Pictures at the Golden Laurel Awards of the Producers Guild of America.

Summer: Shoots *True Crime* in Oakland, his fourth consecutive film based on a best-selling book; Eastwood stars as a reporter who has 24 hours to save a condemned man he believes to be innocent.

## As Director

### *Play Misty for Me* (1971)

Universal/Malpaso; Producer: Robert Daley; Director: **Clint Eastwood**; Screenplay: Jo Heims, Dean Riesner; Director of Photography: Bruce Surtees (Technicolor); Editor: Carl Pingitore; Art Director: Alexander Golitzen; Music: Dee Barton; Cast: **Clint Eastwood** (Dave Garver), Jessica Walter (Evelyn Draper), Donna Mills (Tobie Williams), John Larch (Sergeant McCallum), Clarice Taylor (Birdie), Irene Hervey (Madge Brenner), Jack Ging (Doctor), James McEachin (Al Monte), Don Siegel (Murphy, the bartender), Duke Everts (Jay Jay); 102 minutes

### *High Plains Drifter* (1973)

Universal/Malpaso; Executive Producer: Jennings Lang; Producer: Robert Daley; Director: **Clint Eastwood**; Screenplay: Ernest Tidyman*; Director of Photography: Bruce Surtees (Technicolor/Panavision); Editor: Ferris Webster; Art Director: Henry Bumstead; Music: Dee Barton; Cast: **Clint Eastwood** (The Stranger), Verna Bloom (Sarah Belding), Mariana Hill (Callie Travers), Mitchell Ryan (Dave Drake), Jack Ging (Morgan Allen), Stefan Gierasch (Mayor Jason Hobart), Ted Hartley (Lewis Belding), Billy Curtis (Mordecai), Geoffrey Lewis (Stacey Bridges), Scott Walker (Bill Borders), Walter Barnes (Sheriff Sam Shaw), Anthony James (Cole Carlin), Dan Vadis (Dan Carlin), Buddy Van Horn (Marshal Jim Duncan); 105 minutes

   *And Dean Riesner, uncredited

## *Breezy* (1973)

Universal/Malpaso; Executive Producer: Jennings Lang; Producer: Robert Daley; Director: **Clint Eastwood**; Screenplay: Jo Heims; Director of Photography: Frank Stanley (Technicolor); Editor: Ferris Webster; Art Director: Alexander Golitzen; Music: Michel Legrand; Cast: William Holden (Frank Harmon), Kay Lenz (Breezy), Roger C. Carmel (Bob Henderson), Marj Dusay (Betty), Joan Hotchkis (Paula), Lynn Borden (Harmon's overnight date), Shelley Morrison (Nancy), Dennis Olivieri (Bruno), Eugene Peterson (Charlie), Jamie Smith-Jackson (Marcy), Norman Bartold (Man in Car); 108 minutes

## *The Eiger Sanction* (1975)

Universal/Malpaso; Executive Producers: Richard D. Zanuck, David Brown; Producer: Robert Daley; Director: **Clint Eastwood**; Screenplay: Warren B. Murphy, Hal Dresner, Rod Whitaker; Novel: Trevenian; Director of Photography: Frank Stanley (Technicolor/Panavision); Editor: Ferris Webster; Art Directors: George Webb, Aurelio Crugnola; Music: John Williams; Cast: **Clint Eastwood** (Jonathan Hemlock), George Kennedy (Ben Bowman), Vonetta McGee (Jemima Brown), Jack Cassidy (Miles Mellough), Heidi Bruhl (Anna Montaigne), Thayer David (Dragon), Reiner Schoene (Freytag), Michael Grimm (Meyer), Jean-Pierre Bernard (Montaigne), Brenda Venus (George), Gregory Walcott (Pope); 128 minutes

## *The Outlaw Josey Wales* (1976)

Warner Bros./Malpaso; Producer: Robert Daley; Director: **Clint Eastwood**; Screenplay: Phil Kaufman, Sonia Chernus; Novel: Forrest Carter; Director of Photography: Bruce Surtees (Deluxe/Panavision); Editor: Ferris Webster; Production Designer: Tambi Larsen; Music: Jerry Fielding; Cast: **Clint Eastwood** (Josey Wales), Chief Dan George (Lone Watie), Sondra Locke (Laura Lee), Bill McKinney (Terrill), John Vernon (Fletcher), Paula Trueman (Grandma Sarah), Sam Bottoms (Jamie), Geraldine Keams (Little Moonlight), Woodrow Parfrey (Carpetbagger), Joyce Jameson (Rose), Sheb Wooley (Travis Cobb), Royal Dano (Ten Spot), Matt Clark (Kelly), John Verros (Chato), Will Sampson (Ten Bears), William O'Connell (Carstairs), John Quade (Comanchero Leader), John Russell (Bloody Bill Anderson), Cissy Wellman (Josey's Wife); Kyle Eastwood (Little Josey); 137 minutes
    Academy Awards Nomination: Music (Original Score), Jerry Fielding

## The Gauntlet (1977)

Warner Bros./Malpaso; Producer: Robert Daley; Director: **Clint Eastwood**; Screenplay: Michael Butler, Dennis Shryack; Director of Photography: Rexford Metz (Deluxe/Panavision); Editors: Ferris Webster, Joel Cox; Art Director: Allen E. Smith; Music: Jerry Fielding; Cast: **Clint Eastwood** (Ben Shockley), Sondra Locke (Gus Mally), Pat Hingle (Josephson), William Prince (Blakelock), Bill McKinney (Constable), Michael Cavanaugh (Feyderspiel), Carole Cook (Waitress), Mara Corday (Jail Matron), Douglas McGrath (Bookie), Jeff Morris (Desk Sergeant), Samantha Doane, Roy Jensen, Dan Vadis (Bikers); III minutes

## Bronco Billy (1980)

Warner Bros./Malpaso (see note at end); Executive Producer: Robert Daley; Producer: Dennis Hackin, Neil Dobrofsky; Director: **Clint Eastwood**; Screenplay: Dennis Hackin; Director of Photography: David Worth (Deluxe); Editors: Ferris Webster, Joel Cox; Art Director: Gene Lourie; Music Supervision: Snuff Garrett; Music: Steve Dorff; **Eastwood** sings "Barroom Buddies"; Cast: **Clint Eastwood** (Bronco Billy McCoy), Sondra Locke (Antoinette Lily), Geoffrey Lewis (John Arlington), Scatman Crothers (Doc Lynch), Bill McKinney (Lefty LeBow), Sam Bottoms (Leonard James), Dan Vadis (Chief Big Eagle), Sierra Pecheur (Lorraine Running Water), Walter Barnes (Sheriff Dix), Woodrow Parfrey (Dr. Canterbury), Beverlee McKinsey (Irene Lily), Douglas McGrath (Lt. Wiecker), Hank Worden (Gas Station Mechanic), William Prince (Edgar Lipton); II6 minutes

## Firefox (1982)

Warner Bros./Malpaso (see note at end); Executive Producer: Fritz Manes; Producer/Director: **Clint Eastwood**; Screenplay: Alex Lasker, Wendell Wellman; Novel: Craig Thomas; Director of Photography: Bruce Surtees (Deluxe/Panavision); Editors: Ferris Webster, Ron Spang; Art Direction: John Graysmark, Elayne Ceder; Music: Maurice Jarre; Cast: **Clint Eastwood** (Mitchell Gant), Freddie Jones (Kenneth Aubrey), David Huffman (Buckholz), Warren Clarke (Pavel Upenskoy), Ronald Lacey (Semelovsky), Kenneth Colley (Col. Kontarsky), Klaus Löwitsch (General Vladimirov), Nigel Hawthorne (Pyotr Baranovich); 124–136 minutes

### *Honkytonk Man* (1982)

Warner Bros./Malpaso (see note at end); Executive Producer: Fritz Manes; Producer/Director: **Clint Eastwood**; Screenplay: Clancy Carlile; Novel: Clancy Carlile; Director of Photography: Bruce Surtees (Technicolor); Editors: Ferris Webster, Michael Kelly, Joel Cox; Production Designer: Edward Carfagno; Music Supervision: Snuff Garrett; Music: Steve Dorff; **Eastwood** sings "No Sweeter Cheater Than You," "When I Sing about You," "One Fiddle, Two Fiddle," "Honkytonk Man" (the last performed with Marty Robbins); Cast: **Clint Eastwood** (Red Stovall), Kyle Eastwood (Whit), John McIntire (Grandpa), Alexa Kenin (Marlene), Verna Bloom (Emmy), Matt Clark (Virgil), Barry Corbin (Arnspringer), Jerry Hardin (Snuffy), Linda Hopkins (Flossie), Marty Robbins (Smoky); 122 minutes

### *Sudden Impact* (1983)

Warner Bros./Malpaso (see note at end); Executive Producer: Fritz Manes; Producer/Director: **Clint Eastwood**; Screenplay: Joseph C. Stinson; Story: Earl Smith, Charles B. Pierce; Director of Photography: Bruce Surtees (Technicolor/Panavision); Editor: Joel Cox; Production Designer: Edward Carfagno; Music: Lalo Schifrin; Cast: **Clint Eastwood** (Harry Callahan), Sondra Locke (Jennifer Spencer), Pat Hingle (Chief Jannings), Bradford Dillman (Captain Briggs), Paul Drake (Mick), Audrie J. Neenan (Ray Parkins), Jack Thibeau (Kruger), Michael Currie (Lt. Donnely), Albert Popwell (Horace King); 117 minutes

### *Tightrope* (1984)

Warner Bros./Malpaso; Producers: **Clint Eastwood**, Fritz Manes; Director: Richard Tuggle*; Screenplay: Richard Tuggle; Director of Photography: Bruce Surtees (Technicolor); Production Designer: Edward Carfagno; Music: Lennie Niehaus; **Eastwood** composed "Amanda's Theme"; Cast: **Clint Eastwood** (Wes Block), Genevieve Bujold (Beryl Thibodeaux), Dan Hedaya (Detective Molinari), Alison Eastwood (Amanda Block), Jennifer Beck (Penny Block), Marco St. John (Leander Rolfe), Rebecca Perle (Becky Jacklin), Regina Richardson (Sarita), Randi Brooks (Jamie Cory), Jamie Rose (Melanie Silber), Margaret Howell (Judy Harper), Janet MacLachlan (Dr. Yarlofsky); 114 minutes

*Credited to Tuggle, directed by **Eastwood**. See Introduction.

### *Pale Rider* (1985)

Warner Bros./Malpaso; Executive Producer: Fritz Manes; Producer/Director: **Clint Eastwood**; Screenplay: Michael Butler, Dennis Shryack; Director of Photography: Bruce Surtees (Technicolor/Panavision); Editor: Joel Cox; Production Designer: Edward Carfagno; Music: Lennie Niehaus; **Eastwood** composed "Megan's Theme"; Cast: **Clint Eastwood** (Preacher), Michael Moriarty (Hull Barret), Carrie Snodgress (Sarah Wheeler), Christopher Penn (Josh LaHood), Richard Dysart (Coy LaHood), Sydney Penny (Megan Wheeler), Richard Kiel (Club), Doug McGrath (Spider Conway), John Russell (Marshal Stockburn), S. A. Griffin (Deputy Folke), Jack Radosta (Deputy Grissom), Robert Winley (Deputy Kobold), Billy Drago (Deputy Mather), Jeffrey Josephson (Deputy Sedge), John Dennis Johnston (Deputy Tucker); 113 minutes

### *Vanessa in the Garden* (1985) (Episode of TV series *Amazing Stories*)

Amblin Entertainment/NBC; Executive Producer: Steven Spielberg; Producer: David E. Vogel; Director: **Clint Eastwood**; Screenplay: Steven Spielberg; Director of Photography: Robert Stevens; Editor: Jo Ann Fogle; Production Designer: Rick Carter; Music: Lennie Niehaus (after a theme by John Williams and themes by Richard Wagner); Cast: Harvey Keitel (Byron Sullivan), Sondra Locke (Vanessa), Beau Bridges (Ted); telecast 29 December; 25 minutes

### *Heartbreak Ridge* (1986)

Warner Bros./Malpaso; Executive Producer: Fritz Manes; Producer/Director: **Clint Eastwood**; Screenplay: James Carabatsos*; Director of Photography: Jack N. Green (Technicolor); Editor: Joel Cox; Production Design: Edward Carfagno; Music: Lennie Niehaus; **Eastwood** composed "How Much I Care"; Sound Mixer: William Nelson; Re-recording Mixers: Les Fresholtz, Dick Alexander, Vern Poore; Cast: **Clint Eastwood** (Sergeant Tom Highway), Marsha Mason (Aggie), Everett McGill (Major Powers), Moses Gunn (Sergeant Webster), Eileen Heckart (Little Mary), Bo Svenson (Roy Jennings), Boyd Gaines (Lieutenant Ring), Mario Van Peebles (Stitch Jones), Arlen Dean Snyder (Choozoo), Vincent Irizarry (Fraggetti), Ramon Franco (Aponte), Tom Villard (Profile), Mike Gomez (Quinones), Rodney Hill (Collins), Peter Koch (Swede Johnson), Richard Venture (Colonel Meyers); 128 minutes

Academy Awards Nomination: Sound, Dick Alexander, Les Fresholtz, William Nelson, Vern Poore

*And Joseph C. Stinson, uncredited

### *Bird* (1988)

Warner Bros./Malpaso; Executive Producer: David Valdes; Producer/Director: **Clint Eastwood**; Screenplay: Joel Oliansky; Director of Photography: Jack N. Green (Technicolor); Editor: Joel Cox; Production Designer: Edward Carfagno; Music: Lennie Niehaus; Sound Mixer: Willie D. Burton; Re-recording Mixers: Les Fresholtz, Dick Alexander, Vern Poore; Cast: Forest Whitaker (Charlie "Bird" Parker), Diane Venora (Chan Parker), Michael Zelniker (Red Rodney), Samuel E. Wright (Dizzy Gillespie), Keith David (Buster Franklin), Michael McGuire (Brewster), James Handy (Esteves), Damon Whitaker (Young Bird), Morgan Nagler (Kim), Arlen Dean Snyder (Dr. Heath), Sam Robards (Moscowitz), Bill Cobbs (Dr. Caulfield), Hamilton Camp (Mayor of 52nd Street), Jo De Winter (Mildred Berg), Richard Zavaglia (Ralph the Narc), Anna Levine* (Audrey), Hubert Kelly (Wilson), Billy Mitchell (Prince), Karl Vincent (Stratton), Jason Bernard (Benny Tate), Gretchen Oehler (Southern Nurse), Richard McKenzie (Southern Doctor), Diane Salinger (Baroness Nica); 163 minutes

Academy Awards: Sound, Dick Alexander, Willie D. Burton, Les Fresholtz, Vern Poore

*Billed as "Anna Thomson" in *Unforgiven,* in the role of Delilah Fitzgerald

### *White Hunter, Black Heart* (1990)

Warner Bros./Malpaso/Rastar; Executive Producer: David Valdes; Producer/Director: **Clint Eastwood**; Screenplay: Peter Viertel & James Bridges and Burt Kennedy; Novel: Peter Viertel; Director of Photography: Jack N. Green (Technicolor); Editor: Joel Cox; Production Designer: John Graysmark; Music: Lennie Niehaus; Cast: **Clint Eastwood** (John Wilson), Jeff Fahey (Pete Verrill), Charlotte Cornwell (Miss Wilding), Norman Lumsden (Butler George), George Dzundza (Paul Landers), Boy Mathias Chuma (Kivu), Edward Tudor Pole (Reissar), Roddy Maude-Roxby (Thompson), Richard Warwick (Basil Fields), John Rapley (Gun Shop Salesman), Catherine Neilson (Irene Saunders), Marisa Berenson (Kay Gibson), Richard Vanstone (Phil Duncan), Jamie Koss (Mrs. Duncan), Alun

Armstrong (Ralph Lockhart), Clive Mantle (Harry), Mel Martin (Mrs. MacGregor); 112 minutes

### The Rookie (1990)

Warner Bros./Malpaso; Producer: Howard Kazanjian, Steven Siebert, David Valdes; Director: **Clint Eastwood**; Screenplay: Boaz Yakin, Scott Spiegel; Director of Photography: Jack N. Green (Technicolor/Panavision); Editor: Joel Cox; Production Designer: Judy Cammer; Music: Lennie Niehaus; Cast: **Clint Eastwood** (Nick Pulovski), Charlie Sheen (David Ackerman), Raul Julia (Strom), Sonia Braga (Liesl), Tom Skerritt (Eugene Ackerman), Lara Flynn Boyle (Sarah), Pepe Serna (Garcia), Marco Rodriguez (Loco), Pete Randall (Cruz); 121 minutes

### Unforgiven (1992)

Warner Bros./Malpaso; Executive Producer: David Valdes; Producer/ Director: **Clint Eastwood**; Screenplay: David Webb Peoples; Director of Photography: Jack N. Green (Technicolor/Panavision); Editor: Joel Cox; Production Designed By: Henry Bumstead; Set Decorator: Janice Blackie-Goodine; Music: Lennie Niehaus; **Eastwood** composed "Claudia's Theme"; Sound Mixer: Rob Young; Re-recording Mixers: Les Fresholtz, Vern Poore, Dick Alexander; Cast: **Clint Eastwood** (William Munny), Gene Hackman (Little Bill Daggett), Morgan Freeman (Ned Logan), Richard Harris (English Bob), Jaimz Woolvett (The Schofield Kid), Saul Rubinek (W. W. Beauchamp), Frances Fisher (Strawberry Alice), Anna Thomson* (Delilah Fitzgerald), David Mucci (Quick Mike), Rob Campbell (Davey Bunting), Anthony James (Skinny Dubois), Tara Dawn Frederick (Little Sue), Beverley Elliott (Silky), Liisa Repo-Martell (Faith), Josie Smith (Crow Creek Kate), Shane Meier (Will Munny), Aline Levasseur (Penny Munny), Cherrilene Cardinal (Sally Two Trees), Ron White (Deputy Clyde Ledbetter), Henry Kope (German Joe Schultz), Jeremy Ratchford (Deputy Andy Russell), John Pyper-Ferguson (Deputy Charley Hecker), Jefferson Mappin (Deputy Fatty Rossiter), Walter Marsh (Barber); 130 minutes

Academy Awards: Best Picture, **Clint Eastwood**; Directing, **Clint Eastwood**; Actor in a Supporting Role, Gene Hackman; Film Editing, Joel Cox

Academy Awards Nominations: Actor in a Leading Role, **Clint Eastwood**; Art Direction–Set Decoration, Henry Bumstead, Janice Blackie-

Goodine; Cinematography, Jack N. Green; Sound, Dick Alexander, Les Fresholtz, Vern Poore, Rob Young; Writing (Screenplay Written Directly for the Screen), David Webb Peoples

*Billed as "Anna Levine" in *Bird*, in the role of Audrey

### *A Perfect World* (1993)

Warner Bros./Malpaso; Producers: Mark Johnson. David Valdes; Director: **Clint Eastwood**; Screenplay: John Lee Hancock; Director of Photography: Jack N. Green (Technicolor/Panavision); Editor: Joel Cox, Ron Spang; Production Designed by: Henry Bumstead; Music: Lennie Niehaus; **Eastwood** composed waltz theme "Big Fran's Baby"; Cast: Kevin Costner (Butch Haynes), **Clint Eastwood** (Red Garnett), Laura Dern (Sally Gerber), T. J. Lowther (Phillip Perry), Keith Szarabajka (Terry Pugh), Leo Burmester (Tom Adler), Paul Hewitt (Dick Suttle), Bradley Whitford (Bobby Lee), Ray McKinnon (Bradley), Jennifer Griffin (Gladys Perry), Mark Voges (Larry), Rodger Boyce (Mr. Willits), Lucy Lee Flippin (Lucy), Elizabeth Ruscio (Paula), Dennis Letts (Governor), Margaret Bowman (Trick 'r Treat Lady), John M. Jackson (Bob Fielder), Connie Cooper (Bob's Wife), Linda Hart (Eileen), Wayne Dehart (Mack), Mary Alice (Lottie), Kevin Jamal Woods (Cleveland); 137 minutes

### *The Bridges of Madison County* (1995)

Warner Bros./Amblin/Malpaso; Producers: **Clint Eastwood**, Kathleen Kennedy; Director: **Clint Eastwood**; Screenplay: Richard LaGravenese; Novel: Robert James Waller; Director of Photography: Jack N. Green (Technicolor); Editor: Joel Cox; Production Designed By: Jeannine Oppewall; Music: Lennie Niehaus; **Eastwood** composed theme "Doe Eyes"; Cast: **Clint Eastwood** (Robert Kincaid), Meryl Streep (Francesca Johnson), Annie Corley (Carolyn), Victor Slezak (Michael Johnson), Jim Haynie (Richard Johnson), Sarah Kathryn Schmitt (Young Carolyn), Christopher Kroon (Young Michael), Phyllis Lyons (Betty), Debra Monk (Madge), Richard Lage (Lawyer), Michelle Benes (Lucy Redfield), Tania Mishler (Waitress), Billie McNabb (Waitress), Art Breese (Cashier), Lana Schwab (Saleswoman), James Rivers (James River Band #1), Kyle Eastwood (James River Band #6); 135 minutes

Academy Awards Nomination: Actress in a Leading Role, Meryl Streep

### *Absolute Power* (1997)

Columbia/Castle Rock/Malpaso; Producers: **Clint Eastwood**, Karen Spiegel; Director: **Clint Eastwood**; Screenplay: William Goldman; Novel: David Baldacci; Director of Photography: Jack N. Green (Technicolor/Panavision); Editor: Joel Cox; Production Designed by: Henry Bumstead; Music: Lennie Niehaus; **Eastwood** composed "Power Waltz" and "Kate's Theme"; Cast: **Clint Eastwood** (Luther Whitney), Gene Hackman (President Alan Richmond), Ed Harris (Seth Frank), Laura Linney (Kate Whitney), Scott Glenn (Bill Burton), Dennis Haysbert (Tim Collin), Judy Davis (Gloria Russell), E. G. Marshall (Walter Sullivan), Melora Hardin (Christy Sullivan), Kenneth Welsh (Sandy Lord), Penny Johnson (Laura Simon), Richard Jenkins (Michael McCarty), Mark Margolis (Red), Elaine Kagan (Valerie), Alison Eastwood (Art Student), Kimber Eastwood (White House Tour Guide); 121 minutes

### *Midnight in the Garden of Good and Evil* (1997)

Warner Bros./Malpaso/Silver Pictures; Producers: **Clint Eastwood**, Arnold Stiefel; Director: **Clint Eastwood**; Screenplay: John Lee Hancock; Book: John Berendt; Director of Photography: Jack N. Green (Technicolor); Editor: Joel Cox; Production Design by: Henry Bumstead; Music: Lennie Niehaus; featuring songs by Johnny Mercer; Cast: Kevin Spacey (Jim Williams), John Cusack (John Kelso), Jack Thompson (Sonny Seiler), Irma P. Hall (Minerva), Jude Law (Billy Hanson), Alison Eastwood (Mandy Nicholls), Paul Hipp (Joe Odom), The Lady Chablis (Herself), Geoffrey Lewis (Luther Driggers), Dorothy Loudon (Serena Dawes), Anne Haney (Margaret Williams), Kim Hunter (Betty Harty), Richard Herd (Henry Skerridge), Leon Rippy (Detective Boone), Bob Gunton (Finley Largent), Sonny Seiler (Judge White), Patrika Darbo (Sara Warren), Emma Kelly (Herself), James Moody (William Simon Glover), Michael Rosenbaum (George Tucker), Georgia Allen (Lucille Wright), Charles Black (Alpha), Aleta Mitchell (Alphabette), Kevin Harry (Phillip), Dorothy Kingery (Jim Williams' sister), Amanda Kingery (Amanda, Jim Williams' niece), Susan Kingery (Susan, Jim Williams' niece), Ann Cusack (Delivery Woman), Jerry Spence (Hair Dresser); 155 minutes

### *True Crime* (1999)

Warner Bros./Malpaso Productions/The Zanuck Company; Producers: **Clint Eastwood**, Tom Rooker, Lili Fini Zanuck, Richard D. Zanuck; Director:

**Clint Eastwood**; Screenplay: Stephen Schiff; Novel: Andrew Klavan; Director of Photography: Jack N. Green; Editor: Joel Cox; Production Design by: Henry Bumstead; Music: Lennie Niehaus; Cast: **Clint Eastwood** (Steve Everett), Isaiah Washington (Frank Beachum), Lisa Gay Hamilton (Bonnie Beachum), James Woods (Alan Mann), Bernard Hill (Luther Plunkitt), and Frances Fisher, Michael Jeter, Denis Leary, Mary McCormack, Sydney Poitier, Diane Venora, Francesca Ruth Fisher Eastwood

## As Actor Only

At the beginning of his career Eastwood played small parts in ten films, which we list briefly:

For Universal-International:

*Revenge of the Creature* (Jack Arnold, 1955); **Eastwood** (uncredited) as Jennings, a lab technician

*Francis in the Navy* (Arthur Lubin, 1955); **Eastwood** as Jonesey, a sailor

*Lady Godiva* (Arthur Lubin, 1955); **Eastwood** (uncredited) as "First Saxon"

*Tarantula* (Jack Arnold, 1955); **Eastwood** (uncredited) as jet squadron leader

*Never Say Goodbye* (Jerry Hopper, 1956); **Eastwood** (uncredited) as Will, a lab assistant

*Star in the Dust* (Charles Haas, 1956); **Eastwood** (uncredited) as a ranch hand

*Away All Boats* (Joseph Pevney, 1956); **Eastwood** (uncredited) as a sailor

For RKO: *The First Traveling Saleslady* (Arthur Lubin, 1956); "And introducing **Clint Eastwood**" as Jack Rice, a Rough Rider

For RKO and Universal-International: *Escapade in Japan* (Arthur Lubin, 1957); **Eastwood** as Dumbo, a pilot

For Warner Bros.: *Lafayette Escadrille* (William A. Wellman, 1958); **Eastwood** as George Moseley, a fighter pilot

## Starring/Co-starring Roles

### *Ambush At Cimarron Pass* (1958)

Regal/20th Century-Fox; Producer: Herbert E. Mendelson; Director: Jodie Copelan; Screenplay: Richard C. Taylor, John K. Butler; Director of Photography: John M. Nickolaus Jr. (black and white/RegalScope); Editor: Carl L. Pierson; Music: Paul Sawtell, Bert Shefter; Cast: Scott Brady (Sgt. Matt Blake), Margia Dean (Teresa), **Clint Eastwood** (Keith Williams), Irving Bacon (Stanfield), Frank Gerstle (Sam Prescott), Dirk London (Johnny Willows), Baynes Barron (Corbin), Ken Mayer (Corporal Schwitzer), Keith Richards (Private Lasky), William Vaughn (Henry), John Damler (Private Zach); 73 minutes

### *Per un pugno di dollari/A Fistful Of Dollars* (1964; U.S. 1967)

Jolly Film/Constantin/Ocean Film, United Artists; Producers: Arrigo Colombo ("Harry Colombo"),* Giorgio Papi ("George Papi"); Director: Sergio Leone ("Bob Robertson"); Screenplay: Sergio Leone, Duccio Tessari, Victor A. Catena, G. Schock; Director of Photography: Massimo Dallamano ("Jack Dalmas") (Technicolor/Techniscope); Editor: Roberto Cinquini ("Bob Quintle"); Art Direction: Carlo Simi ("Charles Simons"); Music: Ennio Morricone ("Dan Savio"); **Eastwood** sings "Sweet Betsy From Pike"; Cast: **Clint Eastwood** (Joe, the Stranger), Gian Maria Volonté ("Johnny Wels") (Ramón Rojo), Marianne Koch (Marisol), José Calvo (Silvanito), Wolfgang Lukschy (John Baxter), Josef Egger ("Joe Edger") (Piripero), Margherita Lozano (Consuelo Baxter), Sieghardt Rupp (Esteban Rojo), Antonio Prieto (Don Benito** Rojo), Bruno Carotentuto ("Carol Brown") (Antonio Baxter), Mario Brega ("Richard Stuyvesant") (Chico), Daniel Martin (Julian), Benito Stefanelli ("Benny Reeves") (Rubio); 96–100 minutes

   *Several participants were originally credited under "American" pseudonyms

   **"Don Miguel" in English-dubbed prints

### *Per qualche dollaro in più/For a Few Dollars More* (1965; U.S. 1967)

Produzioni Europee Associate/Constantin/Arturo Gonzales, United Artists; Producer: Alberto Grimaldi; Director: Sergio Leone; Screenplay: Luciano Vincenzoni, Sergio Leone; Director of Photography: Massimo Dallamano (Technicolor/Techniscope); Editors: Giorgio Serralonga, Eugenio Alabiso; Art Direction: Carlo Simi; Music: Ennio Morricone; Cast: **Clint Eastwood** (Manco, the Stranger), Lee Van Cleef (Colonel Douglas Mortimer), Gian Maria Volonté (Indio), Klaus Kinski (Hunchback), Josef Egger (Prophet), Mario Brega (Niño), Rosemary Dexter (Mortimer's Sister), Mara Krup (Mary,

Hotel Manager's Wife), Luigi Pistilli (Groggy), Benito Stefanelli (Rocky), and Aldo Sambrell, Panos Papadopoulos, Roberto Camardiel; 130 minutes

### *Il buono, il brutto, il cattivo/The Good, the Bad, and the Ugly* (1966; U.S. 1968)

Produzioni Europee Associate/United Artists; Producer: Alberto Grimaldi; Director: Sergio Leone; Screenplay: Age, Scarpelli, Luciano Vincenzoni, Sergio Leone; Director of Photography: Tonino Delli Colli (Technicolor/ Techniscope); Editors: Nino Baragli, Eugenio Alabiso; Art Direction: Carlo Simi; Music: Ennio Morricone; Cast: **Clint Eastwood** (Blondy, the Good), Eli Wallach (Tuco, the Ugly), Lee Van Cleef (Sentenza, Angel Eyes, the Bad), Rada Rassimov (Maria), Aldo Giuffré (Northern Officer), Mario Brega (Corporal Wallace), Luigi Pistilli (Father Ramírez), Livio Lorenzón (Baker); 180 minutes (Italy), 161 minutes (U.S.)

### *Le streghe/The Witches* (1967; U.S. 1979)

Dino de Laurentiis Cinematografica/Les Productions Artistes Associés; Executive Producer: Alfredo de Laurentiis; Producer: Dino de Laurentiis; Part Five, "Una sera come le altri"/ "A Night Like Any Other": Director: Vittorio de Sica; Screenplay: Cesare Zavattini, Fabio Carpi, Enzio Muzii; Director of Photography: Giuseppe Rotunno; Editor: Adriana Novelli; Art Direction: Piero Poletto; Music: Piero Piccioni; Cast: Silvana Mangano (Giovanna), **Clint Eastwood** (Carlo); 19 minutes

### *Hang 'em High* (1968)

United Artists/Malpaso; Producer: Leonard Freeman; Director: Ted Post; Screenplay: Leonard Freeman, Mel Goldberg; Directors of Photography: Richard Kline, Leonard South (Deluxe); Editor: Gene Fowler, Jr.; Art Director: John Goodman; Music: Dominic Frontiere; Cast: **Clint Eastwood** (Jed Cooper), Inger Stevens (Rachel), Ed Begley (Captain Wilson), Pat Hingle (Judge Adam Fenton), Arlene Golonka (Jennifer), James MacArthur (Preacher), Ruth White (Madam Peaches Sophie), Bruce Dern (Miller), Alan Hale Jr. (Stone), Dennis Hopper (Prophet), Ben Johnson (Dave Bliss), Bob Steele (Jenkins), L. Q. Jones (Loomis), Bert Freed (Schmidt, the hangman), Michael O'Sullivan (Francis Duffy), Herb Ellis (Swede), Russell Thorson (Mr. Maddow), Rick Gates (Ben), Bruce Scott (Billy Joe), Paul Sorenson (Reno); 114 minutes

### Coogan's Bluff (1968)

Universal/Malpaso; Executive Producer: Richard E. Lyons;
Producer/Director: Don Siegel; Screenplay: Herman Miller, Dean Riesner,
Howard Rodman; Story: Herman Miller; Director of Photography: Bud
Thackery (Technicolor); Editor: Sam E. Waxman; Art Directors: Alexander
Golitzen, Robert MacKichan; Music: Lalo Schifrin; Cast: **Clint Eastwood**
(Coogan), Lee J. Cobb (Lt. McElroy), Susan Clark (Julie), Tisha Sterling
(Linny Raven), Don Stroud (Ringerman), Betty Field (Mrs. Ringerman),
Tom Tully (Sheriff McRea), Melodie Johnson (Millie), James Edwards
(Jackson), Rudy Diaz (Running Bear), David Doyle (Pushie), Albert Popwell
(Wonderful Digby), Louis Zorich (Taxi Driver), Meg Myles (Big Red),
Seymour Cassel (Young Hood), James Gavin (Ferguson); 94 minutes

### Where Eagles Dare (1968)

Metro-Goldwyn-Mayer; Producer: Elliott Kastner; Director: Brian G.
Hutton; Story and Screenplay: Alistair MacLean; Director of Photography:
Arthur Ibbetson (Metrocolor/Panavision); Editor: John Jympson; Art
Director: Peter Mullins; Music: Ron Goodwin; Cast: Richard Burton (John
Smith), **Clint Eastwood** (Lt. Morris Schaffer), Mary Ure (Mary Ellison),
Ingrid Pitt (Heidi), Michael Hordern (Vice-Admiral Rolland), Patrick
Wymark (Col. Wyatt-Turner), Robert Beatty (Cartwright-Jones), Anton
Diffring (Col. Kramer), Donald Houston (Olaf Christiansen), Ferdy Mayne
(Reichsmarschall Rosemeyer), Neil McCarthy (Torrance-Smythe); Peter
Barkworth (Edward Carraciola), William Squire (Lee Thomas); 155 minutes

### Paint Your Wagon (1969)

Paramount; Producer: Alan Jay Lerner; Director: Joshua Logan; Screenplay
and Lyrics: Alan Jay Lerner; Adaptation: Paddy Chayefsky; Director of
Photography: William Fraker (Technicolor/Panavision); Editor: Robert
Jones; Art Director: Carl Braunger; Music: Frederick Loewe, André Previn;
**Eastwood** sings "I Still See Elisa," "I Talk to the Trees," "Best Things," and
"Gold Fever"; Cast: Lee Marvin (Ben Rumson), **Clint Eastwood** (Pardner),
Jean Seberg (Elizabeth), Harve Presnell (Rotten Luck Willie), Ray Walston
(Mad Jack Duncan), Tom Ligon (Horton Fenty), Alan Dexter (Parson),
William O'Connell (Horace Tabor), Ben Baker (Haywood Holbrook), Alan
Baxter (Mr. Fenty), Paula Trueman (Mrs. Fenty), Robert Easton (Atwell),
Geoffrey Norman (Foster), H. B. Haggerty (Steve Bull), Terry Jenkins (Joe

Mooney), Karl Bruck (Schermerhorn), John Mitchum (Jacob Woodling); 166 minutes

### Kelly's Heroes (1970)

Metro-Goldwyn-Mayer; Producers: Gabriel Katzka, Sidney Beckerman; Director: Brian G. Hutton; Screenplay: Troy Kennedy Martin; Director of Photography: Gabriel Figueroa (Metrocolor/Panavision); Editor: John Jympson; Production Designer: Jonathan Barry; Music: Lalo Schifrin; Cast: **Clint Eastwood** (Kelly), Telly Savalas (Big Joe), Don Rickles (Crap Game), Carroll O'Connor (General Colt), Donald Sutherland (Oddball), Gavin MacLeod (Moriarty), George Savalas (Mulligan), Hal Buckley (Maitland), David Hurst (Col. Dankhopf), John Heller (German Lieutenant); 145 minutes

### Two Mules for Sister Sara (1970)

Universal/Malpaso/Sanen Productions; Producer: Martin Rackin; Director: Don Siegel; Screenplay: Albert Maltz; Story: Budd Boetticher; Director of Photography: Gabriel Figueroa (Technicolor/Panavision); Editors: Robert F. Shugrue, Juan José Marino; Art Director: José Rodríguez Granada; Music: Ennio Morricone; **Eastwood** sings "Sam Hall"; Cast: Shirley MacLaine (Sara), **Clint Eastwood** (Hogan), Manolo Fábregas (Colonel Beltran), Alberto Morin (General LeClaire), Armando Silvestre, John Kelly, Enrique Lucero (Americans); 114 minutes

### The Beguiled (1971)

Universal/Malpaso; Producer/Director: Don Siegel; Screenplay: Albert Maltz (as John B. Sherry), Irene Kamp (as Grimes Grice)*; Novel: Thomas Cullinan; Director of Photography: Bruce Surtees (Technicolor); Editor: Carl Pingitore; Art Director: Alexander Golitzen; Music: Lalo Schifrin; **Eastwood** sings the opening folk ballad, "The Dove"; Cast: **Clint Eastwood** (John McBurney), Geraldine Page (Martha Farnsworth), Elizabeth Hartman (Edwina Dabney), Jo Ann Harris (Carol), Darleen Carr (Doris), Mae Mercer (Hallie), Pamelyn Ferdin (Amy), Melody Thomas (Abigail), Peggy Drier (Lizzie), Pattye Mattick (Janie); 109 minutes
    *And Claude Traverse, uncredited

### Dirty Harry (1971)

Warner Bros./Malpaso; Executive Producer: Robert Daley; Producer/Director: Don Siegel; Screenplay: Harry Julian Fink & Rita M. Fink and

Dean Riesner; Director of Photography: Bruce Surtees (Technicolor/
Panavision); Editor: Carl Pingitore; Art Director: Dale Hennesy; Music: Lalo
Schifrin; Cast: **Clint Eastwood** (Detective Harry Callahan), Harry Guar-
dino (Lieutenant Bressler), Reni Santoni (Chico), John Vernon (The Mayor),
Andy Robinson (Killer/Scorpio), John Larch (Chief), John Mitchum
(DiGeorgio), Mae Mercer (Mrs. Russell), Lyn Edgington (Norma), Ruth
Kobart (Bus Driver), Woodrow Parfrey (Mr. Jaffe), Josef Sommer (District
Attorney Rothko), William Paterson (Bannerman), James Nolan (Liquor
Store Proprietor), Maurice S. Argent (Sid Kleinman), Jo De Winter (Miss
Willis), Craig G. Kelly (Sergeant Reineke), Albert Popwell (uncredited as a
bank robber); 103 minutes

### *Joe Kidd* (1972)

Universal/Malpaso; Executive Producer: Robert Daley; Producer: Sidney
Beckerman; Director: John Sturges; Screenplay: Elmore Leonard; Director
of Photography: Bruce Surtees (Technicolor/Panavision); Editor: Ferris
Webster; Art Directors: Henry Bumstead, Alexander Golitzen; Music: Lalo
Schifrin; Cast: **Clint Eastwood** (Joe Kidd), Robert Duvall (Frank Harlan),
John Saxon (Luis Chama), Don Stroud (Lamarr), Stella Garcia (Helen
Sanchez), James Wainwright (Mingo), Paul Koslo (Roy), Gregory Walcott
(Sheriff Mitchell), Lynne Marta (Elma), Dick Van Patten (Hotel Manager),
Pepe Hern (Priest); 88 minutes

### *Magnum Force* (1973)

Warner Bros./Malpaso; Producer: Robert Daley; Director: Ted Post;
Screenplay: John Milius, Michael Cimino; Director of Photography: Frank
Stanley (Technicolor/Panavision); Editor: Ferris Webster; Art Director: Jack
Collis; Music: Lalo Schifrin; Cast: **Clint Eastwood** (Harry Callahan), Hal
Holbrook (Lieutenant Briggs), Mitchell Ryan (Charlie McCoy), David Soul
(Davis), Tim Matheson (Sweet), Kip Niven (Astrachan), Robert Urich
(Grimes), Felton Perry (Early Smith), John Mitchum (DiGeorgio), Albert
Popwell (Pimp), Christine White (Carol McCoy), Adele Yoshioka (Sunny);
124 minutes

### *Thunderbolt and Lightfoot* (1974)

United Artists/Malpaso; Producer: Robert Daley; Director: Michael Cimino;
Screenplay: Michael Cimino; Director of Photography: Frank Stanley
(Deluxe/Panavision); Editor: Ferris Webster; Art Director: Tambi Larsen;

Music: Dee Barton; Cast: **Clint Eastwood** (John "Thunderbolt" Doherty), Jeff Bridges (Lightfoot), George Kennedy (Red Leary), Geoffrey Lewis (Goody), Catherine Bach (Melody), Gary Busey (Curly), Jack Dodson (Vault Manager), Bill McKenney (Crazy Driver), Dub Taylor (Gas Station Attendant), Gregory Walcott (Used Car Salesman), Gene Elman (Tourist), Lila Teigh (Tourist), Burton Gilliam (Welder), Roy Jenson (Dunlop), Claudia Lennear (Secretary), Vic Tayback (Mario), June Fairchild (Gloria); 115 minutes

Academy Awards Nomination: Actor in a Supporting Role, Jeff Bridges

### The Enforcer (1976)

Warner Bros./Malpaso; Producer: Robert Daley; Director: James Fargo; Screenplay: Stirling Silliphant, Dean Riesner; Story: Gail Morgan Hickman, S. W. Schurr; Director of Photography: Charles W. Short (Deluxe/Panavision); Editors: Ferris Webster, Joel Cox; Art Director: Allen E. Smith; Music: Jerry Fielding; Cast: **Clint Eastwood** (Harry Callahan), Tyne Daly (Kate Moore), Harry Guardino (Lieutenant Bressler), Bradford Dillman (Captain McKay), John Mitchum (DiGeorgio), DeVeren Bookwalter (Bobby Maxwell), John Crawford (Mayor), Samantha Doane (Wanda), Robert Hoy (Buchinski), Jocelyn Jones (Miki), M. G. Kelly (Father John), Nick Pellegrino (Martin), Albert Popwell (Mustapha); 96 minutes

### Every Which Way but Loose (1978)

Warner Bros./Malpaso; Producer: Robert Daley; Director: James Fargo; Screenplay: Jeremy Joe Kronsberg; Director of Photography: Rexford Metz (Deluxe); Editors: Ferris Webster, Joel Cox; Art Director: Elayne Ceder; Music Supervision: Snuff Garrett; Music: Steve Dorff; Cast: **Clint Eastwood** (Philo Beddoe), Sondra Locke (Lynn Halsey-Taylor), Geoffrey Lewis (Orville), Beverly D'Angelo (Echo), Ruth Gordon (Ma), Walter Barnes (Tank Murdock), George Chandler (Clerk at DMV), Roy Jenson (Woody), James McEachin (Herb), Bill McKinney (Dallas), William O'Connell (Elmo), John Quade (Cholla), Dan Vadis (Frank), Gregory Walcott (Putnam), Hank Worden (Trailer Court Manager); 114 minutes

### Escape From Alcatraz (1979)

Paramount/Malpaso; Producer/Director: Don Siegel; Screenplay: Richard Tuggle; Novel: J. Campbell Bruce; Director of Photography: Bruce Surtees

(Deluxe); Editor: Ferris Webster; Production Designer: Allen E. Smith; Music: Jerry Fielding; Cast: **Clint Eastwood** (Frank Morris), Patrick McGoohan (Warden), Roberts Blossom (Doc), Jack Thibeau (Clarence Anglin), Fred Ward (John Anglin), Paul Benjamin (English), Larry Hankin (Charley Butts), Bruce M. Fischer (Wolf), Frank Ronzio (Litmus), Candace Bowen (English's Daughter), Danny Glover (Inmate); 112 minutes

### *Any Which Way You Can* (1980)

Warner Bros./Malpaso (see note at end); Executive Producer: Robert Daley; Producer: Fritz Manes; Director: Buddy Van Horn; Screenplay: Stanford Sherman; Director of Photography: David Worth (Deluxe); Editors: Ferris Webster, Ron Spang; Production Design: William J. Creber; Music Supervision: Snuff Garrett; Music: Steve Dorff; **Eastwood** sings "Beers to You" with Ray Charles; Cast: **Clint Eastwood** (Philo Beddoe), Sondra Locke (Lynne Halsey-Taylor), Geoffrey Lewis (Orville Boggs), William Smith (Jack Wilson), Harry Guardino (James Beekman), Ruth Gordon (Ma Boggs), Michael Cavanaugh (Patrick Scarfe), Barry Corbin (Fat Zack), Roy Jenson (Moody), Bill McKinney (Dallas), William O'Connell (Elmo), John Quade (Cholla), Dan Vadis (Frank), Glen Campbell (Himself); 115 minutes

### *City Heat* (1984)

Warner Bros./Malpaso/Deliverance; Producer: Fritz Manes; Director: Richard Benjamin; Screenplay: Blake Edwards (as "Sam O. Brown"), Joseph C. Stinson; Director of Photography: Nick McLean (Technicolor); Editor: Jacqueline Cambas; Production Designer: Edward Carfagno; Music: Lennie Niehaus; **Eastwood** plays piano: "Montage Blues"; Cast: **Clint Eastwood** (Lieutenant Speer), Burt Reynolds (Mike Murphy), Jane Alexander (Addy), Madeline Kahn (Caroline Howley), Rip Torn (Primo Pitt), Irene Cara (Ginny Lee), Richard Roundtree (Dehl Swift), Tony Lo Bianco (Leon Coll), Nicholas Worth (Troy Roker), Robert Davi (Nino), Jude Farese (Dub Slack), John Hancock (Fat Freddie), Tab Thacker (Tuck), Gerald S. O'Loughlin (Counterman Louie); 94 minutes

### *The Dead Pool* (1988)

Warner Bros./Malpaso; Producer: David Valdes; Director: Buddy Van Horn; Screenplay: Steve Sharon; Director of Photography: Jack N. Green (Technicolor); Editor: Ron Spang; Production Designer: Edward Carfagno; Music: Lalo Schifrin; Cast: **Clint Eastwood** (Harry Callahan), Patricia Clarkson (Samantha Walker), Liam Neeson (Peter Swan), Evan C. Kim (Al Quan), David Hunt (Harlan Rook), Michael Currie (Captain Donnelly), Michael Goodwin (Lt. Ackermann), Darwin Gillett (Patrick Snow), Anthony Charnota (Lou Janero), Christopher Beale (D.A. Thomas McSherry), John Allen Vick (Lt. Ruskowski), Jeff Richmond (Freeway Reporter #1), Patrick Van Horn (Freeway Reporter #2), Sigrid Wurschmidt (Freeway Reporter #3), Jim Carrey (Johnny Squares); 91 minutes

### Pink Cadillac (1989)

Warner Bros./Malpaso; Executive Producer: Michael Gruskoff; Producer: David Valdes; Director: Buddy Van Horn; Screenplay: John Eskow; Director of Photography: Jack N. Green (Technicolor); Editor: Joel Cox; Production Designer: Edward Carfagno; Music: Steve Dorff; Cast: **Clint Eastwood** (Tommy Nowak), Bernadette Peters (Lou Ann McGuinn), Timothy Carhart (Roy), Michael Des Barres (Alex), John Dennis Johnston (Waycross), Jimmy F. Skaggs (Billy Dunston), Bill Moseley (Darrell), Tiffany Gail Robinson (McGuinn Baby), Angela Louise Robinson (McGuinn Baby), Geoffrey Lewis (Ricky Z.), William Hickey (Mr. Barton), Frances Fisher (Dinah), Jim Carrey (Post-Nuclear Elvis Lounge Act); 122 minutes

### In the Line of Fire (1993)

Castle Rock/Columbia; Executive Producers: Wolfgang Petersen, Gail Katz, David Valdes; Producer: Jeff Apple; Director: Wolfgang Petersen; Screenplay: Jeff Maguire; Director of Photography: John Bailey (Technicolor/Panavision); Editor: Anne V. Coates; Production Designer: Lilly Kilvert; Music: Ennio Morricone; Cast: **Clint Eastwood** (Frank Horrigan), John Malkovich (Mitch Leary), Rene Russo (Lilly Raines), Dylan McDermott (Al D'Andrea), Gary Cole (Bill Watts), Fred Dalton Thompson (Harry Sargent), John Mahoney (Sam Campagna), Jim Curley (President Traveller), Sally Hughes (First Lady), Clyde Kusatsu (Jack Okura), Steve Hytner (Tony Carducci), Tobin Bell (Mendoza), Patrika Darbo (Pam Magnus), Mary Van Arsdel (Sally), John Heard (Professor Riger); 126 minutes

Academy Awards Nominations: Actor in a Supporting Role, John Malkovich; Film Editing: Anne V. Coates; Writing (Screenplay Written Directly for the Screen), Jeff Maguire

## As Producer Only

### *Thelonious Monk: Straight No Chaser* (1988)

Warner Bros.; Executive Producer: **Clint Eastwood**; Producers: Charlotte Zwerin, Bruce Ricker; Director: Charlotte Zwerin; Director of Photography: Christian Blackwood; Narration: Samuel E. Wright; 89 minutes

### *The Stars Fell on Henrietta* (1995)

Warner Bros./Malpaso; Producers: **Clint Eastwood**, David Valdes; Director: James Keach; Screenplay: Philip Railsback; Director of Photography: Bruce Surtees (Technicolor/Panavision); Editor: Joel Cox; Production Designed By: Henry Bumstead; Music: David Benoit; Cast: Robert Duvall (Mr. Cox), Aidan Quinn (Don Day), Frances Fisher (Cora Day), Brian Dennehy (Big Dave), Lexi Randall (Beatrice Day), Kaytlyn Knowles (Pauline Day), Francesca Ruth Eastwood (Mary Day), Joe Stevens (Big Dave's Driver), Billy Bob Thornton (Roy); 110 minutes

Additionally, the following is "A Malpaso Production":

### *Ratboy* (1986)

Warner Bros./Malpaso; Producer: Fritz Manes; Director: Sondra Locke; Screenplay: Rob Thompson; Director of Photography: Bruce Surtees (Technicolor); Editor: Joel Cox; Production Design: Edward Carfagno; Music: Lennie Niehaus; Cast: Sondra Locke (Nikki Morrison), Robert Townsend (Manny), Christopher Hewett (Acting Coach), Larry Hankin (Jewell), Sydney Lassick (Dial-a-Prayer), S. L. Baird (Ratboy); 105 minutes

**Note:** The five Eastwood films released between 1980 and 1983 were issued without the Malpaso name but were filmed with the usual Malpaso personnel. Most filmographies include them as Malpaso productions.

# CLINT EASTWOOD

## INTERVIEWS

# No Tumbleweed Ties for Clint

REX REED/1971

HE WAS ON THE phone, talking about the matrix and the looping and all the other things directors talk about when they call the Coast. "The sound is 20 frames ahead of the music and the color processing is wrong on the work print." Hitchcock? Minnelli? Well, don't snicker. Would you believe Clint Eastwood?

He was in New York to publicize his new movie, *The Beguiled,* a Gothic Civil War horror film in which a group of predatory females feed him poison mushrooms because he steps on a little girl's turtle. But it was clear that his real interests lay in another film called *Play Misty for Me,* which marks his debut as a director.

"After 17 years of bouncing my head against the wall, hanging around sets, maybe influencing certain camera setups with my own opinions, watching actors go through all kinds of hell without any help and working with both good directors and bad ones, I'm at the point where I'm ready to make my own pictures. I stored away all the mistakes I made and saved up all the good things I learned and now I know enough to control my own projects and get what I want out of actors. So I directed this picture and I'm editing it myself and I think it's damn good.

"In my starving days, I knew a girl who went around knocking on doors trying to get a job as a writer while she worked as a secretary. She wrote a 60-page treatment about a small town disc jockey who meets a girl in a

Published in *Los Angeles Times,* 4 April 1971, Calendar, 50, 62. Reprinted by permission of the author.

saloon one night and even after he goes back to his real girl, this chick
turns psychotic, starts haunting him, murders his maid and turns his life
into a nightmare.

"It's got a lot of action and suspense and I used a small crew and a low
budget of only $800,000, but I think I got more than $800,000 on the
screen. At least I know that if it's a failure it's my own fault and not somebody else's. I've been in enough bombs that were somebody else's fault."

For an actor some people consider a cut-out from the old Hollywood
mold known as "cowboy star, Gary Cooper voice, 6-foot-4, suitable for
framing," the attitude seems startling. But when you talk to Clint Eastwood you begin to discover that his head and his heart are not tied to a
tumbleweed.

Until now, his career hasn't been taken very seriously by the judges and
juries who draw the lines between marketable movie stars and practitioners
of serious art. But at least he's honest about it. "Whatever success I've had
is a lot of instinct and a little luck," he says. "I just go by how I feel."

It's made him a whacking good living, women mob him everywhere, he
turns down 10 scripts a week and—honor of honors—there are Clint Eastwood imitators popping up like ragweed wherever you look. He grins a
boyish grin, throws his legs and arms over the sides of the cushy furniture
in his suite at the Regency Hotel, bites into a chicken sandwich, and phi-
losophizes.

"Hollywood is strange. Everyone is looking for a formula. One year it's
two guys on a motorcycle, the next year it's a girl dying of cancer and they
flood the market with imitations. For years I bummed around trying to get
a job and it was the same old story—my voice was too soft, my teeth
needed capping, I squinted too much, I was too tall—all that constant
tearing down of my ego was bound to turn me into either a better person
or a complete jerk.

"And I know that if I walked into a casting office right now and nobody
knew I was Clint Eastwood, I'd get the same old thing. My voice is still too
soft, my teeth still need capping, I still squint, and I've been compared to a
small redwood tree. But after the westerns I did in Spain I was suddenly
Clint Eastwood and now the other guys who are too tall and squint too
much are the ones cursing me! You go figure it out."

Actually, he was on his way before the Sergio Leone westerns. He had
loped into Hollywood to attend college on the GI Bill after two years at

Ft. Ord where he wafted through basic training teaching swimming. He had been a lumberjack in Oregon and had worked at a variety of odd jobs, from the steel mills to Boeing Aircraft.

At Los Angeles City College, he met a photographer who talked him into doing a screen test and he got a contract with Universal. "I was always the prison guard who brings the guy in to see the D.A. I got $75 a week for 40 weeks a year and I got kicked out after a year and a half, but by then I was determined to do something about a career. I got kicked around the unemployment offices a lot, but I finally got into TV and played a lot of motorcycle hoods and lab assistants, but all that time I never played anyone in a business suit.

"I was very close to quitting when *Rawhide* came along. I was visiting a friend at CBS and an executive saw me drinking coffee in the cafeteria and came over and asked me to test. It was a fluke. It lasted 7½ years. In the sixth year, I had exhausted everything I could do on a horse, so I took a hiatus and went to Spain to make *Fistful of Dollars*. I had nothing to lose. I had a job waiting in TV and I knew if it was a flop nobody would ever see it anyway."

Oh, but they did. *Fistful of Dollars, A Few Dollars More,* and *The Good, the Bad and the Ugly*—better known as "the paella trilogy"—became camp institutions. "They weren't movies you got acclaim for," says Eastwood with a straight face, "but they were harder to do than a lot of the better roles I've had lately. I look back on them as satire, which was difficult to do without lapsing over into slapstick, and I also learned from watching the Italians how to make only a few dollars look like 10 times that much on the screen."

The Italian westerns were remakes of Japanese samurai epics, made in Spain with Americans by an Italian director, but they were the bricks that formed the foundation of the box office phenomenon known as Clint Eastwood. For a Hollywood symbol, he had oddly enough never made a film there. Out of 12 films, 10 were made on location and the remaining two used only partial interiors on sound stages. Nor does he live the Hollywood life.

Shyly, he hides away on a cliff overlooking the San Fernando Valley when in Los Angeles or a cliff overlooking the sea in a small rustic house in Carmel with his wife Maggie and their son Kyle, 2½. "I've been married to the same chick for 17 years. I'd better check my pulse. She's lived through all the changes in me, and she hasn't thrown me out, so I think I'll hang around. I'm just now beginning to find out who I am and what I can do. I know I'll never be a Laurence Olivier.

"With my physical type and my legato personality, I'll never play certain parts. But I still can do things that have some quality. I have never studied acting. Life is a study, film-making in general is a study. There are two kinds of actors — one sits in a dressing room waiting for his call and the other gets out into the business and polishes his craft by absorbing everything. I don't know enough, I'll never learn everything I need to learn. When a guy thinks he's already learned it, he can only go backwards."

Clint Eastwood unhooks his treetrunk legs from around the dainty chair he's been sitting on and smiles that chuckwagon smile that has made him a star. "I thought Geraldine Page was out of my league, being a big star on the Broadway stage and all, but when we started *The Beguiled* she told me she was a big fan of mine on *Rawhide*. I've got no regrets, man, no regrets at all."

# Eastwood on Eastwood

## STUART M. KAMINSKY/1971

CLINT EASTWOOD MOVES QUICKLY. I had been at Universal
Studios, where Eastwood's Malpaso Production Company is headquartered,
for three weeks before I could catch up with him. A few nights before I
made my third try to catch him at his Universal bungalow, I had seen a
preview of *Play Misty for Me*, Eastwood's first attempt at directing.

I got through to Eastwood's producer and associate Bob Daley, who
called across to Eastwood and asked if he could squeeze me in before he
got in his Sting Ray and headed back to Carmel, where he lives. The interview was set for six-thirty that night.

Eastwood's name is not on Bungalow 64, which is about thirty yards
from his friend Siegel's bungalow. The outer office is covered with pictures
of Eastwood from his movies and a large Eastwood poster showing him in
a Sergio Leone picture. There is also a picture of Don Siegel in his role as a
bartender in *Misty*.

Eastwood, wearing a blue pullover T-shirt, greeted me by name, and we
went into his office. He is a nonslouching six-foot-four, as soft-spoken in
life as in his movie roles.

His office is large—comfortable executive conference table at one end,
sofa against one wall, large desk across the carpeted room. On the wall
above the sofa was a huge poster in Italian for *Where Eagles Dare*. Another

Published as chapter 7 in Stuart M. Kaminsky, *Clint Eastwood* (New York: New American
Library, 1974), 80–100. Copyright © 1974 by Stuart M. Kaminsky. First published by New
American Library. All rights reserved. Reprinted by permission of the author.

wall contained a slashed portrait of Eastwood, which figures in the plot of *Misty*.

Popular disc jockey Dave Garver (Eastwood) finds himself at loose ends when his girl friend, Tobie Williams (Donna Mills), unexpectedly leaves town. One night, while drinking at his favorite bar, Eastwood meets Evelyn Draper (Jessica Walter), an attractive brunette who suggests a visit to her apartment and then informs him that she is the girl who regularly phones his radio station to request that he play the song "Misty." By morning, however, it becomes apparent to Eastwood that what he thought was a one-night stand is really a romantic obsession on Evelyn's part; openly pursuing him, she begins dropping in at his home uninvited, at one point disrupting him while he and his co-worker Al Monte are preparing a presentation for station owner Madge Brenner. Further, when Tobie returns and Eastwood resumes their relationship, Evelyn becomes uncontrollably jealous, spying on them during their romantic walks and even cutting her wrists in a desperate effort to win Eastwood's attention and concern. After entrusting Evelyn to the care of Frank Dewan, a doctor friend, Eastwood leaves to discuss a job offer with Madge; but Evelyn interrupts their luncheon and so hysterically insults the older woman that the deal is permanently squelched. Arriving back home, Eastwood finds his cleaning woman, Birdie, almost slashed to death with a razor, his apartment wrecked, and a dazed Evelyn being questioned by Police Sergeant McCallum. With Evelyn removed to a sanitarium, Eastwood sees Tobie again and learns that she has taken a new roommate named Annabelle. But before long, Evelyn phones Dave at the station to tell him that she is cured and on her way to Hawaii — and would he please play "Misty" for her? Then late that night, awakened by the sound of "Misty" coming from his stereo, Eastwood finds Evelyn standing at the foot of his bed. Suddenly lunging, she makes an unsuccessful knife attack and then runs off. A few days later, Eastwood recalls that Evelyn once quoted two lines from Poe's "Annabelle Lee" to him over the phone; remembering that Tobie's new roommate is named Annabelle, Eastwood calls McCallum and asks him to rush to Tobie's apartment. When Eastwood gets there, McCallum is lying dead with a pair of scissors in his chest, Tobie is bound and gagged on the bed, and the deranged Evelyn is once more poised with a knife. In staving off her violent attack, Eastwood hurls Evelyn across the terrace, and stumbling backward, she falls off the edge, plummeting to her death on the jagged rocks below. As

Eastwood unties Tobie and helps her from the apartment, "Misty" once more begins to play on the radio.

With darkness coming over the San Fernando mountains beyond the bungalow, the actor and, now, director sat and talked for a few hours over a couple of beers.

KAMINSKY: *You've done four pictures with Don Siegel as your director. He appears as an actor, the only time he has done so, in the first movie you directed,* Play Misty for Me. *The only other thing you have directed is a short, the subject of which was Don Siegel. What is there about the man that you obviously like so much?*

EASTWOOD: It's a mutual-admiration thing. He likes a lot of my ideas, and I like his. I like his attack on directing. He's very straightforward. His films always have energy. He has that energy as a person. He moves briskly and tries to get right to the point in directing. I've been involved with some directors who are wishy-washy, don't know what they want. Don never starts rolling until he has an attack. We change a lot of things in the middle, but even the changes are positive, forward. I think that's what I like: his forward momentum is always there. He never gets bogged down, even in disaster. I think he's fantastic. We have worked a lot together, and probably will in the future. I feel he is an enormously talented guy who has been deprived of the notoriety he probably should have had much earlier because Hollywood was going through a stage where the awards went to the big pictures and the guys who knew how to spend a lot of money. As a result, guys who got a lot of pictures with a lot of effort and a little money weren't glorified. So Don had to wait many years until he could get to do films with fairly good budgets. He's the kind of director there's not enough of. If things don't, go as planned, he doesn't sit down and cry and consider everything lost, as some directors do.

KAMINSKY: *How does working with Siegel compare to working with Sergio Leone?*

EASTWOOD: Don likes to hear ideas. He has an ego like everyone else, but if a janitor comes up with something, he won't turn it down. He'll take from anybody. He kind of breeds an atmosphere of participation. Sergio Leone, whom I respect very much, would never give me any credit for the style of a film I'd been in with him. Don would and does. This is true even though Sergio and I would hash out ideas together, toss them back and forth. I want to make it clear that I like Sergio, liked working with him. Filmmaking is ensemble work. A director who can have a clear focus in a film, a clear idea of the style he's moving toward, and still draw creative things out of everybody working with him has an atmosphere which will make superior movies in the long run. The director is still the leading force, the captain.

KAMINSKY: *Did your outlook change when you became a director? Do you appreciate the problems of a director more now, after* Misty?
EASTWOOD: No, I knew what I was getting into. I've been in front of a camera for a lot of hours in the last eighteen years. In TV, I saw so much that I *wouldn't* do as a director. I felt prepared.

KAMINSKY: *In* Misty, *I know the first scene you did was the one in which Don Siegel had his acting debut. Did you do that purposely to put him on a spot?*
EASTWOOD: Actually, it just worked out that way. I tell everybody I did it that way because it was my first day on the set, and I wanted somebody to be more nervous than I was, but actually I just started with that sequence because I wanted to start with something moderate, not too rough. We had three days scheduled for it, since it was Don's first acting job, but we did it in a little over a day. He was very nervous during the first few takes, but by the second morning, he was an old pro.

KAMINSKY: *When you work as a director, do you feel you're working the way he does, or some other director, or what?*
EASTWOOD: No, I work my own way, although I've certainly been influenced by the directors I've worked with over the years. Siegel has had influence on my directing, but so has Sergio, and so has Ted Post [*Hang 'em High*]. And so have other guys from the television years, as well as directors whose work I've seen though I've never met them.

KAMINSKY: *What other directors do you admire?*
EASTWOOD: Well, I used to love Hitchcock, some of that earlier stuff.

KAMINSKY: *Why did you decide to do* The Beguiled, *which was so different from everything you'd done earlier?*

EASTWOOD: The studio owned the property, and I was intrigued by it. It's a wild story. I told Don about it and told him I thought it was the kind of thing that could go right to the roof—or right down the toilet. He eventually read it and liked it, and then I had doubts. He was kind of the leading force in getting me to do it, as it wound up. He said: You can always be in a Western or adventure, but you may never get a chance to do this type film again. The studio wanted to do it, so we did it.

KAMINSKY: *Did you think you were taking a chance because it was different from what you had been doing?*
EASTWOOD: Only in the sense that it wasn't a typical commercial film, but we thought it could be a very good film, and that was important.

KAMINSKY: *How would you compare it with the other ones you've done?*
EASTWOOD: I think it was a very well-executed film, the best-directed film Don's ever done, a very exciting film. Whether it's appealing to large masses or not, I don't know.

KAMINSKY: *How did you come to do* Two Mules for Sister Sara*?*
EASTWOOD: I had read the script, which was given to me by Elizabeth Taylor when I was doing *Where Eagles Dare* with her husband. We wanted to do it together, and the studio approved of the combination, but she was going through some deal where she didn't want to work unless it coincided with Richard's working, so we had it set up to do in Mexico while Richard was working there on something else, but then there were some other problems, and I think the studio kind of leaned toward Shirley MacLaine, because they had such high hopes for *Sweet Charity* at that time. It required some writing, and the casting of Shirley stretched the imagination a bit. It would have been ideal for Sophia Loren.

KAMINSKY: *Would you comment on the different styles of Leone and Siegel?*
EASTWOOD: Leone is a very good film editor, and has a good way of making things important. When you build up to an action scene, it's pow! exciting, and then it's back to being very leisurely. Don is a little more impatient. American people are used to shorter films. Don is more direct, though *The Beguiled* was a little more leisurely. It was very smooth; everything sort of folded over nicely.

KAMINSKY: *Do you feel that about particular sequences or the whole film?*
EASTWOOD: The whole film, because it was different. Don usually does those detective-type films. *Dirty Harry* will need Don's kind of energy; it will be very important to that film. I don't think it will be the most exciting I've ever been in, but I do have good feelings about it.

KAMINSKY: Dirty Harry *has so little dialogue.*
EASTWOOD: It's a very physical-moving film. I'm anxious to see the first cut. Don usually makes the first cut and then we run it together and sit and play around with it, and then after he's picked any ideas he has off me, we kick it around, try it and see how it looks, and then tell the studio that's it.

KAMINSKY: *Let's talk about* Play Misty for Me *now. First, why did you stick with the particular song "Misty," since you had so much trouble getting it?*
EASTWOOD: The problem with a new song would have been that you had to play it a lot in the film, and the way the script was designed, you couldn't play the song a lot. I couldn't use it as an underscore. The script was designed by Bob Daley and myself to have most of the music from a source. Now, I needed a song that was not so old that the present generation would say: Gee, I never heard of that. It had to be an old-new song, something that everyone from eighteen on would recognize. The studio wanted me to use "Strangers in the Night," which they own, but it's not a classic, though it was a hit, and there's that dooby-dooby-do at the end. I just thought it wouldn't work. Also, it had already been used once in a movie, and I just didn't like the title "Strangers in the Night" for the movie. It was a square hit song, you know.

KAMINSKY: *Your relationship in the movie with the black d.j. was interesting. At one point, I thought you were going to take him into your confidence and get him to help you with your problem with the girl. The point when I realized this wouldn't happen was when you were sitting at the turntable talking to him while he was getting high in the dark, unseen—was that intentional?*
EASTWOOD: No, though maybe I had underlying thoughts of it that way. I just thought that visually and emotionally it made more sense that the guy is contemplating out loud, he's got somebody to talk to. It was just so much better to take the other d.j. off than to cut back and forth. Dave,

the character I play, just talks freely, thinks out loud. How do you do that when you're looking at somebody? The other guy is there and listening, but he won't help. Of course, he doesn't realize how serious the problem is, since Dave only takes him into his confidence to a certain degree. If he had taken him into his confidence more and been offered some profound advice, I would have brought the other guy into the scene more. Remember, Dave never tells the other guy any of the jazz about the suicide and homicide attempts.

KAMINSKY:  *The only comment the friend makes as he leaves is a joke, a sexual innuendo: "He who lives by the sword, dies by the sword." You do pretty nearly die by the sword [or a knife, technically] in* Misty.
EASTWOOD:  Well, I wrote that line. I did it years ago. There was this friend of mine who was hung up over a chick and trying to get her an abortion, and he was asking me for advice on the telephone. I told him what I thought he should do, and then he said: He who lives by the sword shall die by the sword. And I incorporated it into the films.

KAMINSKY:  *How did you come by that game business you did with Don Siegel in the bar scene?*
EASTWOOD:  It was made up by the writer, Dean Riesner. The moves were just improvised. I had brought in Dean Riesner, incidentally, to work with my role, which was a little soft in an earlier version. The character was apologizing to his girl for things, and he didn't pick up the other girl in the saloon. She picked him up. I just didn't think it was natural. I thought the problems with his girl friend needed some motivation, perhaps the fact that he gets hung up with a fan now and then—you know, d.j.'s in small towns are somewhat big fish in a small pond, and they do get a lot of activity. I thought it would be better if he thinks he's making a deal with the girl in the bar. Anyway, Riesner made up the game. It was certainly an interesting thing. The game does not exist in reality: it was just something Dave and the bartender made up to intrigue women to come over and watch.

KAMINSKY:  *How did you come to choose Jessica Walter as the psychopath?*
EASTWOOD:  Over the studio's dead body. No, I was looking at film on different gals, and I was looking at this film *The Group*, a movie made in

1965, which happened to have in it about three girls who were being pushed by their agents for *Misty*. One was Jessica Walter. She was very good in that film. She plays a frigid gal who talks about sex but is really turned off—and she's with this German guy who's trying to put the make on her and she starts this turn-off, and he just hauls off and slaps the shit out of her. And the look on her face, the transition she makes, the story on her face made me want to get her. I talked to the studio and they named a couple of people who were more well-known, people they could get deals on because business was slow, and I said: I don't want deals, I just want someone who is right for the part. Jessica has certain characteristics as an actress that just made me have a hunch that she would be right. I thought she was very good in *Misty*.

KAMINSKY: *What was Dave's motivation for going in the door at the end after he sees the dead cop?*
EASTWOOD: Well, I think the motivation is justified because the girl-friend is in there, and he thinks: Geez, if this is what happened to the cop, what has happened to this chick?

KAMINSKY: *When the maid is slashed up by the psychotic girl, I expected her to die. Why did you have her live?*
EASTWOOD: Well, if she [Jessica Walter] had killed someone, it would have been just too much that she was released. We'd have to make up some other reason for her getting on the loose again, and we just preferred release to, say, escape. Things like that do happen: there was a case in Palo Alto where a guy went up to a door and just stabbed the girl who answered. She lived, he was put away for treatment for about six months, then released, and the girl was not told. One day he accidentally ran into her at a supermarket, and she really freaked out.

KAMINSKY: *It's interesting that the psychotic girl has no background.*
EASTWOOD: I was advised by lots of people to put in background, but you know, we in the audience meet her the same time the protagonist meets her, and we see her unfold as he does. I didn't see any reason for a scene in which we find out that the mother treated her wrong, the father ran off, etc. When a person finds out that someone is screwed up, knifing

maids and things, unless he's very interested in psychiatry he's not interested in why she's screwed up; he just wants to get out. I think that
audiences are smarter than a lot of producers think they are, and I think
the audience will draw with you.

KAMINSKY:  *Did you want to feel that the protagonist was somehow being*
*paid back for his selfish sexual behavior in the past by being stuck with her?*
EASTWOOD:  No, I don't think he's being chastised by divine scrutiny.
It's just that he's been in some situations, and just when he tries to
straighten his life, this comes as a sort of ironic thing. He probably could
have handled the situation better if this other girl hadn't come back just at
that time. The problems for him are complicated by the one showing up
all the time when he wants to be with the other girl.

KAMINSKY:  *Did you purposely hold off on your physical confrontations with*
*Jessica Walter? The only physically violent thing you do is hit her once, near the*
*end, and of course it works, because the audience is so worked up against her too.*
EASTWOOD:  At the sneak preview, guys in the audience were saying:
"Hit her, hit her." They were also with it throughout, saying things like:
"Don't go in that door." That's very satisfying, but, yes, to answer the
question, that's just the final thing. Here she is, she's killed a cop and is
working him over—I mean, this is it.
   *Play Misty for Me* was taken from a true story. The suicide attempt, the
cutting up of the clothes, the attempt on Dave's life during the night all
were taken from actual incidents (not the knifing of the maid, though, or
the killing of the cop or the becoming roommates with the girl). The roommate part was stimulated by the fact that the woman in the real series of
incidents would dress up, put on wigs, and go into saloons where the guy
was drinking and keep an eye on him and see if he was trying to pick up
someone.

KAMINSKY:  *Was this a story you knew or read or what?*
EASTWOOD:  Jo Heims, who wrote the story, worked it up, fictionalizing
it. What appealed to me about the script is that there are incidents like
this in everyone's life, to some degree, this whole thing of interpretation
of commitment, or misinterpretation of commitment. A girl may say: Sure,

I feel the same way; I don't want any part of marriage. But then next week, slowly, there's that kind of throwing a blanket over a person.

KAMINSKY: *The constriction comes through very well.*
EASTWOOD: It's a very important part of the film, because that's the thing that makes it personal to the audience as opposed to just a horror movie. If you've had any kind of experience in your life where somebody has just tried to move in too fast, or has just held on too hard; I think everybody has had something like that. It's something that could happen.

KAMINSKY: *Yes, a psychological distortion of something we all feel.*
EASTWOOD: A lot of times, with stories about psychotic people, there's no identification factor. In a picture like *Psycho*, the real highlights of the film are strictly the shock and the suspense. It was of course fabulous to have that scene where she sees the skeleton in the basement, but then they almost destroyed everything later with all that unnecessary exposition. Of course, that was eleven years ago, and they used more exposition then.

KAMINSKY: *Obviously your picture will be compared to* Psycho, *and you yourself have just made one comparison. Were you thinking of comparisons when you made the film?*
EASTWOOD: No, I certainly wasn't trying to duplicate *Psycho* in any way. I never saw it that way myself, other than the attacks. Those attacks could be sprung upon the audience with the same kind of suspense and energy as Hitchcock used, I thought, but other than that, I saw it as a story of constriction, the blanket thrown over one, the things we talked about before, the bound-in feeling, the frustration of trying to solve it and not being able to, of having to sit down and calm the person you want to escape from.

No exposition after that is necessary. I heard one person say that he thought the explanation about Tony Perkins by the psychiatrist at the end of *Psycho* was because they didn't want to make it seem like the lead had any homosexual motivation. Nowadays you wouldn't care.

KAMINSKY: *The cutting in and out of the seascape and cliffs, which sort of work into the end—were they part of the original conception?*

EASTWOOD: Well, L.A. has a hundred disc jockeys and stations. So, in the first place, I know that area where we shot. I live up there, and I knew a disc jockey up there. Disc jockeys know everybody in a small town. They're big stars in their areas. So here's a guy who is quite successful working for a small station in a small town, and he has ambitions to do television and better things, and this is all destroyed because of this relationship, too.

KAMINSKY: *What about the seascapes, specifically? In editing, you keep coming back to sea, birds, and cliffs.*
EASTWOOD: It's just because the sea is so much a part of the whole thing, not just because it was the place of the conclusion of her life [Jessica Walter].

KAMINSKY: *The movie contains two breaks. First, when Jessica Walter goes to the hospital, there is that love sequence with the other girl, followed by the jazz-festival sequence. Both, I assume, are used to show passage of time, yet both go on longer than would be necessary just to show passage of time. Was it that you liked the sequences, or were you trying to make us forget about the mentally disturbed girl, or what?*
EASTWOOD: A little of both. The real motive was temporarily to take us away from Evelyn [Jessica Walter]. People were also suggesting that the part of the other girl, Tobie, needed strengthening and there should be some sort of love scene. Well, I hated the idea of a dialogue sort of love scene, bullshit dialogue, and I was trying to look for a visual way to show life was really falling into place for these two people. I heard this song, "The First Time," going to work one day, on this FM station, and I said: God, that just tells the whole story, so I went out and bought the song, not just the song but the whole record and just took the master tape and played it, and I edited the scene to that, because I thought it told the whole story. There was nothing else around, no human life, aircraft, automobiles, etc. in that sequence. It showed that things were really working well for them. That was the only non-source music I used. Then we went to the jazz festival and back into his profession with a little bit of music, music which was more into the rhythm of the film, and then I figured: boom, I could go back to the station and the phone call. Bingo, here's this little fairy tale with a wrench stuck in the wheels.

KAMINSKY: *There's one shot in there which is one of the most beautiful I've ever seen, and that is the orange-ish sea with the sun going down. But as far as plot in those two sequences, all we know is that Dave's girl has a new roommate.*
EASTWOOD: Well, it's just a thing that grates on the guy. It was a very tough thing to set up that roommate thing without setting up so much that you tip it off. If you talk too much about it, you tip it off. So there has to be a first discussion of it, and then you meet one of them, and then there is the jazz festival, which is the last time roommates are mentioned. I had to do that in a very brief way. I don't doubt that a good percentage of the audience did guess what would happen.

KAMINSKY: *I think the normal reaction is that when Tobie calls to the room-mate and says, "Annabelle," what you expect is nobody to come out because Evelyn has killed Annabelle, but this isn't what happens. Evelyn walks out and is accepted as Annabelle.*
EASTWOOD: Yes, that's when everybody starts lighting up their cigarettes.

KAMINSKY: *I came into the movie cold, not knowing what it was about. Do you think that publicity and word of mouth will hurt the picture, and did you think of this in making the movie? The critics of course will screw things up too by giving away the plot and direction.*
EASTWOOD: Yes, I have to hope that there's just enough entertainment value there regardless. If it is effective, even if they know what is going to happen, people will stay with it.

KAMINSKY: Psycho *is an example of this: everybody knows what will happen, and it's exciting anyway.*
EASTWOOD: Yes, the first thing everyone talks about is the shower sequence.

KAMINSKY: *I was watching your knifing scenes closely, and you actually show a couple of slashes, unlike* Psycho, *though the feeling of revulsion and pain is similar.*
EASTWOOD: Well, I just preferred to make it a little more...maybe I'm not as subtle as Hitchcock is.

KAMINSKY: *How long did it take you to make the film?*

EASTWOOD: We shot it in four and a half weeks. We had a five-week schedule. We were two and a half days under schedule.

KAMINSKY: *Would you say it was expensive or inexpensive?*

EASTWOOD: Inexpensive. We shot it completely away from the studio, one-hundred percent natural locations. We just rented houses, moved in, and shot. We rented a house for Dave, for example, and decorated it some, because there was stuff that had to be carved up and broken. Bob Daley is a very sharp guy on costs, and he didn't let too many false charges stack up. The studio would have liked it to have been even more expensive, but we were trying to prove something: that we could make something of entertainment value without exorbitant fees tacked on. I did have complete freedom on the picture, so if it doesn't work, it's my fault, and that's fine. I was given a chance to fail or do it right.

KAMINSKY: *Do you do what Don tries: go for a usable take the first time?*

EASTWOOD: Well, I do rehearse. I use a different technique than Don, a video-West technique. We used Panavision equipment, which goes through the same lens as the camera, and I can go back and look at the scene afterwards. Jerry Lewis uses a similar method, a TV camera which goes parallel with the movie camera. My method is superior in that even the focus is the same, so even if the focus operator misses the shot, you can see it. It's black and white, but you can see how the scene will be set up. It's terrific on zoom shots.

KAMINSKY: *I also noticed that you use a lot of the people that Don Siegel uses, for example Carl Pingitore was your editor, Dean Riesner your writer, Bruce Surtees your cameraman.*

EASTWOOD: Well, as far as Bruce goes, I'd worked with him three times as an operator, and Don and I promoted him for *The Beguiled*, which he did, but even before he did *The Beguiled*, Bruce was set for *Misty*: we had talked about it and he'd read the story.

KAMINSKY: *You directed several sequences of* Dirty Harry. *Was that your first real experience of directing?*

EASTWOOD: No, I had directed *Misty* first and also a short subject on Don Siegel. Actually, I can't take as much credit for directing the latter. The editor/writer was more or less the brains behind the thing. I thought it was pretty good. We slapped it together in about a day. Had to use still pictures and everything.

The reviews of *Play Misty for Me* were among the best Eastwood had received as an actor, and his debut as a director was generally admired, though there were strong dissenters.

Andrew Sarris in *The Village Voice* called the film "a surprisingly auspicious directorial debut for Clint Eastwood . . . one of the most effectively scary movies of this or any year."

Joseph Gelmis said in *Newsday*: "Eastwood's first crack at directing is remarkably effective. . . . Throughout, Eastwood resists overreaching [and] keeps his cool very nicely on both sides of the camera."

Most critics did complain about the idyllic sequence in which Eastwood and Miss Mills roamed about to the music of "The First Time Ever I Saw Your Face." Ironically, the song, which was several years old at the time, became a top hit of 1971 and 1972 after *Play Misty for Me* reintroduced it.

# Clint Eastwood

## PATRICK MCGILLIGAN/April 1976

THE MALPASO COMPANY IS no longer at Universal City—some chagrin over miserable promotion there. Instead it is located in a Spanish style bungalow on the Warner Bros. lot. There is nothing like its serenity in all of madly urgent Hollywood, with its ascending leafy-green plants and muted crossworks of brown timber, and a kitchen with water cooler and strewn-about books on Indian folklore. Relaxed, friendly, almost mellow, as different as Southern California is from Northern California, Malpaso takes on the qualities of its number one star and executive, Clint Eastwood, who gravitates between the two distant worlds. He commutes. Usually—most happily, one presumes—he is with his family several hundred miles north in Carmel—far away from Hollywood. Today, on a late Friday afternoon, he is working on post-production for *The Outlaw Josey Wales,* his latest picture, a western he also directs. He agrees to an interview. He is dressed in a white T-shirt and blue jeans—brown, sinewy, rangy and handsome. The obligatory press agent is dismissed (a rarity) and Eastwood sprawls into an easy chair in his inner office decorated with posters of Coogan, Dirty Harry, the Man with No Name, etc. A secretary enters, pours herbal tea, exits. Sunlight arrows into the room through tiny shutter apertures, making

Published in *Focus on Film,* no. 25 (Summer–Fall 1976): 12–20. Reprinted by permission of the author.

funny kaleidoscopic patterns on the darkened ceiling. Eastwood
says that he does not like to talk. But in a surprisingly soft and
composed voice, coming from across the room, he effortlessly
talks the afternoon away. . . .

*Can you tell me a little bit about* The Outlaw Josey Wales?
This film I just finished is a little like *The Good, the Bad and the Ugly,*
although it's not satiric. It's a saga. It's about the character I play, whereas
in *The Good, the Bad and the Ugly* the only character you got to know—
somewhat—is the Eli Wallach character. In other words, Josey Wales is a
hero, and you see how he gets to where he is—rather than just having a
mysterious hero appear on the plains and become involved with other
people's plights.

*Are you reacting against the mysterious hero?*
No, it was just written that way. I'm not sure that this wasn't written
under unique circumstances. This was written by a guy who had never
written a book before, a half-Cherokee Indian with no formal education
including grammar school. He's a terribly self-taught person who became
famous as an Indian poet and teller of stories. Somebody talked him into
writing one down. So he wrote this western, and it was published down in
Arkansas by a publishing company called Whippoorwill Publishing. They
put out about seventy-five copies—that's all—hard cover.

He sent it to me unsolicited. Sometimes you don't like to take unsolicited scripts without having them registered with the Guild or an agent,
because of possible plagiarism. Anyway, this was sent to me. It sat on my
desk with several other things. It was called "The Rebel Outlaw: Josey
Wales." The jacket on it was not too interesting but there was a letter attached to it. My associate, Bob Daley, read the letter one night after I left
the office. The letter was such a reaching-out kind of thing—it had such a
nice feeling about it—that he figured, "Well, I've got to give this at least a
twenty page read and see if it's going anywhere." So he sat down to read it
and ended up reading through dinner and reading through the night. He
called me the next morning and said, "God, this has so much *soul* to it
that it's really one of the nicest things I've read." I was up in Monterey at
the time—at Carmel. So I said, "Get it up to me right away, I'll read it." I
read it and felt the same way about it. We called down there where he was

living at that time—then in Arkansas, now he lives in Texas—and bought
the screen rights.

*What is his name?*
Forrest Carter.

*Is he an older man?*
About 46. After we bought the screen rights and began to make the picture,
Delacorte brought it out as a paperback and they changed the name to
"Gone to Texas."

*I like "Rebel Outlaw."*
I didn't like "Gone to Texas" [as a title] because it puts it into a specific
region. "Rebel Outlaw" I didn't like because there are so many AIP pictures
about motorcycle gangs.

*Your westerns always seem to be more allegorical, more mythic in a sense, rather
than specific to a region or history.*
I'm attracted to that sort of thing, although I don't think this one is—as
much. This one is more of a saga, rather than *High Plains Drifter* where the
hero drifts in, you don't know anything about him and you don't know
where he comes from. In this one, you pick him up prior to the Civil War
on the Kansas-Missouri border, when the people of Kansas were talking
about going to the North and the people of Missouri were talking about
going South. He becomes an outlaw because of the war; it shows what the
war has done to him.

*Are you tending more towards directing nowadays?*
I have been for the last few years, but I've started to pull back a little bit. I
ended up doing this one because of various circumstances.[1] I like the story
very much too. It just depends. I don't intend to direct every picture I make.
In fact, I'd like to lay off a bit, directing. It's a terribly mind-fatiguing job
to be both actor and director. Just being a director is a very consuming
job—the pre-production and post-production especially. It really isn't the

---

1. Philip Kaufman began the direction but left, apparently after quarrels with Eastwood
over his handling. —Ed.

eight or nine weeks it takes to shoot the film that is the problem—it's all the time afterwards. If you direct films, you really can't act in too many films.

*You'd rather act?*
There's no way you can set a plan; scripts come and go, ideas change and you see one you'd like to direct and another you'd like to act in. Right now, my feeling is I'd like to hold back for a year or two on directing, and then—unless I find something along the way I want to do—eventually pull out of acting and just direct. If I was doing a part that was more of a departure, a larger challenge, maybe I would prefer not to direct. But, for instance, to do a film like *High Plains Drifter* wasn't that difficult—because I had been familiar with that character for a long time. There was no problem.

*When did you first decide you wanted to direct?*
Back when I did *Rawhide*. I went to Eric Fleming [co-star of the series] and said, "Eric, would you be adverse if I directed an episode? I would like to ask the producer to direct an episode." I'll tell you what started it...

When I was up on location one time, we were shooting some vast cattle scenes—about two thousand head of cattle. We were doing some really exciting stampede stuff. I was riding along in the herd, there was dust rising up, and it was pretty wild really. But the shots were being taken from outside the herd, looking in, and you didn't see too much. I thought, we should get right in the middle of this damn stampede. I said to the director and producer, "I'd like to take an arriflex [camera], run it on my horse and go right in the middle of this damn thing, even dismount, whatever—but get in there and really get some great shots, because there are some beautiful shots in there that we are missing." Well, they double-talked me. They said, "You can't get in there because of union rules"—which isn't true at all, because if you're doing a shot the normal camera operator can't do, if he's not a horseman, then there's no reason in the world why you can't do it— in fact, I've done it a lot of times and there is no union rule against it. But they kind of double-talked it away. I could see they didn't want to upset a nice standard way of movie-making.

Finally, later on, I asked Eric Fleming, "Would you be adverse to my directing?" He said, "Not at all, I'd be for it." So I went to the producer and he said great. Evidently he didn't say great behind my back; but he said great at the time. He said, "I'll tell you what, why don't you direct some trailers for us—coming attractions for next season's shows?" I said, "Terrific. I'll do it for nothing and then I'll do an episode." And I did the trailers. But they reneged on the episode because, at that time, several of their name actors on other television shows were directing episodes, not too success-fully. So about the time I was getting set to do it, CBS said no more series actors could direct their own shows. So I called it a day.

Then I went over to work with Sergio Leone. He didn't speak any English, I didn't speak any Italian. So my agreement with the producer of the show was that I could rewrite the story. The stories were all the same, but the dialogue was terrible because it was interpreted by an Italian into English. I said, "You've got to let me rewrite some of this stuff." They said, "Fine." So I got more actively involved in the production over there. Leone had only done one movie before and we got along terrifically. I started getting interested—because he was a younger man than some of the guys I'd been working with, and a little more imaginative. And working on the European scene sort of inspired me to get back into directing.

*A lot of established Hollywood directors were working in television in the early Sixties. Do you remember observing any particular director or directors?*
There were a lot of people who had made very nice films—like Tay Garnett (who made *The Postman Always Rings Twice*), Laslo Benedek—guys from another era who had done some nice films along the way. After seven-and-a-half years—different people every week—200-some odd episodes—you get to see a lot of people. You get a lot of ideas about what to do and about what not to do, because you come across a lot of turkeys—at least, in my opinion—guys that didn't know as much. You end up seeing how they paint themselves into corners.

*Is Leone an extremely classical director? Does he plan every shot with enormous care?*
Leone isn't the most planned guy; he's very flexible. He's not super-planned like, say, Vittorio de Sica. He [de Sica] and Siegel are the two most planned-out guys I've ever heard of. They're very flexible guys, but they're extremely well organised. Leone isn't that organised but he has a very good concept of what he wants. He's very good with compositions; he has a nice eye. He's very good with humour, a very funny guy—his humour is very sar-

donic. He's not very good at directing actors, he's only as good as his actors are—but most directors aren't very good at directing actors. The most a director can usually do with actors is to set up a nice atmosphere in which to work.

*Did he work with you in terms of your acting?*
No. We couldn't even communicate or speak the same language.

*Do you communicate today?*
Today, I speak Italian in the present tense and he speaks English in the present tense.

*It's amazing to think of* A Fistful of Dollars *or* The Good, the Bad and the Ugly *being put together by people who don't even speak the same language.*
The first picture was a German-Spanish-Italian co-production. The German co-producers were down there and I could speak with them because they could all speak English. I didn't speak any Spanish. I had never taken any languages.

*Was the entire mythic quality of the "dollar" westerns written into the original script,* A Fistful of Dollars?
Yes, it was fairly written into the script. I brought all the wardrobe and everything from here, and I had ideas about the character. The character talked a lot more in the script; I took a lot of his dialogue out. My point of view was, the more the leading character talked, the less mystique he had, and the more dissipated the strength of the film. There were many more expository-type scenes written that we took out.

*That's the character's real strength—you just wait for him to do or say something, anything.*
You are mystified by him. It was played approximately the same way in *Yojimbo,* which it was stolen from or taken from.

*Were you conscious of that at the time?*
There was never any doubt. When we got over there, they told me it was a re-make of *Yojimbo.* I said fine. When I first saw *Yojimbo,* I thought, geez,

this would make a great western, only nobody would ever have the nerve to make it with this style. And then when the script came through several years later, I thought this might be an interesting project. A European might not be afraid of it — like Leone — where an American would be afraid of approaching a western such as *Fistful of Dollars* with that kind of style.

For instance, there were rules in Hollywood years ago, unspoken rules, that you never tied-up shots of a person being shot. In other words, you never shot a tie-up shot of a man shooting a gun and another person getting hit. It's a Hays Office rule from years ago, a censorship deal. You'd cut to the guy shooting, and then cut to a guy failing. That was alright — the same thing — the public isn't counting the cut. But you could never do a tie-up. We did because Sergio didn't know all that. He wasn't bothered by that. Neither was I. I knew about it but I couldn't care less. The whole object of doing a film with a European director was to put a new shade of light on it.

*Even before* Rawhide, *were you attracted to the western?*
I always liked them, even as a kid, and that's the only way I ever judge a film.

*Are you aware of qualities about the western that attracted you, and that you can articulate?*
It's a tough question. I don't know whether I could answer it, although the western is one of my favourite genres. I don't know whether I can intellectually answer it, because I don't try to approach things on that sort of vein. I try to approach film emotionally, how it moves me. But particularly, in retrospect, I think there's a certain escapism, like to a less-complicated era, a more do-it-yourself era, so to speak. And the excitement of the movement lends itself . . .

*Did you, for example, like John Wayne when you were young?*
I liked him as a youth, depending on the film, but I was never a fan of any one particular actor outside of James Cagney.

*That surprises me.*
I've only met him once.

*Robert Redford told me the same thing: the only actor he admires is James Cagney.*
I love him. I love his early films, I always try to watch them on television.

*That's funny. In a sense, he's the opposite kind of actor from you — he's convulsive and you're so restrained.*
He isn't at all like me. When I first started out as an actor, all the secretaries used to call me Coop, because they thought I resembled Gary Cooper, kind of a backward kid — quite a few years ago.

But Cagney... I always liked Cagney's style and energy. He was fearless. Most of those guys were, though: they were fearless. Going back to the most famous thing, sticking grapefruits in people's faces, they weren't afraid to do things that were outrageous. A lot of actors get wrapped up in images.

*Do you have any sense of working in the same tradition as people like Gary Cooper and John Wayne?*
I've approached things totally differently, and I think I come off extremely differently than they do. My films are distinct from theirs — in their time, I mean, because who knows what they might be doing if they were in my generation today? They might be doing similar things. I don't know.

*But although you say you approach film emotionally, many of your westerns have an intellectual or satiric quality about them.*
I can intellectualise, sit down and talk about them for hours with somebody if they want to sit and exchange symbolism or whatever. But I don't approach it that way; I start out on an animalistic level, and after I've got the script totally in mind, then I can move to it on almost any kind of level. But I prefer to be drawn to it on that emotional level; if you start out on an intellectual level, I think you're starting without the nucleus. The instinct and motivation is the thing that will tell you whether it's going to be successful or not; if you have good instincts about a play and it moves you on that level, then obviously your audience is going to be moved on that level, because the vast majority of the audience doesn't want to intellectualise it, they want to emotionalise along with it. They may want to intellectualise afterwards, particularly if they are film buffs.

*Obviously, you yourself intellectualise though to the extent of pondering the distinctions between saga and myth. Have you ever reflected upon what you, Clint Eastwood, mean to people?*

I think I appeal to the escapism in people—the characters I play, let me put it that way. I like those characters myself; that's why, maybe, I carry them to other extremes than my predecessors. In other words, in the complications of society as we know it today, sometimes a person who can cut through the bureaucracy and the red tape—even if I'm playing in a modern film—a person who thinks on that level is a hero. A person who can do that, such as a "Dirty Harry" character, a man who thinks on a very simple level and has very simple moral values, appeals to a great many people. I think that's one of the great frustrations in the world. People see things as becoming more complicated. Every time you go to do something—every time you go to register your car—it becomes more complicated. You're waiting in longer lines every year.

For major drama, for major conflicts like crime, they like to see a guy who can hack his way through all that. A very self-sufficient human being is almost becoming a mythical character in our day and age.

*Does a sense of history intrigue you about the western?*

Yeah, I think so. It's always nice if you can tie it in—although a film like *High Plains Drifter* didn't have to be a western, it was just a small morality play. It's probably been done in other forms and fashions over the years— it just seemed as if it played itself out well as a western. It wasn't intended to be a true saga western—the winning-of-the-West kind of thing—the saga of men and women who pioneered the West; it was just a vignette of a certain attitude.

*Do you do a great deal of historical research?*

No. I read books on the West a lot and sometimes, on a certain film, I'll look for something specific. On *Josey Wales,* we tried to find as much information as we could about the outlaws of Kansas. We've all heard about the Missouri guerrillas—a lot has been written about that, Bloody Bill Anderson and the group down there—but there hasn't been too much written about the Kansas Red-Legs. They were actually sanctioned—legal—by Kansas; they were a state militia. They were like a vigilante group who, under the guise of protection, did a lot of bad deeds.

*Can you articulate what you've learned from Don Siegel?*
Well, I'm a very good friend of his, and I think I've learned a lot from him in the sense that he's a man who does a lot with a little—so therefore our philosophies are pretty much akin. He's a man who's done a lot for very little money with budgets over the years; he's a very lean kind of director—he usually knows what he wants and goes in and shoots what he has intended to shoot, and doesn't protect himself like a lot of guys; there's a lot of guys that shoot thousands and thousands of feet, many and many takes of the same thing. They cover themselves every which way so they can't make a mistake. Siegel laughs about that himself. He says, "Those guys always end up making the 'Best Picture.'" He was brought up to work under a certain economics; he had never been what Hollywood considered a "name director," the handful of guys who always got the big stars.

*Are you a faster director than Don Siegel?*
Yeah [*laughs*]. I'm very fast, faster than Siegel. We kid a lot. I cover a fraction more than he does because I think he covers too lean. He thinks I do something else too much. I do things a little differently. We don't direct at all alike. Yet maybe we do. I've taken from hundreds of people I've met over my life. I don't know who my influences are, but I was probably influenced by hundreds of other people, same as he was.

Coogan's Bluff *is very underrated as a picture.*
That's the first picture we did together. It was a fun film to do in the sense that it started out with another director, and Don and I didn't know each other. We started out a little butting heads together and, as it turned out, we ended up with a great working relationship.

*Coogan's Bluff* started out as a story, not a complete story, but I thought it had potential and so I signed a deal with Universal to develop it. It was assigned to a guy named Alex Segal, who just won an Emmy, I believe, for doing *Death of a Salesman*. He and another writer sat down, we had a meeting and put some pretty good work in on it, but we got to a certain point and were stymied. They didn't know where to go with the character—I never did find out the full details. We had a limited time in which to shoot the damn thing—and the agency and the studio said, "You've got to find another director."

So they said, what about so-and-so, naming two or three guys; then they said, "What about Don Siegel? You're out of European films and, although he isn't, he's got sort of a cult following in France; he's well thought of in those groups." I said I'll look at anybody. So we looked. I said I liked his work—I had seen several things he'd done, he'd obviously shown that he could execute certain things. He heard that I was looking at his films, and he hadn't seen the "dollar" films, so he said, "Fine, but let me see his work." It was kind of an ego thing [*laughs*]. So he looked at mine and liked those films, we got together and talked.

Then he went off to New York and wrote a script with kind of a different concept on it that I liked. Originally, they were playing the guy much more as a bumbling type—I'm not saying that's wrong, it might have worked out. The writer working with the first director saw the guy as a guy who's always losing his wallet and being taken by all the people in the big city. Well, I thought that had been done a lot in the past, with James Stewart and a lot of guys. I felt, what happened if it doesn't mean anything that he's a small-town guy? Maybe he was in the war in Korea, he's travelled a little bit around the world, and he's been exposed to other things—just because he's not a New Yorker doesn't mean he's a clod. Plus the fact that maybe his kind of prairie cunning might work well for him against a big city background. We got together, hashed it out and Siegel liked that idea. I liked some of his ideas, we kicked it around and came to a meeting of the minds.

*But he was the only director to do shooting?*
Oh, yeah. In fact, somebody had told me about Mark Rydell and I was talking to him as a possible director for it. And Rydell asked, "Who else are you considering besides me?" I said, "Don Siegel and a couple of other guys." He said, "I'll tell you something: if you want to do it in a month's time, there's only one guy that can do it. I can't do it—I don't have the knowledge or the background to do it." He said, "Don Siegel would be the greatest." I thought that was rather admirable to say that, because other guys would say, "Give me another month or two of preparation and I'll do it." But Mark Rydell said, "No, in the amount of time you want to go, there's only one man who is really capable of doing that, Siegel. He'll do it much better than I would."

*I think* Dirty Harry *is Siegel's best film.*
I thought he did a nice job with *The Beguiled*. Of course, I was the one who hired him for *Dirty Harry*. When I came over here [to Warners], it was tied

in to somebody else and the script was going in another direction. I got
Siegel involved. My agreement with Warner Brothers was, "I'll do it if you'll
let me hire a director like Don Siegel and we'll take the story back to its
original concept"—which was Harry Julian Fink's screenplay. They had
taken it off in another direction.

*I wonder if you know that a lot has been written about the film—pro and con.*
To emotionalise things doesn't mean I drop any sort of intelligent thought
about it. A lot *has* been written about it, pro and con. There are people
who line themselves up with the political overtones of the film. But there
are none really. Those people are crazy.

*Even Siegel has said that, ultimately, it's a very liberal film, as opposed to being
right-wing in nature.*
The people who call it a fascist film don't know what they're talking about.
They're just mouthing off . . . there's nothing like that in there. The guy
was just a man who fought bureaucracy and a certain established kind of
thing. Just because he did things a little unorthodox—that's the only way
he knew how to handle it. He had so many hours to solve the case and as
far as he was concerned, he was more interested in the victim than the law.

He says, in the picture, he is a man of high morals. Then the law is
wrong if this person [the killer] can be let off on a technicality like that.
Well, the laws are changing—they're always changing back and forth in
the courts, the pendulum is always swinging back and forth, right and left.
Once in a while, the court gets too loose on one end, too conservative on
the other, and it changes every ten years.

We, as Americans, went to Nuremberg and convicted people who committed certain crimes because they didn't adhere to a higher morality; we
convicted them on that basis—that they shouldn't have listened to the
law of the land or their leaders at that time. They should have listened to
the true morality. We sent them to jail on that basis. This is how it is with
this man. Somebody told him this is the way it is, too bad, and he said,
"Well, that's wrong. I can't adhere to that." That isn't fascist, that's the
opposite of fascism.

*I understand Dirty Harry III is in the works. Will Siegel have anything to do with
it?*

Well, I don't know. It depends on his availability. We're still at a script stage right now. If it works out script-wise, we'll do it, and if it doesn't, we won't. I don't want to do a character just to continue it.

*Is it fair to say that Dirty Harry and the Man with No Name are essentially the same character with many common qualities?*
No, I don't think so. But they're both moved by passions. Dirty Harry is a man who is callous, seemingly hard on the surface. I think the Man with No Name is much more satiric, it plays more on traditions of the West, and breaking the taboos of the West. Dirty Harry had a much more straight mind—he had a job to do that he became emotionally involved with. The only thing similar about them is that you don't know too much about the background of Dirty Harry, although you get a hint of it—you get a hint that he's had a certain personal life. The Man with No Name—other than in *The Good, the Bad and the Ugly*—doesn't develop too much, and you don't know anything about his background at all. That wasn't always true. In the original *Fistful of Dollars*, we did have a background scene—it was kind of a prelude to the film—but it was better without it.

*The thesis of a book I wrote on Cagney is that an actor's work can be approached as seriously as a director's, and that an actor's personal life can often be traced in relationship to his films. Cagney, for example, was very socially involved as a young contract player, and his Thirties films, such as* The Public Enemy, *reflect that. By the Fifties—thanks to the patriotism of World War Two,* Yankee Doodle Dandy, *and the fact that he is getting richer and more comfortable in life—Cagney's films change greatly. It seems to me that, to a certain extent, your career can be understood this way. You are the Man with No Name in your private life, an enigma to people, and very often a reflection of the character you play in film.*
Certain things that come out of the collage of characters you play *are* you; certain elements of the person can't be withheld. I suppose I feel that way, I suppose that's why I play it well. Other people can't play that. Open people, more extroverted people maybe, can't play that kind of a character because they don't feel that way. They don't feel alone, and they're lonely alone, if you know what I mean—they're not happy alone. They act real well in circumstances where, maybe, there are a lot of people and relationships going on. I guess that's somewhat because of the way I am. My

personal life...I just don't care to have it exploited, I get no satisfaction out of having it exploited.

*I've seen you in movies as far back as* The First Traveling Saleslady *(1956) but I'm not aware of your acting background. Did you go through any formal training that made an impression?*
I've gone to a lot of acting schools, the same as anybody else. I drifted around in my early days before I could get jobs. That area you're talking about—*Traveling Saleslady*—before then, and even after then, I went through periods where it was very hard to get work, but I would go to acting classes at night and work on various projects and scenes in groups.

*Are you aware of any influences or techniques that you have inherited from that experience? From a coach or another actor?*
I've never felt myself influenced by any particular actor, no. I've never felt I played a scene like anybody, otherwise I'd probably be acting like Cagney—but that wouldn't fit with my physiognomy or total being. I've always interpreted things the way it felt to me, not the way it came from an outside source. I've studied in acting groups, but the basic fundamental of learning acting is to know yourself, know what you can do. That's one big advantage of doing a series, if you can. You get to see yourself a lot, get to see what you can do wrong or right. You get to looking at yourself on film so much that you can almost step away with a third eye or as a second person.

I think if you take all the books written by Stanislavsky, Chekhov or whoever right down the line, the basic function of any teacher is to teach yourself. There's no way you can learn out of a book. You can learn to learn it—if you know what I mean—by learning certain techniques or tricks, the basic concentration. I went through all that scene. And I managed to live through the Fifties when everybody was imitating Marlon Brando. There was a period there when every actor, whether they were playing neurosurgeons or not, always talked like ex-fighters.

Brando's very good, he's a terrific actor. I think he's done some of the finer performances on the screen—especially *On the Waterfront*. But there was a tremendous imitative thing starting with Dean and moving on down that they have got away from now. This is an era more akin to the Twenties and Thirties when every individual had their own thing. You take the major personalities in the business today: they are much more distinctive as personalities than they were in the Fifties. The guys coming on are not as influenced by one guy.

Did you see the [Paul] Mazursky picture *Next Stop Greenwich Village*? I saw it the other night. It's so very true. He hit it right on the nail. The whole deal where the character (Larry Lapinsky) lied about having been at the Actors Studio . . . because everybody was with that, since Brando had been there a month or two. Everyone was on that scene.

I was up for a picture once and the producer said he really wanted me for it. But he said, "I have to give the director the last choice." I think Sterling Hayden and Anita Ekberg were the stars; this [part] was for the younger brother. I thought I was really right for it, everybody thought I was really right for it. But the director got some plumber who got off the train from New York, some guy who *[mumbles]* and the director said, "Man, he's great, put him in the film."[2] They snapped this guy up and it's typical of what Mazursky is saying there. You got to the point where, after a while, you said, Jesus, do I have to say I'm from this funky studio to get a job? Everybody had to say that to be anybody, to be in on the vogue of the moment. I didn't do that, but I saw it happen, I lived through that era. It was very true the way Mazursky laid it down.

*On the other hand, it strikes me that Dirty Harry is almost an entirely different person from Clint Eastwood in some ways — the Clint Eastwood who, for example, practices transcendental meditation. The character on the screen is like part of a split personality.*

Well, it's a character you play, and sometimes you play a character, it has a certain impact, and people think you are that character. It's a left-handed compliment, in a sense, because you do the character to the point where they think, Hey, maybe he's a mad-dog killer, I really believe him, that's the way he is, he's gotta be that way. The Man with No Name, same way. Wow, he must be like a guy who never says anything. Maybe I am. There are elements of privacy in my life but, obviously, I can shoot my mouth off if I get feeling in the mood. I've got to admit I'm moody about it, though.

---

2. The film must have been *Valerie* (1957) in which Peter Walker played the brother. — Ed.

*Getting back to directing, what is your relationship with your producer?*
When I first started as a contract player at Universal, Bob Daley was in cost
analysis. Then he became a first assistant and a unit manager. He always
thought the way I did, trying to keep as much of the cost of the film on
the screen as possible, rather than having it in limousines, etc. So, when I
was forming this company to do films like *Hang 'em High,* I needed somebody like a producer in the old sense who knew budgets and schedules.
There was a period there where producers were just promoters; they would
go out and buy a story and put their names on it as producer and sell it.
Today, a producer is a guy who produces—who knows something about
the film-making aspect. So I hired a guy who had a good background in
film rather than just a salesman I didn't need.

*When was Malpaso Company formed?*
Right after *The Beguiled.* He was working with me during *Beguiled,* preparing for *Misty.*

*What does "Malpaso" mean?*
"Malpaso" means "bad pass" in Spanish, like a bad pass in the mountains.
Or "bad step"—like if it looks like you're going to trip over something.

*Let's talk about* Play Misty for Me. *When I was in college, that film was a very
big money-maker on campus. Funny, I went to school at the University of Wis-
consin in Madison, which is or was a hotbed of the New Left. Yet your movies
were always popular.*
The only time I've been associated with anything political is by innuendo
or by people's assumptions that I have certain political aspects. Probably—
actually—I'm the most moderate person, politically. After Watergate, I'm
like everybody else—thinking, Oh Jesus, politics, keep me away from it—
I'm reticent. I've supported Democrats and Republicans in California. It
depends on what the guy stands for at the moment.

*Didn't you support Nixon in 1968? I seem to recall your picture on a poster, along
with people like Henry Aaron and Wilt Chamberlain.*
Yeah, that was a while back. Like everybody else, you vote for who you
think is right, with the limited amount of knowledge you have at the
moment.

*Anyway* Play Misty for Me *has an unusually good script.*
That was written by a friend of mine, a girl, Jo Heims, who, surprisingly, writes both men and women well. She did *Breezy,* too. She wrote the man's part in *Breezy* very well; she captured the whole feeling of a divorced businessman's doing fairly well, swinging along with chicks, but totally disconnected with everything, who sort of rediscovers life through the eyes of this young girl.

I had optioned *Play Misty for Me* when I was doing *Where Eagles Dare.* I talked to the author and optioned a sixty-page treatment. Then I went to Europe, doing *Where Eagles Dare,* and she had an opportunity to sell it — I had just an option on it, very little money, so she called me and asked if she could sell it, she needed the dough. I said, "Go ahead, because I don't know when I'm going to get out of here or what I can do with it." I had taken it to Gordon Stulberg at CBS, and he said, "We're doing a film here called *The Sterile Cuckoo* with Liza Minnelli. It's too much like that." I said, "It is? Okay." I took it to Universal — they said, "I don't think so." I took it to David Picker at United Artists and he turned it down. Everybody turned it down. At that time, I was just starting to come into my own with my films, but I was still the kid from Europe. I didn't have quite enough juice to pull it off.

I was working in Oregon on *Paint Your Wagon,* then I came back down to do *Sister Sara* for Siegel at Universal, and I signed a deal to do three or four films with them. All of a sudden, it hit me one day: "Whatever happened to that *Play Misty for Me* that you guys bought?" They said, "Well, it's on the shelf, it's not going anywhere, nobody's going to do it anymore." I talked to Jennings Lang and said, "You know, I'd like to make that film." I didn't tell him I wanted to direct it at that time. He said, "Jesus Christ, who in the hell wants to see Clint Eastwood play a disc jockey?" I said, "Who in the hell wants to see him play anything? I don't know... it just seems like a good story. It's got a lot of conflict; elements of it could happen — elements of it have happened to me." I identified with it...

So I went to Lew Wasserman and told him, "You've got a thing on the shelf here that I'd really like to develop and I think I can make it very cheap, all on natural sets." He said, "Great, take it and run with it." I know exactly what they were saying behind my back, probably saying, "We'll let the kid fool around with it. He'll do that and then he'll probably do a couple of westerns for us, or some other adventure-type film that will seem more commercial at the outset." The other thing they weren't pleased about is... they said, "Why would you want to do a film where the woman is the best part in the film?" I said, "Well, what difference does it make? The guy is the victim, he's the subject certainly. I think it's maybe more conflicting to have a man who handles himself in a more physical situation stuck in a situation where he can't handle it physically, a frustrating situation. But they didn't see any of that.

Then I went to Don Siegel and I told him, "Don, I've got this little picture that I'm working on now, and I'm really thinking seriously about directing it." Siegel said, "Go ahead, I think it'd be great. I'd kind of like to sign your director's card." You have to have two guys for you to join the union. So I have to say that Siegel was very influential.

So I went to Wasserman again and said, "I've got the script fixed. I want to do a good film and I want to direct it." I had to haggle with him to do the film at a certain price. They said, "Well, would you act in it for nothing, just on a percentage, instead of your regular deal, since we don't consider this a commercial property?"

I said, "Fine, I just want to do the picture." They were pleased. My gross percentage turned out to be better than if I had taken the salary. *Misty* came out and did well, despite their advertising. There wasn't much concentration put into it; it was just out. It had tremendous re-release, too; the exhibitors I talked to said they had great luck with it on the second or third run. And they got a really good television sale on it, because the film took off. It made a lot of money, they were happy and I was happy.

*Breezy was also poorly distributed, although many people like the film very much. Wasn't it shelved by Universal and then released a year later? Some bad reviews, initially, virtually killed it.*
You can't blame it on reviewers because, if the film's good and the reviewer doesn't see that it's good, that doesn't mean the public will stay away from it. The public stayed away from it because it wasn't promoted enough, and it was sold in an uninteresting fashion. Good reviews would have helped that type of film. There's some films that reviewers can unanimously rap and still do business. But this was a small film—it was just the story of the rejuvenation of a cynic. I thought that was an interesting subject, especially nowadays in the era of cynicism...

*William Holden gives a strong performance, and Kay Lenz is really a terrific, underrated new actress...*
Yeah, she was nice...

*Did you do* Breezy *deliberately to break pace with* Dirty Harry *and the Man with No Name? Are you interested in other genres?*
I'm interested in them but, at the same time, you have to be constantly conscious of the fact that you want people to see the films. One of the films that got the best notices of those I did was called *The Beguiled*. It was a disaster at the box office, very poorly distributed and very poorly advertised. That had a lot to do with its lack of success but the fact is they sold it to the Man with No Name audience—it would do good the first few days and then fade out terrifically. Because they never sold it to the audience who would like that kind of film.

That's Universal. They have a terrible advertising department, they're not smart. Look what they're doing now to *Gable and Lombard*. I don't care what kind of film it is. The ad campaign is terrible. No particular logo or anything, just a spread-out bunch of squares. Horrible copy: "They had more than love, they had fun." That's just about the worst copy I've ever read in my life.

*Do you try to oversee your own advertising as much as possible?*
I try to keep an eye on it but there [Universal] it was a harder thing to do. Here [at Warners] it's easier, because they're much better. For instance, the *Dirty Harry* and *Magnum Force* campaigns, both made here at Warners, were, I thought, laid out very nicely.

*The script seems very weak in your latest picture,* The Eiger Sanction, *although the visuals are very exciting.*
It was more on a visual plane than *Play Misty for Me*. It didn't have the kind of a story you could tell with that kind of impact and excitement. The only excitement you could do was on a visual level and that is the way it was written. I would have liked, in a way, to have done *The Eiger Sanction* as a not-so-satiric, maybe serious adventure story with tremendous characters, and conflicts between the characters, and still do it with that same visual thing. You could really make something special. This bordered on a Bondish sort of thing in certain areas.

*Play Misty for Me,* on the other hand, was fun because it had elements of a Hitchcock-type thing, but at the same time it was unlike Hitchcock. A lot of time in his films—like *Psycho*—the story part doesn't mean anything until you get to the impact of the psychotic thing. In *Misty,* you have that interpretation of commitment between individuals and how this interpretation takes people in certainly different directions. I think it was a much more contemporary thing for people today, because so many people go through this in various relationships—not just, as in the case of the picture, where the man is a victim, but there are women too who become suppressed or choked by an individual just because somebody has different ideas about a relationship.

*Did you get into* The Eiger Sanction *too quickly to develop any ideas in the story, thematically? The characters all seem to be so thinly, almost absurdly, drawn.*
That is just the way it was done. I took a book Universal owned—a bestseller—and I couldn't figure out what to do. The book has no ties. In other words, the character who is killed at the beginning has no relationship to anybody else. I just took it and tried to make the guy relate to the hero so the hero had some other motivations. The way the book was written, he had no motivations for anything. He just went there (to the Eiger) strictly for monetary gain, no other motivations, period. At the end, he's not with any of the people he started with—including the girl. It just rambled on that way.

But it was a book (Trevanian wrote it) that was especially popular with people who like escapism.

*The visual aspects are impressive, nonetheless; I thought there was a long shot the movie might get nominated for an Oscar.*
If you wanted to get on that kind of a bandwagon, but it wasn't that kind of a movie. The music was almost up [for an Oscar]. But they had a panel that chose and they chose *Jaws,* because *Jaws* was the movie of the year. The same guy [John Williams] did this score and it was probably better than *Jaws.*

Also, the challenge of it for me was to actually shoot a mountain-type film on a mountain, not on sets. The only ones done in the past were all done on sets; the mountains were all papier-mâché mountains.

*I understand that a technician died during the filming...*
Yes, we lost someone...the Eiger is a mean mountain. So it was a great challenge to pull off that type of film—it was a tough film to make. *Josey,* which I just finished, is a much more intelligent story—in a classic mode. It isn't what you would call a standard western, it has a classic saga feel— I'm not too articulate...

# Eastwood Direction

RICHARD  THOMPSON  AND

TIM  HUNTER/1976–77

(THIS INTERVIEW WAS CONDUCTED in the summer of 1976 and in December 1977. Jack Shafer generously contributed key suggestions. Dick Guttman arranged the interviews. The authors are grateful to both.)

*How did you start directing?*
I first got interested when I was doing *Rawhide*. We were shooting a stampede on location, 3,000 head of cattle, and I was riding right in the middle of it, dust flying, really dramatic looking. I went to the director and said, "Look, give me a camera. There's some great stuff in there that you're not getting because you're way out here on the periphery." I got all kinds of static about union problems. As usual, everybody's afraid to try something new. Finally, they threw me a bone: I directed some trailers. I was so disappointed with the whole damn thing that I let it drop.

*What made directing so important to you?*
It's a natural progression, if you're interested in films. The overall concept of a film was more important to me than just acting. I'd done second unit work for Don Siegel and enjoyed it—not so I'd want to do it in every picture, but whenever one came along that stuck in my mind when I read it.

---

Published as "Clint Eastwood, Auteur" in *Film Comment* 14, no. 1 (January/February 1978): 24–32. Reprinted by permission of the authors.

*You have a remarkable sense of your own material, more objective than most stars have.*
You mean: which ones to act in?

*To act in, and which ones of those to direct yourself in.*
Just instinct. If I thought about it too long, I'd probably change my mind and do something wrong. I try to think about it in terms of the end, not in terms of the character I play. Hopefully, the story takes over and brings you into it, as you want it to do for the audience. If I have a virtue, it's decisiveness: I make decisions very fast, right or wrong.

*Do you get your shots with few takes?*
I'm always trying to get it on the first take—a Don Siegel technique. After directing awhile, you get an instinct about it, but you have to be able to trust your own feelings. Invariably, two-thirds of the way through a film, you say, "Jeezus, is this a pile of crap! What did I ever see in it in the first place?" You have to shut off your brain and forge ahead, because by that time you're getting so brainwashed. Once I commit myself to a film I commit myself to that ending, whatever the motivations and conclusions are.

*Do you have a main flaw as a director?*
Tons of 'em, probably. Sometimes I slough myself too much when I'm acting a scene. It's difficult to make the changeover from directing the scene to stepping into it as an actor.

*You're at the center of the challenge to the hero in this decade: what do you think about heroes?*
I was one of the people who took the hero further away from the white hat. In *A Fistful of Dollars,* you didn't know who was the hero till a quarter of the way through the film, and then you weren't sure; you figured he was the protagonist, but only because everybody else was crappier than he was. I like the way heroes are now. I like them with strengths, weaknesses, lack of virtue.

*And humor?*
Yeah. And a touch of cynicism at times. In the old days, with Hays Office rules, you never drew until drawn upon. But if some guy is trying to kill the character I'm playing, I shoot 'em in the back.

*Pauline Kael has tossed you some antimacho barbs.*

Well, she's out of line there. Some of the points she made I agree with, about the changes of movies over the years, and Vietnam. She goes on and on about the need for showing the weaknesses of men, and that's all right—there's a place for that. But why isn't there a place for escaping into the era of some would-be person you'd like to have the ingenuity of?

She's obsessed by something else; you see it in the films she likes. I've talked with her about it. Her image is being outspoken, so she has to be outspoken about something. She picked macho-ism, because that's the name of the moment. In the Sixties, it was racism; who knows what it'll be next. It doesn't bother me, because my films don't do any less well because of what she's talking about. *Josey Wales* will outgross *Nashville*.

*John Milius claimed Pauline Kael was in love with him because she kept talking about him all the time.*

Oh, I said that. Just for laughs, I called a psychiatrist and read him the article. He said, "That's what you call 'reaction formation,' a defense mechanism. She wants to fuck you." And I said, "I don't believe that." And he said, "Well, it may not be the case, but it's fun to think about, anyway."

*Macho is very much under fire now.*

Oh, yeah. The way Jack Nicholson plays the guy in *Cuckoo's Nest*: Super macho. One of the guys she praises—and he's terrific in it. It's the style. She'll go on to something else in a couple months. In a year or two, everybody'll look back and say, "God, sure wish we had one of those films again." Obviously, I'm not like those characters. I'm not shooting people down in the streets.

*What's left for that hero now?*

I don't know. Take Josey: unlike the High Plains Drifter or those other characters who come and go, picking up their vengeance or motivation along the way, you see what makes him the way he is, gradually growing. But I don't think of it in terms of the hero—I think of it in terms of person. He *becomes* heroic, as heroic as I've presented him to be.

*Anthony Mann said that the audience liked to see someone accomplish something; they didn't like to see someone fail.*

I think that's true. The one picture I failed in was *The Beguiled*. It was good for me personally, critically well-received, but it was very poor for the company that spent the money to produce it. Maybe it couldn't have been successful, because the hero failed. He tried to do everything through the back door. He wasn't such a bad person; he was just trying to exist. It showed the sicknesses of war, and what war does to people.

I think people still like the guy who accomplishes. I just think that nowadays they want him to accomplish it in a different way, maybe not so pseudo-virtuous, if there is such a word.

*Play Misty for Me (1971), Eastwood's first film as director, shows a remarkable sense of place, an eye for interesting interior design — especially modern — and an ability to fix characters through visual description of an environment. His talent for tailoring landscape to fit a film's mood and theme is unsurpassed among recent American directors. His films are also superbly paced: unhurried; cool; and giving a strong sense of real time, regardless of the speed of the narrative.*

*Eastwood's pictures come from the male point of view, but this very one-sidedness gives them a certain truth and conviction beyond politics. Of all his films,* Play Misty for Me *best reveals Eastwood's need to test and compromise his own image, pushing it toward the limit of personal honor.*

*The movement of the plot is simple: as Eastwood tries to win back* fair lady *Donna Mills (a woman with whom he can be satisfied without putting out a lot of emotion),* spurned *dark lady Jessica Walter goes crazier and crazier, finally plotting to kill him. Eastwood sees the story as being about "misinterpretation of commitment," and his character as essentially victimized — but* Play Misty for Me *works on darker levels.*

*Walter is the exact opposite of Eastwood: impulsive where he is controlled, passionate where he is complacent. Consequently, we admire her a little, sensing some justice in her attack at the base of his self-satisfied life. She is nearly his alter-ego, a projection of his suppressed furies and fear of love — a pull toward death and self-destruction that he must battle and exorcise within himself. In this sense,* Play Misty *is a companion piece to Siegel's* The Beguiled *(in which the anti-hero surrenders to dark passion and does die). They are Eastwood's two sexual meditations; both films show women archetypically as Innocent or as Corruptor. In* Play Misty for Me, *violence is equated with sex, and women with life (pulling man out of his isolation) or death. The film plugs into the main stream of the male, American romantic tradition and exerts a fascination well beyond the limits of the plot. If* Play Misty *benefits from these subconscious implications, it is finally satisfying because Walter is such a wonderful villainess: a personal devil for Eastwood to fight equalled only by Andy Robinson's prime psycho in Siegel's* Dirty Harry. *Regarding alter egos, one remembers how that film and its ad campaign stressed the similarities between hero and villain; in* Play Misty for Me, *as in all his films, good triumphs in the fight with evil— but rarely has the devil lived so close to home.* —R.T. & T.H.

*You can work with a fine range of directors. How do you pick the films you want to direct?*

I had optioned *Play Misty for Me* as a treatment. It was written by [Jo Heims,] a gal I knew in the old days when she was just a secretary and I was an actor. I couldn't sell it. Couldn't get UA to do it: David Picker didn't think it was commercial. Tried Gordon Stulberg, at CBS-Studio Center; tried Fox, who said, "No, we're doing something too much like this with Liza Minnelli"—which I didn't see was like it at all, but that was their reason. I went away, lost the option, and forgot about it. Somewhere in there, Universal bought it.

Then I started thinking about what had happened to it. But I didn't know any directors particularly; Don Siegel was busy. Anybody could have done it, with a lot of different concepts. It was a small enough picture, small cast, not overly difficult—not like starting out with a massive thing.

So I went to Universal and told them I'd like to develop this picture and act in it. Then I went to Don Siegel and said, "I have a pretty good idea of what I want to do with this; I want to direct it. What's your advice?" He said, "Yeah, do it, I'll sign your DGA card." I told Universal—I had a three-picture deal with them—and they said, "OK, if you'll do it for nothing." So I said OK. As it turned out, they're paying more than if they'd hired me at straight salary, because the film did all right.

*When you knew you were going to direct it, how did you prepare?*

I worked on the script: I got Dean Riesner, a guy I'd worked with before. I wasn't going to get a big name cast: without overhead costs, the picture was only about $740,000, maybe a little more. I came in quite a bit under that. I compared all the shots in my mind, laid everything out, made notes to myself, looked at film, cast Jessica—the key role—cast the other people, went to the jazz festival and got permission to shoot at no cost. Just normal preparation, following logical sequence. Coming from acting to directing, you're used to working on a set with lots of people, whereas writers or editors turning director are used to working by themselves. Gives me an edge on problem solving.

*Interesting that you optioned* Misty *so long before you made it; what was it about the story you related to?*
The idea of suffocation. I'd seen a lot of psychotic films, like *Psycho.* But if you think of *Psycho,* you never think of its story. You think about the tremendous scenes: where Marty Balsam got it on the stairway, or Janet Leigh in the shower. If you ask people about the plot line, they have a hard time telling it.

   This was an opportunity to do a film that had that kind of element and at the same time a story which everyone knows—it's not polarized one sexual way or another; it could be man against woman or woman against man—about suffocation, that misinterpretation of commitment. One person's casually dating the other, who's saying, "Forever and ever." I thought a lot of people would identify with that. It happened to me when I was younger, not quite to that degree. This girl who wrote it took it from a real person. That person didn't commit homicide, but did everything else that was in the picture plus other things. She'd dress up in wigs, disguise herself, and go to saloons hoping this guy'd walk in so she could catch him with another gal. She cut all his clothes up in the closet. Really insane things.

*Did studio people tell you it wouldn't go because it was so uncharacteristic for you at the time?*
The studio first said, "Who the hell wants to see Clint Eastwood play a DJ?" I said, "Who the hell wants to see him play anything? It just seems like a good idea to me." They said, "Why would you want to do a part in a picture where the woman has the best part?" "I don't give a crap," I said; "I'll look out for me. The guy is the subject of what's going on, so what difference does it make?"

*The scene in the outdoor restaurant, when she comes in and makes trouble, totally blew my mind. Until then, you know it's rational, it can be solved by communication; that's the scene where you think, "Oh, Christ, she's never gonna let him out."*

You just can't believe it. The guy I played couldn't, and the audience couldn't believe there were people that far off. That combination made an interesting idea for me to tackle, plus I thought I could do the film all on location without ever setting foot in the studio, which I didn't.

*How did you pick jazz arranger Dee Barton for the music?*
I just happened to hear him and ask him if he'd like to interpret some old music that MCA owned — we had to use all their standards in order to get by, budget-wise; the only big expense was paying for Errol Garner.

I had to fight Universal on that too. They wanted to call the film *Strangers in the Night,* because they owned that tune. But it had already been used in a film [*A Man Could Get Killed*], and it hadn't been a success then. I needed a standard that bridged several generations. I didn't want to use "Stardust": it goes too far back and doesn't hit the newer generations. I finally crammed "Misty" down their throats.

*Did you go through a formal process like storyboarding for* Play Misty?
I just have the shots down, marking in my script what I want. The only board I have is the scheduling board of the assistant director's.

*About visual composition. Do you draw sketches?*
I have a pretty good idea what I want, but it always has to adjust to what's happening. Sometimes you get out there and say, "Jesus, the light's lousy," and you want to change it around the other direction to get it backlit. There's a million different reasons why you might have to change it. So I go out and line it up in my mind, just looking around to get the general idea. Then if an actor has a hangup about moving to that side, I can adjust. I've found that if you explain to the actors what you're trying to do, you never have any problem with anybody. I keep them abreast of what I'm trying to accomplish as a movie.

*The real inspiration of* High Plains Drifter *(1973) is its conception of the town, a sparkling clean main street that looks as much like a new condominium in Northern California as it does the movie western towns of the past. This town, built on an oasis-like lake in the middle of a scorched desert, ably serves the allegory of the film. Both it and Eastwood's man-with-no-name hero appear completely cut off from the world.*

*This is Eastwood's best revenge picture, and the most skillful thing about it is that we never really know why he's taking revenge, even after the picture's over. The people in the town are so corrupt, though—worthy of Brecht and Weill's Mahagonny—that one can take special pleasure watching Eastwood get most of them killed. The overtones of Sodom and Gomorrah are deliberate, as is the devil quality of Eastwood's anti-hero—not to mention the film's homage to Japanese ghost-revenge melodramas.*

*The contrast of dark brown interiors and blinding white light exteriors added to the strikingly different look of the town, gives* High Plains Drifter *a stylized visual originality that goes beyond the expressionistic CinemaScope shots influenced by Sergio Leone and Don Siegel. The pacing casually makes the most of the action. Of all the films he's directed,* High Plains *has the best stylization of violence, with a laconic shooting from a bathtub especially memorable.—R.T. & T.H.*

*When* Breezy *came out, I was booking a college film society. Picking up prints at a Universal exchange one day, the people there told me how much they loved the film and how pissed off they were at the head office for not pushing it. I don't know if you knew the little people were behind you.*

I knew it—you could just tell. That's one of the reasons I'm not at Universal for every picture. They didn't push *Play Misty* either, but it took off in spite of them. I'd get calls from execs saying, "Goddamn, that picture's doing well." I'd say, "Why shouldn't it do well?" They'd say, "Well, I don't know, it isn't a Western and you're not a cop." Their eyes were really channeled.

*Did the rep* Play Misty *built improve your bargaining position when you came around to direct a second picture?*

Yeah, on the second picture they left me completely alone. But it was a western, *High Plains Drifter.* They argued with me very little. Their first suggestion was that we make it on the back lot—they always do, because Universal owns the back lot. With smog. So I say, "Nope, we're gonna go away and build this very inexpensive western town, looking sparse." So Ferris Webster [Eastwood's house editor] and I went up to Mono Lake and did it, even did initial editing there; we did final editing back in L.A.

*Did you know then that* High Plains *would be the second film you'd direct?*

No. That came to Universal as a nine page treatment called *Mesa* or something. I made a deal with Ernest Tidyman to make a script out of it.

I wanted to get an off-look to it rather than a conventional western look. It was written for a typical, middle-of-the-desert, Monument Valley town. I was trying to find someplace on the water: I looked at Lake Powell, Pyramid Lake, and Mono Lake. Mono Lake has a weird look to it, a lot of strange colors—never looks the same way twice during the day. And it has such a high saline content, nobody'll put a boat in it, so you don't have to worry about waterskiers in the background.

I picked a spot up there and we built a little town, interiors, exteriors, all together. Shot the picture in five weeks.

*An abstract-looking town: no railroad, no industry, no reason for the town to be there.*
Just that it's fresh water, and most towns would be on water as opposed to the conventional western where the town is out in the middle of some-place nobody'd want to live.

*People felt your film was an homage to Leone.*
No, I don't think so. I didn't shoot it like he does; I used a different style. The character might resemble his hero.

*Did you work out the style ahead of time? What style did you want?*
I just saw the film clearly. That's why I decided to direct it. I had two westerns in preparation at that time, *High Plains* and *Joe Kidd.* I didn't par-ticularly like the story on *Joe Kidd,* so I let somebody else [John Sturges] direct it—it had some pretty good elements to it, but I didn't visualize it as strongly as *High Plains.* I visualized *High Plains* so strongly I figured I'd bet-ter do it, just to make sure; you hate to hire someone and then impose a total concept on them, it's not fair to them. I've found that out since then.

*Do you collect images, ideas for shots?*
You mean prior to having a story? Sometimes. For instance, I was in a barn the other day, showing my kid a chicken ranch. There were chickens peck-ing away, zero space in between. I thought, God, what a great shot. I don't know what to do with it, but someday I'll need the shot and have to go into that chicken barn.

High Plains *reminds me of Japanese ghost-story films, particularly the way you leave the door open for that reading at the end, when the hero rides out of town*

*and the midget sidekick asks him who he is. Did you ever make a decision in*
*your own mind as to who he was?*
Yeah, to me he was the brother. But I presented him . . . [trails off, pauses].
The way the whole town was, no children, kind of strange: it's a weird situation. As far as me justifying the role, he was the brother. But as far as the
audience is concerned, if they want to draw him as something a little more
than that, that's fine.


Breezy *(1973) is the only film Eastwood has directed in which he didn't star;*
*its commercial failure minimizes the possibility for another directing-only pro-*
*ject. Following* High Plains Drifter, Breezy *is again an allegory, with Eastwood*
*still concerned with the hypocrisies and failed values of middle class society — in*
*this case, L.A.'s idle* nouveau riche. *Directly, effortlessly, Eastwood conveys*
*(and satirizes) the impotence of this* dolce vita *cocktail set, and this lack of*
*equivocation gives his simple tender love story a special grace quite different from*
*the cold new crop of romances released since* Breezy.

Breezy *has the biting, moralistic wit of this period in Eastwood's work; one*
*feels that here, in* High Plains *and in* Play Misty, *Eastwood enjoys stripping the*
*mystique from the leisure class.* Breezy *evokes the spirit of his homeground,*
*Carmel, more than it does the Laurel Canyon-Hollywood-West L.A. setting of the*
*story. The use of the setting is rich. William Holden's elegant but lonely house —*
*natural woods, rough boulder walls, indoor/outdoor jungle — is the perfect mirror*
*of his soul in the balance. The* mise-en-scène *is so transparently simple, closest*
*in style to* Play Misty for Me, *that* Breezy *overtly becomes an actor's showcase.*
*Probably because he wasn't starring in the film, Eastwood gives freer rein to his*
*sentimental streak; one of the many pleasures of the film is the degree of self-pity*
*allowed the Holden character as well as the unabashed hippy corniness of Kay*
*Lenz's Breezy.* — R.T. & T.H.


*What attracted you to the story?*
It was written by Jo Heims, who wrote *Play Misty.* She wrote the man and
woman's characters so well I thought, I don't know if I'm going to act in
it, but I'd sure like to make it. I liked the whole comment on the rejuvenation of a cynic, living around L.A., divorced, making good dough but
hating it, then finding out about life through a seventeen-year old. She
teaches him more about it than he teaches her. It's a mutual exchange, but
it doesn't go on forever and ever, and she doesn't die of some exotic disease.

*Breezy* was a big risk at the time, in the sense that I knew I was making it at Universal, who were doing me a favor in letting me make it. It wasn't an expensive film, so they didn't have that much to lose; but they didn't feel it was commercial, subject-wise. It cost $725,000 direct, then they tacked on the overhead. They're not very adept at promoting films, especially that kind. I think here, at Warner Brothers, the film might have had a chance. When we four-walled the picture, it seemed to do well; word of mouth was good, people liked it. Universal was writing it off before they even released it, as they occasionally do. It's just deciding to exist and see what happens. What's wrong with existing?

*How was Holden?*
Terrific. Technically very astute as an actor, he understood the role completely, so it was easy for him to play. After he'd signed for the part—I'd just met him—he told me, "You know, I've been this guy." And I said, "Yeah, I thought so." A lot of people have been this guy at one time or another in their lives. The actress, Kay Lenz, was young, so I had to work a little more with her. Holden was very, very gentle with her, even during the screen test. I tested ten gals, and he shot all the tests; most guys would say, "Get some kid." Holden's a snap.

*The scale of the production was perfect for the material—it's an actor's film.*
It was. There's nothing in it to overshadow the people. The main thing for the director to do is set up an atmosphere to work in, move on, and keep everybody involved with the plot. Some scenes I'll rehearse quite a bit, if they're technically complicated, but others I'll improvise. Depends on the actor or actress, too: Jessica Walter liked to improvise and shoot the first take. The big advantage of film is that you can always reshoot it if it's wrong. But if it's just right in rehearsal and you didn't shoot that, you may not see it for awhile, six-eight-ten takes down the road, if ever. Through the years, I've seen too many good takes left on the rehearsal floor.

*Now,* The Eiger Sanction: *Did you get to do it with the condition that you would star in it?*
The studio had it and they offered it to me. I said I'd try to make a script of it; then the agents couldn't agree on a price, so it went to another director. He couldn't get a script together either, and it came back to me.

When I began planning it, I went out climbing. When you get into mountain climbing, you realize there's just no room for a crew hanging around—literally no space on the mountainside. So I figured I had to at least do the climbing sequences.

I didn't totally visualize *Eiger Sanction*. It was difficult to place the way the story should be told—whether to go completely outlandish like James Bond, or to go for the middle line. There was tremendous room for the adventure part, which was the big challenge as far as I was concerned. I got wrapped up in wanting to be the first guy to shoot totally on the side of a mountain, not papier-mâché rocks—outside of documentaries, that is. We did everything, dangling 2,000 feet over the first splatter.

*That's some shot where you fall into the frame and are jerked short by your safety rope.*
We hung off the cliff and built a ladder out from it for the downshot. I had to cut myself loose. That was a psychologically damaging thing to do.

*Why psychologically?*
It's just against your nature. You do it and for three days afterward, you're just staring off. You don't say much.

*Part of Eastwood's strong appeal is that he seems too large for society. He embodies a dream: that a man can rise above the treadmill of bureaucracy and act on his own law. But the price of this independence is isolation. Eastwood's films often focus on this theme, as if to say that good can triumph in the world only when set apart from it.*

*Leone and Siegel nurtured Eastwood's image as a cutthroat anti-hero who could play dirtier than anyone as long as his motives justified his means. Treading the line between hero and devil in the characters he plays, Eastwood selects stories about bounty hunters, policemen, and revengers—all subjects where character motivation turns murky and paradoxical. With all moral values so compromised, Eastwood has only to maintain a tiny edge of purity so that the audience can identify with the self-righteousness that allows him to set himself above the rest of the world and act on his own predatory impulses. Regardless of director, the movement in all his best films is toward a dichotomy between the Eastwood character and, at the opposing pole, everybody else.*

*His recent films have moved toward softening this polarity, testing it through wider interaction with other characters and a continued belief in the potential of romance. From all indications, Phil Kaufman would have made a more sincerely communal* Josey Wales *than the one Eastwood finally made, one which would have incorporated Eastwood more completely into the whole. The crisis undoubtedly arose because Eastwood, conscious of "shorting" himself when he directs, felt he wasn't being covered well. The final version points up the standard dichotomy of his films even more than those which play off it more overtly. Closeups of Eastwood as Josey Wales are less well blended into the style of the overall film than usual. An increasingly abstracted stylization of violence doesn't quite mesh with the theme of the film and its desire to be a tapestry or Breughel scene of the West. Despite a certain lack of tension,* Josey Wales *is an admirable attempt at broadening his scope and—no puns intended—the best thing about this visually sumptuous movie are the remarkable Panavision master shots, and an ease with the medium that gains in assurance as it looks for new challenges and directions in choice of subjects—*R.T. & T.H.

Every picture takes on its own style. I get into the film and then I get the look of it as it comes, rather than having a constant style that goes through each film, putting a mark on it. I think each picture should have its own mark.

*How did you become involved in* The Outlaw Josey Wales?
This one was a book submitted to me. It was written by a Cherokee Indian who had never written a book before but who was a well-known poet in Indian circles. My associate, Bob Daley, was so taken by his cover letter that he took the book home to read and couldn't put it down. It was written in a very honest fashion. The character seems like he's destined to become a loser. It's an episodic kind of story. It just read beautifully—even the dialogue jumped off the page.

It's fun to do a saga-type film: introduce a lot of people...hope the audience will get to like them and miss 'em when they're gone. When the kid dies, I think people are genuinely lost for a minute, as the Wales character is, riding through the forest of vines and drizzle.

*How long did* Josey *take to shoot?*
About eight-and-a-half weeks. *Josey* was difficult in the sense that we shot in Utah, two different locations in Arizona, and in California—we had to

move a lot on that one, 'cause it's a saga—you have to feel the travelling in the land.

*Playing against conventional expectation in scenes is a strategy throughout the film. For instance, when the bounty hunter comes through the door and you say, "Look, it doesn't have to be this way," and he goes back out the door.*
That was all the book, very intelligently written. My favorite line in the movie is when one of the bounty hunters says, "Man's got to do *something* for a living these days," and Josey answers, "Dyin' ain't much of a living." He [Forrest Carter, the novelist] understands the guy completely.

A lot of guys have done Quantrill and the Missouri guerrillas on film, but nobody's ever done the Kansas Redlegs, who were a lot like carpet baggers. When the winning side of the war came, they were always seen as heroic, even though they were just as much renegades as Quantrill.

*As the director, you play yourself as actor down to give Chief Dan George the focus in quite a few scenes. He's very funny, wry.*
Like when you think the Indian girl is Josey's, and then she and the Chief become involved instead. Our hero just keeps losing out all the way. Not that he wants to get involved; he even says, later in the picture, trouble just follows him. Chief was very good in those scenes.
When I read the book, I knew Chief Dan George was the only person to play that character. He's got a face you never get tired of looking at. You put a camera on it and you just can't do wrong. One minute he looks like a puppy dog and the next minute he looks like a very aristocratic king. Magnificent face. I love the last scene where he comes up to Josey; all he says is, "You're up kind of early," but he knows Josey is leaving, he reads the whole situation. A lot of pro actors can't move you that way. He gives you gold. He says the simplest thing and it sounds like an important statement; everything has importance.

*(Sondra Locke, who played in the film, and was present during this part of the interview, said:* "I was commenting on how I didn't have any dialogue in the film and Bruce Surtees [the cinematographer] said, 'Well, it's much better to be that way. You notice the Chief talks so slowly that you listen very closely to hear his next word, because you don't know when it's going to come. Same thing with you: if you don't talk, they'll be waiting for a word.'")

I did that for fourteen pictures, then finally I had to utter one and blew the whole thing.

*We understand that Phil Kaufman was set to direct and even began shooting* Josey.
Yeah, he shot a week of it. He did marvelous work on the script. It was just a matter of how the shooting was going down, so I just took it over and re-shot stuff. I hated it; it was the worst moment of my life. I've never fired anybody. It was just a disagreement.... He did some really good writing. I'd seen his first two films [*The Great Northfield, Minnesota Raid* and *The White Dawn*] and thought he'd be terrific directing *Josey*; but it was larger, less documentary, and more episodic, a very difficult film for a person who's done a lot of films, much less a few. It was my fault: I should have prepared and done it myself, but after *Eiger*, I was kind of weak, mentally, and wanted to get somebody else to do it. Then, as I got into it, I began to visualize it differently.

*You've worked with Bruce Surtees, the cinematographer, on five films* [The Beguiled, Play Misty for Me, Dirty Harry, High Plains Drifter, The Outlaw Josey Wales]; *what made you use him on this one?*
I used Surtees in this picture because his photography has a hard light effect and I wanted that. I wanted to backlight the whole movie; a lot of guys are afraid to do it.

*He'll shoot very dark, too; darker than most.*
Yeah, I didn't want to pump light in the faces. That's the conventional thing to do, but I wanted to backlight it. It's very easy to do if you shoot in the fall. It's the best time to shoot a western: the sun stays low and you've got cross-light; it's not overhead and flat all the time.

*It takes the star quality out of the film, when you can't see features—when faces aren't lit and made up for glamor.*
You lean forward to get into them rather than having them bombarding out at you. I love that cross-lighting; in November, the sun stays low all the time, never really gets overhead. It rained every time I wanted it to—I willed it. Especially for the opening montage of the war, I didn't want any sunlight. It gives it a much more sombre effect. The first part of the film showed a kind of idyllic light; then all of a sudden it goes to a very sombre

tone. Then it gradually gets to a nicer tone as his life gets better when he gets to the ranch and starts winning—going from a loser to a winner. That was the way it was planned, and fortunately The Head Gaffer Up Above stayed with us.

*We're struck by the boldness of your widescreen composition and your free-and-easy construction of sequences.*
I felt good with it. It has a lot of scenes with two people, and then it has a lot of scenes with things going on in towns. The easiest thing is to shoot long shots and close-ups; the hard part is in between, the connective tissue. It's how you connect the scenes with the camera, how you tie it all up.

I shoot reverse masters: masters one way, masters the other way. Drives 'em crazy sometimes, but I like to flop between masters and not worry, where a lot of older directors are afraid to flop people from side to side in the frame; for them, everybody starts out on one side of the camera and they stay there, unless they cross during a shot. But I'll jump around, go through here, then go right through there, reverse this way, break the composition up. And in my coverage, there are the kind of mistakes that if you make on purpose are OK—if you make them *without* knowing it, you get yourself in a corner, painted in tight.

One of the most important things on this film, after it was all over, was the lab timing, which Spanky Surtees doesn't sit in on. I sit in on it with the lab to make sure that I have a very good timer. There are so many light changes between shots. You have to make the light change evenly and then balance it up. In the old days, guys like George Stevens would wait around a year till the light was perfect. I can't afford a year, wouldn't want a year. Nine weeks is OK, eight weeks is terrific, six weeks is even better 'cause I like to be moving.

*It seemed to us that the film in some ways is more democratic than your other films. You've tried to share it more with your other characters, although you are the main focus.*
I know what I can do and what I can carry, I think; but at the same time, it's the ensemble and all that periphery—those little characters, even the ones that come and go, like the river rats—that make for a rich tapestry as opposed to just a quickie, where you do the plot and get out of it. I like the other people in *Josey Wales*.

*Also, more people save your life in this film than usual.*
Exactly.

*Eastwood has just directed* Gauntlet, *which is a Christmas release (as were* Dirty Harry, Magnum Force, *and* The Enforcer). *It's a couple-on-the-run, paranoid chase film. At $5 million dollars—including overhead—it's his most expensive to date, and his most technically complex: $1.25 million for special effects. The cast includes Eastwood, Sondra Locke, Pat Hingle, and Bill McKinney.*

*Judging from the production stills,* Gauntlet *moves away from the elegant visual style—post-genre painting, with a bow to the Brandywine School—of* Josey Wales, *to locate itself within a contemporary L.A. art tendency involving kinetic, environmental, and event art ideas, in which domestic icons are transformed by barrage violence, a movement obviously taken from demolition derbies. The point of this sort of art is not to exhibit the finished object, but for the viewers to witness the progressive cruelty visited upon the subject until it is, indexically, finally exhausted of surface/textural potential to absorb any more. This process is preserved on film as the only significant record of the art work, as Tinguely's work has been, or that of many other event artists.*

*In* Gauntlet, *two of these events are:*

*1. Police surround a bungalow and lavish so many rounds on it that it implodes, leaving only a cubic yard of fresh barkdust (the idea that the house becomes its own negative space).*

*2. A Greyhound SceniCruiser runs a downtown Phoenix gauntlet of officers until it becomes a* Guiness Book of Records *item (how many heavy-caliber bullet holes can one bus contain?).*

*Eastwood was kind enough to take time out from preparing a release version of the film for the lab to discuss* Gauntlet *in a phone-call; the film had not yet been screened.*

*FILM COMMENT wants to run the interview. They're gonna put your kisser on the cover.*
Great balls of flame!

*Did you have Dean Riesner work over the script?*
No. It was written by Dennis Shryack and Michael Butler. It was in very good shape. There was a minor amount of rewriting, a lot of it deletions; I did it myself.

A cop starts out to fly an extradited witness from Vegas back to Phoenix for trial. Everything goes wrong—there's this group of people who don't want him to get back. She's a hooker, and he's a cop who hates hookers, but they grow together as they go—via car, via foot, via motorcycle, via train, via bus, you name it. They're just on the run. It's a strong woman's role like in the old days, *It Happened One Night*. The gal stands up to the guy, and because of that, it makes both characters more interesting.

*Do they both live through the film?*
Yeah, we both make it.

*You seem to avoid making the same type of film twice.*
Right. This isn't like anything I've directed before. It's a detective story, but very unlike the [Dirty] Harry Callahan character. This guy, Ben Shockley, has the same determination as Harry, but he isn't as all-knowing. There's a vulnerability factor in *Gauntlet* that isn't there in the Callahan hero. Well, there is some in Callahan, very subtly.

*His grim commitment to victims and little people?*
Yeah. There's a sadness about him, about his personal life, about his smart-alecky fight with the bureaucracy: that's a lot of fun, but there's a lot of sadness behind it, too.

Ben Shockley in *Gauntlet* is a guy who's never had the big cases Callahan's had. The big case is happening to him right during the movie; that's where they're different characters. Shockley fumbles through a few situations that Callahan would have handled much slicker.

What attracted me to the story was that it was a good relationship story. It's an action picture with a ton of action, but at the same time, great relationships. The girl's part is a terrific role, not just token window-dressing like in so many action films. Her part is equal to the male part, if not even more so. It's in *The African Queen* tradition: a love-hate thing that turns out to be a love story. It's a bawdy adventure, too.

*All your films have major women's roles, in which the hero-heroine relationship is used to define each character.*
Good ladies' roles are always important; *Play Misty, Breezy* ... it's a nice way to define characters.

*What did you want to emphasize about the characters?*
There are little moments, gestures between them as they grow together, that become symbolic—but they're not overt gestures. He never goes to bed with her even though she plays a hooker, and that would have been the obvious thing to do. It's a relationship built on another plane. A cop who's had a lot of disappointments, never had a personal life that reached any heights—it becomes a very pure love affair, with great friendship, great regard for one another.

*Do they become partners in the fight for survival?*
Yes. And they have this dream, very idealistic discussions of what their lives should be together. They go on this suicidal mission which they don't think they're going to come out of; then, you don't know what they go on to—they could go their separate ways, you know.

*Do you consciously choose to protect certain private areas of your characters' lives from the audience?*
Oh, sure, definitely. I do that consciously: it's much more interesting for the audience to write with you, to draw with you. In *High Plains Drifter*, they could draw in many endings. At the end of *Josey Wales*, who knows what's going to happen? The audience is rooting for him to go back, but you don't show him going back into the arms of the girl he's left. He's just riding off in that direction, into the sunrise rather than the sunset. Hopefully, it gives you the feeling. The audience is willing him to go back there. That's their participation.

*When you plan a film, how do you think about the place of the audience?*
I think they must participate in every shot, in everything. I give them what I think is necessary to know, to progress through the story, but I don't lay out so much that it insults their intelligence. I try to give a certain amount to their imagination. I try to play straight across with the audience.

I don't like expository scenes, unless they have an important payoff. I hate to have the scene where you take a break, sit down, and tell the audience what's been done up to that point because they're not smart enough to understand it. That's playing down to the audience. As a rule, I always shy away from exposition.

*Do you have a dream film you'd like to direct, if you could do anything at all, no restrictions?*

No. I wouldn't know it till I read it. I wish I had the talent to sit down and say, "I'll write this, and that, and that," but I can't do it.

*What is the gauntlet?*

They run the gauntlet at the end. Their bus travels down through town and is just ripped to shreds. Hence the title.

*Is this the strategy of displacing violence against people with violence against expensive objects such as cars that television took up a few years ago?*

Yeah. This isn't a terribly violent film in the sense of gruesome violence. There's a lot of action, but not a lot of killing per se.

*When you began planning* Gauntlet, *did you have a particular visual look you wanted?*

Yeah, but it wasn't one I could compare with anything else. We had a lot of night shooting, and one thing I knew I didn't want was a lot of forced shooting. In the night sequence in the cave, when we weren't in light, I wanted the screen black—*real* black. With forcing, it's all grey: they low-key light, they force-develop, and then it all comes out milky.

*You've been spoiled by Bruce Surtees.*

Yeah, he likes hard light. Frank Stanley, on the other hand, likes soft light, which is OK, and which worked well for a film like *Breezy*—I liked that look. For *Josey,* the hard light worked much better. I wanted it very natural, for the sets to be unlit looking.

When I build a film, I build a lot for the sound, too. I'm always con-scious when I'm shooting of how it's going to sound. I'm not sitting around like a lab technician, saying "Oh God, the color's off, the light's too low, you're not going to be able to see enough of the scene, nobody'll know what it's about." Well, they're gonna hear and they're gonna feel it—there's a lot of other elements that are not limited to just photograph-ing a blank shot. You always picture the end result while you're doing it.

# Director Clint Eastwood: Attention to Detail and Involvement for the Audience

RIC GENTRY/1980

"MAKING A GOOD MOVIE takes a good cast, a good story, and everything else," Eastwood begins. "But what it comes down to, whether it's going to be any good or not, is how disciplined you are in keeping the overall concept through the assembling. And it's tough to do because you look at the film over and over again, and you have to go back to your original instinct in making subsequent decisions."

And that's the primary reason Clint Eastwood likes to work fast once he begins a film, to minimize the duration between the "original instinct" and the final cut. The second reason is, of course, economic, and the combined momentum of both factors allows him to finish *every* project ahead of schedule and under budget. So an Eastwood budget is low—while the returns are extremely high. The comparatively scant $3.5 million needed to produce *Every Which Way but Loose,* for example, spawned over $87 million, and the $6.5 million for *Bronco Billy* has already made $28 million and still is rising, as it circulates to accolades overseas.

More than Eastwood's implicit box office magnetism goes into the success of his work and his production company, Malpaso Films (recently Robert Daley Productions, for legal reasons). Cost-effective filmmaking is one part of it. The other is having a sense of what the public wants. "You have to trust your instincts to be in sync with the audience, " he says.

Eastwood is largely an intuitive thinker, as that comment and his working methods might imply. When he directs a film or chooses a project to

Published in *Millimeter,* December 1980, 127–33. Reprinted by permission.

appear in, he has very firm "emotions"—not reasons—for knowing how to proceed. Working quickly keeps these emotions intact.

"Because half-way through every movie you always say to yourself, 'Gee, I wonder if I should do this?' or even, 'Do I like this?' But you have to grab yourself and say, 'No, this is what my first feelings were about it. I'm committed to this ending and this development of the story and I'm going to stick with it.' Because you're dealing in an emotional art, a visual medium which has its own logic, and so you're telling a story in a way that accords with that. Film is mostly an expression of how we feel and think. So if you sit and analyze why you're having these thoughts, then you're distancing yourself from the emotions. You just have to go with those first emotions."

When Eastwood reads a script he visualizes it, both in terms of shots and composition. But pre-eminent is the mood gleaned from the material, the overall sensuous texture of environments and movements that have implicit emotional resonances. Thus, he does not transfer his impressions into a shooting script, an intermediary repository of those impressions which could tempt a reconsideration of the mental pictures, while intricately plotting them.

Instead, Eastwood first seeks a confirmation of the mood, or the nearest approximation of it, in an appropriate location. It is no coincidence, then, that one of his salient features as a director is his penchant for landscape, the widest concentricity of a dramatic center. Moreover, his intimate knowledge of the topographical United States, particularly the West, contributes to his distinction as a director of certified American tastes.

"I scout locations in different ways," he explains. "*High Plains Drifter* I scouted by myself, just me and a pick-up truck, hauling around through Oregon and back down through Nevada and California. . . . But you have to find spots that read into the story. Sometimes you just have to keep looking because there's always a million other places you could do a picture, some maybe better, some maybe not. The location just has to correspond with the concept of the film, to the atmosphere created by the story."

For *Play Misty for Me*, his first film as a director in 1971, Eastwood chose the irregular and diverse territory of Carmel and Monterey, California, the area near his home, to suit the unstable psychology of the characters. In *The Outlaw Josey Wales* (1975), it was northern Arizona and southern Utah that communicated the sombre, sometimes Gothic tones of the post-Civil War saga. For *Bronco Billy* (1980), the story of a modern day Wild West Show entrepreneur, his most recent directorial venture, he situated the production in Idaho for several reasons.

"It was written for Oklahoma or Kansas," he explains, "but if you're familiar with that area you know everything's the same. And I'd been through Boise, Idaho and Ontario, Oregon, that area, and up in the mountains nearby while vacationing in McColl. As I drove through it, going through the eastern Oregon plains, there, which were only a few miles away, I saw that it was the same kind of country as middle America. And then with the mountains nearby, I chose Boise as the central location because it gave us a lot of variation within a few miles. Though it was West, it could have been anywhere in middle America, the plains of Kansas or Illinois or Oklahoma."

Boise was first of all practical, enabling the backdrops to change as they needed to change to conjure the wayfaring of the traveling show. But another reason was thematic, for the open spaces reflect the protagonist's need for freedom, Billy's escape from the one-room tenement in New Jersey where in an earlier life he was a discontented shoe salesman.

Another crucial factor in establishing mood for Eastwood is, of course, cinematography. But unlike most directors, he does not choose a cinematographer for a specific style, but rather an able and creative technician who is as adaptable as Eastwood is as a director. "I try to get the cinematographer involved with the story, I tell him what I want to accomplish and try to convey a feeling for what I think it should look like, because the style grows out of the material, and so the style changes really with each picture."

Consequently, Eastwood will keep the same cinematographer for several films. David Worth for example, who shot the lush, sometimes piquant colors for *Bronco Billy,* is reportedly doing something much different for *Any Which Way You Can,* the sequel to *Every Which Way but Loose* (to be released shortly) which Buddy Van Horn is directing.

An even better example is perhaps Eastwood's five-film relationship with Bruce Surtees, which produced some extraordinary visual diversities and innovations, all of which marry the cinematography to the respective stories with such distinction that no two even resemble each other. *The Beguiled,* directed by Don Siegel with Eastwood in the lead, is composed of almost Expressionistic distortions of color, with red the over-riding tint. In *Dirty Harry,* another Siegel film, Surtees strips the look of all stylization to better view the harsh realism of the story.

It is with *Josey Wales,* however, that Eastwood and Surtees teamed up to do some of their most imaginative work. "Bruce came up with a suggestion that I thought was very innovative," Eastwood recalls. "At that time they were going to stop manufacturing a certain film stock, a much slower stock than is used presently. We were scheduled to begin shooting in the fall of the year, which is a great time to shoot a Western because the sun stays low in the sky, though you do run the risk of an early winter setting in. But Bruce said, 'Why don't we use this slow stock? We'll have to use a little more light for certain scenes, but for outdoors it gets richer blacks. The only trouble is they're running out of it.'

"Now, I love rich blacks in a film. I can't stand it when the blacks go grey and come out milky. In fact, I worked with one cinematographer who wanted to force everything, but I didn't have the patience for the way the blacks would curdle and go milky. But Bruce doesn't do that. He has a hard light effect and I wanted to backlight the whole movie. He knew what I liked, the blacks and the contrast, and he wanted to use this stock. So I said, 'OK, let's buy up enough stock to use for this picture.' So we did." They bought the stock they needed and stored it in the basement of Eastwood's office on the Burbank lot. "It was the last of the old speed," he says. "If you were to duplicate that look now, you'd have to do it through an entirely different technique."

But there was still another problem on *Josey Wales.* "We got to the final sequence of the picture and the scene was to be shot at dawn, the scene where Josey has his final encounter with the Cherokee chief (Chief Dan George) before he rides off at sunrise. Bruce said, 'Maybe we should just shoot it in portions, do a piece of it at dawn every day.' And I said, 'That's just prohibitive. In the first place, when I'm in a sequence I want to stay in sequence. And secondly, I don't have that much to fill up the rest of the day.' So I said, 'Here's what I want you to do. I've never seen a film shot day-for-night that looked like night. At best, it looked like dawn. So I want you to shoot that sequence as if you were shooting it for night, just like a day-for-night sequence, and it'll come out dawn.' So that's the way we did it."

Similarly, Eastwood shot another scene, where Josey has a final confrontation with the bounty hunter who's been pursuing him throughout the film, "at sunset as if it were sunrise. At sunset you get that very heavy cross light and it was like the first light of the day. I just did it out of order, so the sun would be at a certain angle at a certain time, which is very tricky and requires preparation because it happens so fast and the shadows get longer rather than shorter."

Another practical habit Eastwood has is to designate scenes that require bad weather and then withhold them until they actually happen—breaking the continuity of the shooting schedule at that point to accommodate the inclemency. For *Bronco Billy* there is a scene early in the film where rain is needed to bolster the humor and the pathos of an argument Billy has with his five cohorts in the show, along the roadside in the middle of nowhere. "All along I wanted to play with this rain sequence," he recalls, "and on that day it was just colder than a well-digger's ass. Every actor in the scene was just praying that he wasn't going to be the one to forget his lines so we'd have to start over. But we shot it real quick, with one camera, moving from set-up to set-up as fast as we could.

"I laid it out, shot by shot, as a cover set, as you would normally on a day for rain, setting it aside so that when it did rain we could shoot the scene. It was raining, but very lightly, and we added to it from a creek we found nearby in order to have it pouring. We just went and threw a lot of water on it, but the light was consistent because it really was an overcast day, so the lighting is flat. It was wet in depth. The highways were slick in the distance and not just wet around the camera. Everything worked to our advantage that way. And it's a good position to be in, to have a sequence where you want bad weather, because inevitably you get some. We just continued along until it looked like a storm was brewing."

Once the mood is established, Eastwood works extensively with the script, "until you see the total picture, and all the perspectives of the character." In *The Gauntlet* he rewrote several scenes, and in *Bronco Billy* he added an entire sequence. Wearing his sharpshooter six guns, Billy is in line to cash what is surely a meagre check when two masked men suddenly enter to hold up the bank. One of them knocks over a little boy who drops his own savings to the floor. And it's then that Billy takes action, preventing the robbery and becoming an instant local hero.

"I felt the script needed that because of the sequence later on where the sheriff humiliates Billy when he's trying to bail his friend out of jail. Because the sheriff taunts him about who's quicker on the trigger, you've got to know that Billy can be very cool and quick-witted and good with the guns so that the audience is really rooting for Billy to blow the sheriff away. It's important that he doesn't, though, because he's more interested in his friend than in his own pride at that point. To be more commercial, you would have had him draw on the sheriff. But as far as the statement of the movie goes, it wasn't appropriate. Clint Eastwood fans are maybe saying, 'Yeah, take 'im out.' But in terms of the statement, what that scene has a lot to do with, loyalty and sacrifice, Billy couldn't do that. The main thing he had to do, no matter how the sheriff humiliated him, was to get his friend out of jail."

More often than not, however, Eastwood subtracts from the script rather than adds. One of the primary strategies of his films is to minimize the background information about the characters and to let gesture transmit the nature of the character to the audience. The less revealed, he contends, the greater is the participation of the audience. The technique originated with his creation of "The Man with No Name" in the Sergio Leone film, *A Fistful of Dollars,* the film that gained Eastwood his international status.

"Originally it was written with just pages of dialogue," he points out, "all of it explaining the background of the character. But I wanted to play it with an economy of dialogue and to build a whole feeling through attitude and movements. So I said to Sergio, 'Let's keep the mystery of the character and just allude to what happened in the past.' Sergio argued with me, though he did agree in a way, but it was just much harder for the Italian mentality to accept. They're just used to so much more exposition and I was throwing that out. Finally he accepted it, but then the producers thought something was really awry. They said, 'Christ, this guy isn't doing anything. He isn't saying anything. He doesn't even have a name! And that cigar is just sitting there burning.' They just didn't know what the hell was going on. But when they saw it all assembled, they realized what it was, and then how it went over on the public. The 'No Name' guy soon became a very imitated character."

And the mystique transfers to narrative structure, for just as all but the most pertinent exposition is deleted, so is the final destiny of Eastwood's characters. The action finishes, the dramatic elements are resolved, but there is still the sense of the protagonist still at large. "I like to leave them that way," he says, "still in the process of finding their way. You're not ending with a person's demise and you're not telling a life story. It's the nature of films maybe. In a Scott Fitzgerald novel you might do an entire life span, almost start with a flashback and then bring it up to the present and proceed from there. But these movies are really incidents. *Dirty Harry* was just an incident in one man's life. *Josey Wales* is more of a saga, covering a longer period, but you felt that he was going back to the group he collected along the way."

Eastwood recalls an argument he had with his editor regarding the open-ended conclusion of *Josey Wales*. "He felt that I should literally show him returning to the girl and the group after he has that final talk with the chief. And I said, 'No, you don't need to show him going back. You see him riding off at sunrise and that's enough.' He said, 'Yeah, but how will the audience know that he's going back to the girl and the others?' And I said, 'Because they're *willing* him to go back there. The audience is taking him back there.' It's the audience's imagination and participation that makes a film work. You don't have to tell them everything."

Perhaps the most vivid demonstration of excluding expository material to heighten audience participation is *High Plains Drifter*. The film begins with one of Eastwood's most dazzling visual flourishes. A lone rider emerges from the desert through a dance of lights and haze that, through the use of an extreme telephoto lens and the mirage-effect of the wavering heat, renders the impression that he is gliding through the sky. It is the virtual arrival of an Apocalyptic Horseman. As he reaches the isolated town of Lago, he gradually subjugates the populace to his authority and finally wreaks havoc upon them for reasons we never really learn. The Drifter then leaves as mysteriously as he arrived, crossing the desert once more and disappearing.

"It was originally written that the Drifter was the brother of the murdered sheriff, but I played it as if it could have been some apparition. You're not quite sure, but you know that he has a strong interest in making this town suffer for their sins and that it ties in with their complacency with the murder. But the only clue is when the Drifter lies down (later in the hotel) and has this dream of the sheriff being whipped to death, and you know from there that he's tied in some way, but you're not sure how. That way you keep the mystique and the whole atmosphere is mysterious. To me, if the Drifter comes to town and immediately says, 'I'm the brother of the murdered sheriff,' right away you draw the conclusions. Instead, once he takes the town and humiliates them through his own methods, you're asking, '*Who* is he? *Why* is he doing this?'

"The traditional way of doing it," Eastwood continues, "was to just lay everything out. You know, right away, as the guy rides into town—using the Western as an example, but it could be any kind of film—he rides into town and sees a man beating a horse. He interferes with it, punches the guy out, so you know immediately that's the antagonist with whom the hero is going to resolve a conflict later on. Then he sees the school marm on the porch and she gives him a stare or whatever, and you also know that they're going to be romantically involved. And you can almost draw the ending right there, in the first five minutes. The audience should never be able to anticipate that far ahead where it's going, because otherwise they sit there waiting for the movie to catch up with them."

*High Plains Drifter,* basically a morality play, also benefits considerably, if not definitively, by the location, the Mono Lake district of northeastern California. The story was originally situated in Monument Valley, the grandiose site of so many John Ford films, but, Eastwood says, "that wouldn't have provided the same mood I got from the story. I needed a place that would correspond with that mood and Mono Lake is what I finally found. It's a dead lake. It has some very interesting outcroppings and the colors almost change moment by moment, so it gave the film an elusive quality.

"The visuals at the beginning were to set up the mood of the rider. I took a piece of the heat wave out of the corner of the shot and blew it up so it was the same texture in the whole frame. As it was initially, I couldn't get back far enough with the lens to get the rider out of sight, so I just started with a blank screen and dissolved through it. With the heat wave you don't notice the dissolve. Things like that just set the tone for the film, but from the very beginning I saw the film very clearly. It was the reason I decided to direct it."

Again working with Bruce Surtees, Eastwood shot *Drifter* with unusually wide apertures to intensify the outdoor brightness, so that everything in the town appears visibly scorched by the light, almost flaming. (And the effect precipitates the later incident when the Drifter coerces the people to paint their whole town red and re-title it "Hell.") By contrast, the interiors are composed of deep browns, sienna, and burnt orange, with a proclivity for underexposure to render a sense of decay.

Eastwood describes the difficulties—and the importance—of establishing a continual spatial relationship between the indoors and the outdoors, and vice-versa. "It was part of the elusiveness again, because you never felt stable with what you saw. The colors changed, the clouds changed, and the exposures jumped at you. In one instance we started with the Drifter in the saloon, a very dark room, and then had him walk out the door into the light, so there's a huge exposure change. As you get to the front door you have to start changing it for the outside or you just get a giant flare. It's not unusual, but it was a bit tricky, and in the film it worked quite effectively."

In addition to narrative vacancies and character distillations, Eastwood also strives to include the audience within a complete use of space to focus on the action. He has no compunction about breaking the 180° rule for camera placement, a visual stylistic that only Japanese directors are really comparable to. "I'm not afraid to reverse master shots, to shoot on both sides of the actors. A lot of older, more traditional directors would never do it. For them, the camera stays on one side of the actors in a scene unless they cross during a shot. But I like to break up the composition. I think you involve the audience more by changing perspective freely, not binding them to their seats that way. One reason I like location shooting is that you don't have to worry which side of the actors you're on at any point, and are not limited to a set, which dictates where the camera goes."

And he does fully exploit the advantages of being on location, availing himself of stimulations in the environment and improvising when inspired. In *Bronco Billy*, the pivotal moment in the film involves a scene where Billy decides to single-handedly rob a diesel train. The absurdity is self-evident as the train goes roaring by and Billy gives chase, but the moment is not only the culmination of his frustrations with the struggling Wild West show, it's also the clearest example of his commitment to the romantic ethos of his cowboy fantasies. So the scene itself, as Eastwood suggests, had to be very carefully constructed and sufficiently understated. "It can be very dangerous in a scene like that," he says, "because if it isn't done correctly, you can just blow the whole momentum of the picture." The scene had to make you laugh and evoke your sympathies at the same time.

But instead of playing it safe, Eastwood added something which more than summarized the thematic intentions while it jolted our perspective of the scene. It occurred to him about a half-hour before he did it. "What happened was that it was cold outside," he explains. 'It was real sunny, but it was real cold. I was on the train with the extras and I saw this little kid, a kind of extroverted little guy and his mother was sitting there. He was asking her a lot of questions and I started thinking that I should get a point of view from the train. So I just made up this little deal. I said, 'You just look out there when I come riding up, and say "Cowboys and Indians." ' " So I got him real excited about it and then had the mother take the opposite tack, of 'Uh, yeah, OK,' as if she's hardly paying him any attention. But it just gave the ultimate irony to the whole thing, because his imagination is going wild just like Billy's. They're both intrigued by this thing with the Old West because, after all, Billy's like a kid himself."

It has been suggested by Sondra Locke, now in her fifth film with Eastwood, that in directing actors, he communicates motive for character through the position and angle of the camera rather than through effusive verbal cues. "I'll let the actors create their own roles," he says, "find what it is in the material that means something to them, what connects for them emotionally. Casting, though, is already a designation of character. And I've worked with almost all these people before, so I know what they can do.

"But camerawork is like penmanship; there is as much expressed in the way you write as in what you write about. And so the camera works with the actors for a cumulative effect. The camera is not a neutral eye, and the actors aren't the whole scene either." What is the scene more than anything else is the moment of its articulation, when the whirr of the camera heightens the activity like adrenalin, and the long nurtured sense for mood is brought into focus with the greatest discrimination.

"I think that directing a film is *seeing* it, when you see it there live, when it's happening right there in front of you. The guy walks in and then the girl walks in and the scene just goes, right at the first instance of the first take. A lot of times it's a shock. You say, 'Jesus, that worked terrific.' But you have to be able to say, 'That's what I want,' and walk away. And if it's not working, you have to work until it *does* happen, even if it's the tenth time. But if it works immediately, you've got to have enough wherewithal to say, 'That's it. That's good. That's what I want.' You have to have the picture there in your mind before you make it. And if you don't, you're not a director, you're a guesser."

Significantly, Eastwood's films are extremely well paced—unrushed, relaxed—with a strong sense for real time, regardless of the force of the action or the speed of the narrative. He ascribes much of this to the "proper punctuation" of scenes during the cutting, but it would also suggest a faithfulness to the rhythm of things as they were experienced during the shooting—so that the editing is in accord, not manipulative of the moment of visual record.

Obviously, style is a result of technical mastery, the implicit use of the elements of production to cohere with one's vision of the material. Eastwood was never content to express himself solely as an actor, and as a regular on the TV series *Rawhide* some 20 years ago, he strove to increase his creative contribution. The channels proved limited, however, and the most he was permitted to direct were some trailers. But working on the show from week to week gave him the opportunity to acquaint himself with the technology and then to think with the director, weighing his decisions and considering his strategies. "I would always ask myself, 'How would I do it?' If it was something impractical I would make a point of never getting myself into that position, but rather than second guessing, just disagreeing with what he was doing, I tried to come up with a viable alternative, a real solution and not just a complaint.

"But I think you pick things up from people just as you pick up your own ideas as you go along. I've always said that you learn something from almost everybody you work with—every director, actor, or actress, you always learn something. They do something particularly interesting or well that you've never seen before and you always remember it. And on the other side of the scale, you see a director do something that impresses you negatively and you always remember that too. You think, 'Shit, don't ever do that.'"

Eastwood is specifically critical of directors who are either hypermeticulous in their methods or, for lack of decisiveness and therefore virtually without methods, those who repeat a single set-up to the exhaustion of the actors and the energy of the film. Furthermore, such counter-productive habits, which he sees advancing to epidemic proportions today, skyrocket costs and infringe on the potential for other features. "Anybody can make a film if you shoot 40 or 50 takes on everything. If you run off enough footage you can put all that together and get something out of it. But whether it's any good or not, has any soul to it, is another thing again. It's like firing a shotgun. You can hit a lot more things with that than you can with a rifle, but it takes a lot less skill and it has a lot less impact.

"There was a thing in the *Hollywood Reporter* recently, in that regular feature they run about things happening 40 years ago on this date, that just shows you the irony implicit with all these guys doing all these takes and exposing a million feet of film per picture. It said that John Ford had just finished *The Grapes of Wrath* and he had exposed the least amount of film for a feature up to that time, which was something like 37,000 feet. Now here's a guy who makes a classic, that people want to see forever. Long after the man's dead people will be running it, for years and years, and he did it with a record low of exposed film for that time, and that's because Ford knew exactly what he wanted and knew when he had it. He didn't go out there for six or eight months or a year and do 50 takes on everything. When he saw the prints that he liked he went off to the next thing. . . . *The Grapes of Wrath* had tremendous energy and it's a classic on every score. What makes you think you're going to make any more of a classic by exposing 50 times the amount of film he did? It just doesn't make any sense."

Another way that Eastwood facilitates the celerity and economy of the production is to have a crew that is compatible with quick decisions and set-up changes. "You have to be able to move and have everybody move with you," he says. "But most of the people I work with are in sync with it." He has worked with virtually the same crew for the last five films. Moreover, and no doubt recalling his years as a stifled talent on *Rawhide*, Eastwood is highly receptive to their suggestions on the set. In fact, all the outward signs of either authority or star status are removed in order to encourage camaraderie and equality. There are no director's chairs, no extravagant preferential treatment for the actors, nor any exclusive cliques to stratify the community, which a full production unit implicitly comprises.

"It's definitely a democracy," says Eastwood. "If I have any qualities that work as a director, it's that I try to stimulate everybody to be as creative as they possibly can. I like them to contribute to the film and not just do their jobs by rote. It makes for a better atmosphere and ultimately for a better film. If I come in and play big shot and say, 'This is the way I want it and you guys just do this. You do the slate. You run the sound. And I don't want to hear anything but what I tell you,' I mean, that's so short-sighted. I think that's what a lot of people think auteur directing is. But there's no such thing as 'auteur' in my mind. It's an ensemble. Somebody leads the ensemble, there's a lieutenant to the platoon or something, but that doesn't mean all the other people aren't being innovative. Rather than just having them pick up a brick and laying it in, they're all being creative with the design in a certain way. And as long as that doesn't deviate too far, that's great, because I turn down as many suggestions as I accept, but I do take some good ones." And similarly, no one in the industry can be said to have provided so many new talents with opportunities to advance their careers. Michael Cimino, Philip Kaufman, Bruce Surtees, John Milius, writer Jo Heims, David Worth and numerous others from within his own production ranks have benefited from Eastwood's trust and encouragement. Veteran stunt co-ordinator Buddy Van Horn is making his debut as a director on the upcoming *Any Which Way You Can*, a step forward that led to other offers before the film was even started.

But all of this coincides with Eastwood's philosophy of choosing roles and material for himself. "You've got to take chances. You've just got to. If I don't take chances, then I don't deserve to be where I am to some degree because what's the point of getting into a position where you can make certain films and not make others? I could sit and go through scripts and say, 'Now that's not commercial,' or 'That's not what I built as an image.' When I went to make *Every Which Way but Loose*, my agent, my attorney, and a lot of people were against it. They said, 'This isn't Clint Eastwood.' And I said, 'What do you mean it isn't me? None of these other guys are me either.' There are elements maybe, but you do it for different reasons. You can do a picture with the idea of doing it for straight entertainment, but then, I've proven I can make pictures that make a buck here and there. But there's other things I've got to prove in my life, too, just to myself as a person, to make comments that are of other natures." He even goes on to say that he would consider projects adverse to his own political position or of highly controversial nature if they offered both a relevant alternative to a public issue and a generally accessible story.

"You've got to keep stretching out and trying other stuff," he adds. "I could have chosen a lot of scripts that were different than *Bronco Billy,* that were less of a challenge. But *Bronco Billy* was just worth trying. If it doesn't work, it doesn't work, but it's worth trying." The receipts on *Billy,* one of Eastwood's most unusual and complex films, would certainly indicate that it does work. But more than that, the plethora of critical writing that the film has inspired would also suggest that it's a film that will be looked at for a long time to come.

"I hope so," he concluded. "It's really gratifying to make a film like *Josey Wales* or *High Plains Drifter,* that people have a long range interest in. I get a whole lot of cinema groups who want to talk about those films. And I really enjoy that, when they want to come back and go into it years down the line, to learn what made it tick and how it evolved. It means you did something right. But you've got to trust yourself, trust your instincts."

# Eastwood: An Auteur to Reckon with

## CHARLES CHAMPLIN/1981

SUCCESS BEGETS POWER, BUT power does not necessarily beget more success in turn, or corporate life would be very dull. The question of what the successful will do with their powers is somehow more suspenseful in the movies than anywhere else because the answers are so visible — ponderous failures or daring and imaginative leaps to further success.

Clint Eastwood, in his deceptively low-keyed and laid-back way, has used the star power generated initially in other people's pictures to build an independent production company with a success record that is probably second to none in its return on investment.

By electing to do what he wants to do, Eastwood has, it turns out, done exactly what his public wants him to do, sometimes confounding his critics, the local man included.

Having been a laconic man of action, he became a good-hearted slapstick man of action, feeding second-banana lines to an orangutan in *Every Which Way but Loose,* a loose-jointed farce the public clasped to its bosom in a frenzy of pleasure. In last year's *Bronco Billy,* he took the comedy a long step further and played a sweet-hearted and gentle idealist, a man so in love with the heroic myth of the West and a man of such goodness that he would not even seek revenge on the corrupt and nasty sheriff who had humiliated him.

By an irony that did not escape Eastwood for a minute, it was the critics, who had previously been as eager to scoff as to praise, who now embraced

*Bronco Billy* in a frenzy of admiration. It was the customers who initially weren't so sure (possibly put off by an artful but ambiguous ad campaign). But virtue triumphed in the end and *Bronco Billy* has done nice, steady business ($15 million gross domestically so far) and is, Eastwood calculates, safely into profit.

*Any Which Way You Can,* the sequel to *Every Which Way but Loose,* is one of a handful of runaway box-office successes of year-end. At last count it had taken in something more than $50 million at the box office. It is the same Eastwood, but a new and younger orangutan. "Two years in the life of an orangutan is a lot," Eastwood said the other day. The original had grown as if aspiring to be King Kong, no longer pal-sized.

The script of *Every Which Way but Loose* had been around for a long time, rejected by everyone, Eastwood says. The script itself was dog-eared and food-stained. "Most sane men were skeptical about it; there were conflicts about it in my own group. They said it was dangerous. They said it's not *you.* I said, it *is* me. Nothing on the screen yet has been me. It's a left-handed compliment when people say, 'That's him.' If you make people think that, you've done a lot."

*Bronco Billy* came in over the transom on a friend's recommendation, not from an agent. Eastwood was going to send it back to writer Dennis Hackin but was caught by the title, glanced at a couple of pages and couldn't put it down.

"My first thought was that Frank Capra or Preston Sturges might have done it in their heyday. It had some values that were interesting to explore in contrast to the '60s, Vietnam and Watergate and so on.

"Here was a guy who was a loser but who wouldn't acknowledge it and who was a holdout against cynicism. It wasn't old-fashioned but in a way it was.

"The guy was fun to play because he had to be stripped bare of all his dignity, like the character in *It's a Wonderful Life,* to make the transition and end up all right."

There was nervousness, not to say dissension, within the ranks of Eastwood's Malpaso Co. about *Bronco Billy,* particularly about the unavenged humiliation.

"I knew it wasn't a commercial attempt," Eastwood says. "There were suggestions we add more action and some sex, but I stuck to the writer's intent. If that's what we had to do to be a slam-bang commercial success,

I didn't want to. I don't have to prove my commercial value at this point in my career. I didn't pay off the bad sheriff. I suppose a 'normal' Clint Eastwood picture would have."

If the budget had been $12 million, Eastwood admits, that would have been another matter; he is not a spendthrift with his own money or anyone else's. But he brought *Bronco Billy* in for a dirt-cheap, by present standards, $5 million.

"When I started directing in 1970, whoever would've said $5 million would be a very modest budget?" he asks.

The spiraling cost cycle, however, is one Eastwood has seen before. Watching *Paint Your Wagon* swell to $20 million as far back as 1969, Eastwood decided it needn't be and started his Malpaso production company to do it more efficiently.

"*Bronco*," Eastwood says, "wasn't hard or expensive to make in this day of overblown budgets and jaded regard for the financiers. I always think, what would Jack Warner say in this situation? You can say what you will, those guys watched the store, and they pulled the plug when it ought to be pulled. I'm told that the production costs get out of hand because some of the executives know other things but not film making. What I ask is, if they don't know film making, what is their function?"

Eastwood keeps Malpaso small and loose. "Nobody looks at you sideways if you make a suggestion or argue about a point. Just tell the truth is all I ask."

He has developed a sort of repertory company of supporting players, like the marvelous veteran Scatman Crothers who played the ringmaster in *Bronco Billy* and who entertained the crowd extras in Boise so Eastwood could film reaction shots. Geoffrey Lewis, another expert farceur, is also an Eastwood regular, and Sondra Locke is Eastwood's costar onstage and off.

What Eastwood would most like to do now is another Western. His *The Outlaw Josey Wales* seems to have been the last really successful Western — excepting, perhaps, *Blazing Saddles,* which was a bit off-trail as Westerns go. The recent fate of Westerns is not encouraging, but then again they have not had Eastwood and they have not had the mythic quality that classic Westerns have had and that Eastwood as the laconic loner carries with him like a saddle blanket.

But if the Western is alive in his mind (a script is being developed, one of three projects he has in the works), Dirty Harry is dead.

"I'm not sure what you could do with Dirty Harry now," Eastwood says. "I don't know where else to take him. You could do one for commercial satisfaction, maybe, not for personal satisfaction. That's why I'd like to do a Western; I'd love the challenge of people saying you can't do it."

One of Eastwood's first acting jobs was as one of the flyers in William Wellman's *Lafayette Escadrille* (Tab Hunter and Tom Laughlin were others). His regret, as an intense lifelong film buff, is that he didn't get to work with Raoul Walsh, King Vidor, William Wyler and other great directors. "I came along just a bit too late," he says.

His own career, he has no doubt, will ultimately be as a director. He directed *Play Misty for Me* and had a grand time. "One of the executives at Universal said, 'Who the hell wants to see you play a disc jockey?' I said, 'Who the hell wants to see me play anything?'" Eastwood liked the double duty and says, "I was talking to George Lucas about some things the other day and I know he does not like directing. He said that just before *Star Wars* he was thinking of getting out of that part of it altogether. But I kinda thrive on it. It leaves you zapped, but it's worth it."

Now Eastwood has had the honor of a retrospective tribute at the Museum of Modern Art. "Usually it's some great Yugoslav director. This time it was a commercial, or sometimes commercial, director. And it was *Bronco* that pushed them over the hill into doing it."

A young audience one afternoon went crazy over *Misty*, Eastwood reports. "Those kids analyze everything we took for granted in our day. They can dazzle you with their information and their questions. They can also read in more than there is there, as the critics did on *Dirty Harry*. But the young people are into movies, and that's something."

Eastwood learned directing from watching, reading about and then working with masters, of whom Don Siegel in Eastwood's book is one. "Other directors will say, let's try it once. Don always said, 'I'm never trying for the second time. I'm always trying to make it right the first time.' De Sica would say cut in the middle of a speech. He had enough; he knew what he needed. He'd say, I'll allow you a little lead-in when we do the other shot."

Not long ago, in a "40 Years Ago" column, Eastwood read that John Ford had shot just 36,000 feet of film on *The Grapes of Wrath*, an astonishingly small amount. "I then thought about the 2 million feet Mike Cimino did on *Heaven's Gate*. I gave Mike his first feature chance on *Thunderbolt and Lightfoot* and I thought he did a very good job. But one's a director, the other's a guesser."

Eastwood plays his hunches about what he wants to do and what he thinks will work and enjoys the power to play the hunches, but he is not a guesser and in his quiet way he has become an auteur to reckon with.

# Cop on a Hot *Tightrope*

DAVID THOMSON/1984

CLINT EASTWOOD KEEPS THE same old bungalow at Warners, with subdued light and brown décor, where he can stretch out on a sofa in a T-shirt, jeans, and sneakers, yarning away for a couple of hours about doing his movies. It's all kept at an amiable, easy-going, unpretentious and un-alarming level—hey, come on in, let's talk. Yet Eastwood is more likely to extend that invitation to Norman Mailer than to *Time* or *Newsweek*. In the last two years, Clint was covered by Mailer for *Parade,* and he was the sub-ject of a lengthy article in *The New York Review of Books*. Something in the long, lean loner hankers after respectability.

You don't have to look too far ahead to see him getting an Oscar for overall career excellence, or even the AFI's Life Achievement Award. Mean-while he has to get along with being the most famous and successful movie star of the last 20 years. There is word at Warners, coaxed out of the dis-creet woodwork by Joe Hyams, an executive "with special responsibility for keeping Clint happy," that $800 million in rentals have come in on Clint's name since *The Outlaw Josey Wales*. Eastwood is too cool to be count-ing, though there are stories of him putting on his spectacles at the end of every day to go through the books ("Make my day—show me an error").

And if counting counts, then you'd have to add in the Universal period (with *Dirty Harry, High Plains Drifter, Play Misty for Me,* and *Thunderbolt and Lightfoot)* plus the spaghetti Westerns (and Clint had ten percent of *The*

Published in *Film Comment* 20, no. 5 (September/October 1984): 64–73. Reprinted by per-mission of the author.

*Good, the Bad and the Ugly*), not to mention the durability of his films on TV reruns and his newfound supremacy on video-cassette. Nearly all of his work has been done for his company, Malpaso, meaning "bad step—like if it looks like you're going to trip over something." Eastwood has always explained Malpaso as a way of making his own mistakes. But it has been the knife to cut out a fat share of the rentals.

What is he like?

Let Norman Mailer answer that, in the talking-to-himself format of his *Parade* article:

"Do you like him?

"You have to. On first meeting, he's one of the nicest people you ever met. But I can't say I know him well. We talked a couple of times and had a meal together. I liked him. I think you'd have to be around for a year before you saw his ugly side, assuming he has one.

"It would take that long?

"Well, he's very laid-back. If you don't bother him, he will never bother you. In that sense, he is like the characters he plays in his films."

Mailer needs heroes. I think disillusion might come a little quicker, like 364 days quicker. You *have* to like Eastwood: he has Magnum charm, he is very impressive physically—as he nears 55, the beauty hardens; it is edged with frost now, instead of suntan. He is very natural, very strong; his mind is very made up. You don't have to be too imaginative to see the rock against which some of your questions break. It is startling and intimidating when an actor has so little need of your love, and not much softened if he still wants your respect.

Eastwood runs a small, tight unit at Malpaso, and I doubt if there are too many screw-ups or too much Latin tolerance for them. Over the years, there have been reports of his regular gang, headed by producers Bob Daley and Fritz Manes, looking at new young directors as if to say "Prove yourself." It is equally legendary that Eastwood does not rehearse and favors first takes—all of which contribute toward the economy of his operation (*Honky-tonk Man* was shot in five weeks for $2 million in below-the-line costs).

The most evident streak of Eastwood's hardness, and his greatest limitation as a screen presence, is his unwillingness to push beyond his own gut reactions. If it felt right to Clint, a director might have a tough time going for more takes. Moreover, his briskness onscreen sometimes imparts a feeling that he is not bothering to think too much about a moment or a situation, but just wants to get it done. Equally, the famous narrowing of the eyes, the hiss of the voice—call it intensity or sudden impact—is a mode that fends off subtlety as surely as the squelching one-liners. Eastwood *can* be ironic about his act, but he keeps going back to it.

Whether from boredom, recklessness, creativity, or the insolence of confidence, he keeps on testing the limits of his own antiheroism. *Bronco Billy* and *Honkytonk Man* were considerable extensions of the self-mockery that emerged in *Josey Wales* and the orangutan pictures. They showed Clint as a self-destructive fraud, and *Honkytonk Man* proved his greatest failure as well as the spur to *Sudden Impact*, which reconfirmed him as number one to all those who want number ones. All of that aside, he is still the most interesting tycoon in Hollywood today, still hidden after all these years.

The penchant for taking risks perseveres. While he has his eye on the box office target this December with *City Heat*, with Burt Reynolds (originally a Blake Edwards project reassigned to Richard Benjamin after Eastwood stepped in), Eastwood did a dark variation on Dirty Harry Callahan in *Tightrope*, released in August. It was a hit-and-miss movie, made too fast and too sketchily for the good of its own material. Written and directed by Richard Tuggle (who wrote *Escape from Alcatraz*), *Tightrope* is often disturbing. No other big star, I think, would have risked it. For it's about a New Orleans cop on the track of a sex killer who is himself subject to many of the same contorted, violent urges that might make a man lately divorced (like Eastwood) into such a killer. Moreover, the role of the cop's eldest daughter, played by Alison Eastwood, is one of the most ambiguous things in its stripping of a star persona.

*Tightrope* may have shocked some Eastwood purists. It could have frightened anyone, and with a more searching script and a greater readiness to explore its characters' depths, it could have been far better—along the lines of *In a Lonely Place*. Eastwood's problem could be that the comfort of keeping the Malpaso gang around doesn't stretch him enough. He has made remarkable excursions into vulnerability. But the pictures are put together in such a sure-fire mood of confidence and efficiency, Eastwood is kept from the rawness of his characters. It would require a very forceful director, and very good material, but Eastwood could play a greater range than he has ever attempted, even without the slightly brutal detachment that he maintains toward his films. He is a cautious conservative, but Harry Callahan is a hero in whom our fantasies about lone sufficiency turn into psychosis—

not really that far from Gary Gilmore in *The Executioner's Song*, a role Mailer realized Eastwood was made for.

*What do you think happens to the central character, Wes Block, in* Tightrope *after the film ends?*
Well, you can draw in lots of little subplots. But I assume he continues his relationship with this girl [Genevieve Bujold]. She's the first woman that he has felt something more than just a passing, sexual night kind of thing, like he comes across so many times, in the seamy atmosphere of his work as a New Orleans police officer. I think he wants the stability. And hopefully he can soothe the trauma in his two daughters and go on with someone in a normal life.

*Was Wes involved with prostitutes during his first marriage? Could that have had anything to do with the break-up?*
It might have, but he states in the script that he never had those kinds of friends until just after his wife left. I think the marriage disappointed him a lot. I think he placed a lot of himself emotionally in the marriage. And when it went sour—for whatever reasons—he became very disappointed and he just reached out to whatever's around. Being in the type of work he was in, he ran across a lot of bizarre ladies.

*But he has feelings for them that are perverse or strange. And clearly there is a moment in the film where he wonders whether he could be a sex killer. And there are even moments where you're not totally sure he isn't the killer.*
We definitely wanted that. I stressed that even more in the film than in the screenplay. But I always liked that aspect: is this guy, or isn't he? How does he fit in? I even looped the lines of the actor who played the killer at the beginning, though I changed the voice slightly. Not that I wanted to play all the roles, but I just wanted a little bit of the thing, "Is that Eastwood? Is that him?" You can tell it isn't me, but on the other hand there's just enough familiarity to tie in with the shoes and just kinda getting it going that way. And then later on, when you know it isn't him . . .

*. . . You also know it could have been.*
Yes. It could very well have been him, and even his thoughts about the cop when he talks about him one time, it's like, "This guy is as screwed up

as I am." Who knows what happens? He's got involved with enough of these gals that maybe he felt like it.

*I'm sure the audience will say, "Clint Eastwood couldn't be the villain." But I wonder to what extent Clint Eastwood is intrigued with teasing the audience? It's a brave film in a lot of ways. Some of your hardcore fans may be shocked.*
The hardcore fans, I could just bombard them with the same kind of character for the rest of my career. But that wouldn't be as interesting. I think the more astute fans—I hope some of them are astute—will find this provocative. Because in contrast to the obsessed cop, Dirty Harry, Wes has these other emotions. Not just solving the thing he's obsessed about, and the inequities of the legal profession, the courts, and all that. He just does a job and does it the best he can, and he's got all these sideline characters.

*Did you think it would be brave or risky, compared with* Sudden Impact?
Yeah. I think if on the surface you gave the studio these two, one in each hand, they'd say *Sudden Impact.* That's a lot of money. But I thought it was bold. If it's exciting and bold, that's fine; if it's bold and dull, that's another thing. Hopefully, those people who like suspense and action films will be intrigued by the climax... but along the way they're going to have to bear with this character.

*You've also let yourself look bleaker in this film than ever before.*
Well, that didn't come out of any particular makeup or anything, it just came out of the attitude. It *should* look that way. If I sat there and thought, "What do I look like?" then I'm thinking about the wrong things. I've got to think of the character. You've got to donate yourself to the character. You can't say, "Jeez, will I look as sharp as I have in some films?" Like in *Honky-tonk Man,* I'm playing a consumptive—like you're purposefully putting on a type of Kabuki makeup. But I don't usually wear makeup in films, so the character in *Tightrope* is just that way out of his feelings and attitudes.

Tightrope *is the most extreme case, but there have been others in recent years in which you might have been saying to your fans, "Well, don't fantasize about being Clint Eastwood too much. He gets old, he has personal problems, he doesn't conduct his life like Harry. He's beaten sometimes." How conscious are you of doing that with your fans?*

Well, I don't know if I'm conscious of doing it. I think it evolves out of love for the story. The story's given to me, and I like the character and feel it's a challenge. I can't just do—regardless of some fans—the mysterious kind of character who has everything under control. That's fun to play, but I've done it a lot. I'll do it again, probably, but I have to broaden the scope.

But it's been successful. Everybody in the world advised me against doing *Every Which Way but Loose*. They said, "That isn't a Clint Eastwood film: the girl dumps you, you give up the fight, and you've got this silly orangutan," that sort of thing. I said, "Yeah, but it's kinda interesting." It's comedic, and yet it's different. And if I hadn't felt in a broadening mood, I might have said, "Yeah, you're right, that isn't me. I'd better do another Harry, or a cowboy." Which is fun—I like to do that. But you have to broaden out.

Sometimes it doesn't work. *The Beguiled*, years ago, wasn't a success. It disappointed people. It was unfortunately sold to appeal to people who liked another kind of Clint Eastwood. *Tightrope*, I hope, will sustain the fans—because he does win out at the end—but it's a tougher win for him than it is for Dirty Harry. This guy isn't inept, he's just more vulnerable. His personal life has affected him more.

*Did you want the* Dirty Harry *admirers to think again about him? I wondered how far the obsessiveness in the Harry character has to do with him having virtually no sex life.*
Yeah, Harry's wife is dead. Several of those films touch lightly on his disappointments in romance, and he's definitely a loner and a lonely character. But Wes is lonely because of the shallowness of his existence, though he loves his daughters. He succumbs to a lot of things in the evening, and he gets involved with a lot of girls Dirty Harry wouldn't be involved with. Not that Harry's asexual or anything, but they're not the kind of gals he'd go for. He'd find some nice secretary, or whatever, and date her, or somebody—a working or professional gal. But this guy doesn't know what he wants.

*Was there ever a moment in the planning of this film where someone said, "Suppose we did make him the killer?"*
No, I never thought of that, but if you'd read the first screenplay we definitely indicated more. [Richard] Tuggle wrote it and then had second thoughts about it. I liked the parallel between him and the killer, and I liked the not knowing. And I felt the more we could lead the audience to think

that maybe this was it, the more it gives them somewhere to go. They live with his insecurity and his strife, but at the end there it's okay, enough of all this, now do this, get the guy. He becomes as determined as Dirty Harry is normally.

*Years ago—this must have been just after* Coogan's Bluff*—Don Siegel said that he had never met anyone with such an obsession to be an antihero. Is it still true?*
I think so. In *Dirty Harry,* after shooting the guy, actually torturing the confession out of him—that was my idea—and his feeling was that most actors conscious of a certain image would be afraid to do that. But I felt it as the immediacy of the character. At this point, I don't care about his motivation.

And if there is any secret to my success—and I've never sat down and tried to be analytical about it—I think it's that the audience rides along with me. They either sit forward in their seat as to what you're doing, and the intensity with which you're doing it—or, if the audience senses that you're throwing out to them, almost looking to the camera, then they sit back. I've always felt that they're just at the window. Now, I don't want my aunt in Des Moines to think I'm a sadist. I give her credit for being intelligent enough to know I'm an actor playing a part. If they're not that smart, if they think it's really me, then obviously there's something wrong with them.

*You give less sense of wanting the public to love you than most actors.*
Yeah. That's what intrigued Don.

*Do you want them to dislike you?*
I don't want them to dislike me, overall, but a certain aspect of the character. In *Tightrope,* maybe Clint Eastwood wouldn't do some of the things this character would do. I'm just an actor portraying a role.

*You give the impression onscreen of being a lot more secure than other actors.*
That's the way I feel. I don't approach it thinking, What are they going to think behind the camera, or in the theater? I approach it by thinking, What do I have to do here? I'm not smart enough to be aware of all these things at once. I'm not that diverse in my concentration. I have to do what the role has to do.

*If five or six films in a row went wrong and no one wanted to make Clint Eastwood films, would it trouble you?*
No, it wouldn't trouble me.

*Would it trouble you if you couldn't direct?*
It would trouble me not to work again. But I feel that . . . audiences are smarter than most people give them credit for. Though sometimes they don't always respond in the way you'd like 'em to. For instance, the two times I've died in films, *Beguiled* and *Honkytonk Man,* the audience has never really enjoyed it. And though I knew in *Honkytonk Man* it was going to be very, very risky, because the other time that happened it didn't work out that well—it didn't work out that well there either! But in certain countries, certain viewers, France, they treated it kindly. Still, nobody ran to it, like they ran to *Dirty Harry* or any of the other films. And I don't know about *Tightrope,* either.

*I felt about a year and a half ago, in* Bronco Billy *and* Honkytonk Man *you'd tried to do different things, and in its way* Firefox *was different—you'd never done a special effects film. Those three pictures marked a faltering in your box office. Have you been under pressure to do another Dirty Harry film? Is that what happened with* Sudden Impact?
(Chuckles.) Well . . . not really. *Firefox* did pretty well. There was sort of a consensus that *Bronco Billy* wasn't a success, but it was a very inexpensive film and I loved the story, loved making it. I think it's one of the best films I've made. It was one of the more enjoyable ones. It did pretty good, it just wasn't in the league following *Every Which Way but Loose.*

*You have the reputation in the business of being very cost-conscious, even down-right stingy. Are you proud of that?*
Yeah. I don't consider it stingy, though. We pay pretty decent. It's just that we try to organize the films and make them in the least amount of time. We're talking about an industry where there's so much waste, and so much faith put in people who have very little experience. Even in the executive strata, not too many of them have the film knowledge of the past generations. Once they've made the deal they turn it over to a film person, and maybe he's experienced, maybe not.

*But the budgets on your films are startlingly low.*
I think so, but that's to do with planning. We use the very best people, who are philosophically aligned at getting the most for the money. If a picture cost $5 million, I hope it looks like $10 million on the screen. If it cost $5 million and it looks $3 million on the screen, then that's a failure to me. There's an awful lot of pictures that cost $20–30 million that look to me like $6–7 million.

*Is it also part of your wish not to seem soft?*
I don't know. Maybe it's a certain pride in workmanship or respect for someone who's going to put his money up and who I do right by. A studio like Warner Brothers will do *Honkytonk Man.* They know Clint Eastwood's not hunching around or shooting up. They're still putting in faith that I'll make the best picture I can. So I try to show them some respect. It's easy to fall into the pattern, I've seen it happen, once you're sucked into a movie it's too late. Jack Warner would have said, "Get back on schedule."

*Have you ever been in a situation, as actor or director, where you got a notion for a whole new scene not in the script?*
Oh, yeah. I change pictures as I go. I just use a script as a framework. A lot of times I'll send out page changes on a script.

*Do you think you're a reasonable actor now for other people to direct, or do you notice you have ideas and can't keep quiet about them?*
I've done so many of my own films I haven't had that situation you're talking about. But I'll offer suggestions, and if the person doesn't like them it doesn't make any difference to me—they're just suggestions. If I'm working with a director and there's something that needs to be added to the script, I'll try to clarify it before we ever shake hands to do the thing. So that there's no surprises. I don't want some guy to turn around and say, "Now you play some transvestite!" I'll have ideas along the way and hopefully that's all hashed out. On *City Heat,* Richard Benjamin seemed to like the contributions. Don Siegel loves participation.

*What determines now whether you direct a film or only act in it?*
It's just a mood thing. Some films I see them kind of vividly, either a story I like very much and want to direct, or I see it clearly and I don't want to

have to work with another guy and explain to him. Then there's other scripts where I say, "Well, someone else can have just as good a tack on this." Maybe there's a production problem. On *Every Which Way but Loose* and *Any Which Way You Can* I needed to work out and train up a lot, I just didn't want to take on the job. I wanted somebody there to act as captain of the ship, and I could work with the animals and whatever needs to be done.

*What happened on* Josey Wales *with Phil Kaufman?*
Well, I had . . . I liked him as a writer. I bought this book and owned it myself, and I had my own money in the project, and he liked it when I gave it to him, and I thought it would be interesting to have him direct. And he did bring some very good contributions to transferring the book into the screenplay. We were both in sync all the way down the line on that. But when it came to shooting, he just had a little bit different ideas of the style of the film. And I did have my own money in it, and I bought the book from scratch, and I just felt I didn't want to see it portrayed that way. So it was strictly a point of view. Nobody will ever know, but for all we know his ideas might have been the best. I just had a line on it and loved the project and didn't want it to be done the way he was going to interpret it. And he didn't want to do it the way I wanted to do it. There wasn't any animosity or disrespect for him in any way, shape or form.

*Can you put your style into words, your way of telling a story and directing?*
Well, there is no particular way. Most of my films have a different look, depending upon what the film calls for. It's a combination of pace and an eye for composition. I can't explain exactly what it is, because there isn't as much a style to my films—an individualistic style—as there is to those of Don Siegel. Mine vary. *Play Misty* varies greatly from *Breezy,* from *Josey Wales,* from *Bronco Billy.*

   I think what has happened these days is that an awful lot of people direct movies in a style they'd direct commercials in. Where they just kind of float around all over the place. Being an actor has one advantage—you don't need to make your presence known. Your presence is already there. So I'm not trying to feature any tricks as a director. I'd say a director who is pretty straight on is Sidney Lumet or Martin Ritt. Guys who never try to intrude themselves. They try to feature the story, because directing is an interpretative art, as opposed to writing, the creative art. Those are guys who've told the story very well.

*When you first saw the Sergio Leone films, was there a big shock? Or did you know they'd be so stylized?*
Yeah, I think I played my character in sync with the style. I spun off Sergio, and he spun off me. I think we worked well together. I like his compositions. He has a very good eye. He wasn't a real experienced director. He'd only done one movie, a thing called *Colossus of Rhodes*. And if you look at that, it doesn't have any of his style. I liked him, I liked his sense of humor. I can't speak for him, but I feel it was mutual. He liked dealing with the kind of character I was putting together. The character was written quite a bit different. I made it much more economical. Much less expository. He explained himself a lot in the screenplay. My theory to Sergio was, "I don't think you have to explain everything. Let the audience imagine with us." I'd sort of coerce him into going for it on that level, like a B picture. But he did go for it. He wasn't really coerced, he liked the style.

I think the producers of the film were a bit shocked. They didn't know what was going on. They said, "Jeez, this guy doesn't do anything, doesn't say anything, just stands there with the cigar." They were used to Italian films—*Divorce Italian Style*, flamboyant, a lot of things happening. But Sergio, he kinda stayed with it, and he embellished it as he went along over the three films.

He's offered me other films since *The Good, the Bad and the Ugly*, but at that point I felt like he was looking for a different thing in films than I was. I was looking for more character development and maybe a smaller film, and he was looking for more panorama, a David Leanesque kind of thing. So we just drifted, though it was very amicable.

*Did he ever ask if you were interested in* Once Upon a Time in America?
Yeah. He started thinking about that project back when we did *The Good, the Bad and the Ugly*. And he had this idea about doing a gangster movie. He said, "What about Irish gangsters? You could play an Irish gangster." Long before *The Godfather* and all these things came out. But he never developed it. It was always just there, hanging there. And a lot of times Sergio would

just want to go with an idea. But through the years of television I'd been reading the story too much. Though I did sort of go along with *The Good, the Bad and the Ugly* on a treatment.

But as time went on I didn't think it was a wise thing to do, with him or anyone else. I like to know the joke. I don't want someone to tell me a joke and not give me the punch line. I like to know where I'm going; and I'll improvise, and be as crazy as anyone wants, but I just want to have a clear line on where I'm headed. But he talked to me about doing *Once Upon a Time in the West* and what became *Duck, You Sucker,* but they were just repeats of what I'd been doing. I didn't want to play that character anymore. So I came back and did a very small-budget picture, called *Hang 'em High,* which had a little more character. Maybe it was time, too, to do some American films, because even though these films were very successful, the movie business for some reason was still thinking of me as an Italian movie actor. I can remember the field guys at Paramount years ago said they'd talked about using me but all they got was, "He's just a TV actor." I wasn't marked to be accepted. There were a lot of other actors who were marked to succeed more than me. Same with the press. I wasn't marked in their estimation. I was never a darling of that group.

*These days people go from one lot to another. For eight years you've been Warners' most successful product. They're anxious to keep you, and you look comfortable here. It's a little like the Thirties.*
I wouldn't have been happy with that, as far as being an actor is concerned. Those guys were contract players and they had to do many films they didn't want to do. You couldn't step back for two years. And you had no control over it. The reason I started Malpaso in the first place was I saw a lot of inefficiencies, and I thought I can screw up as good as the next person. I'd rather be the cause of my own demise.

*But you also like to keep a settled team.*
Yeah, I do. I like working with the same people. I've done a lot of films with other people along the way, and sometimes I'll use actors I've used three or four times. Like *Bronco Billy*—everybody in it I'd used before. And it was great fun. Behind the camera, too, a lot of the people have been with me a long time. It's very relaxing to know that certain people are very,

very good at their job. A lot of that aspect of the old days I like. Everybody moved at a good clip. Studio heads were tough and obstinate, but they knew about film. But there was no competition then. All movies made money, more or less. A movie actor today is making a tremendous competition.

*Do you think the public sees you as an actor playing parts or as a fantasy figure called Clint Eastwood?*
I think the public understands that you're playing different characters. But there is a fantasy in this era of bureaucracy, of complicated life, income tax and politicizing everything, that there's a guy who can do certain things by himself. There'll always be that fantasy. I think there's an admiration for it. Maybe certain groups will try to suppress it or advocate against it. But that fantasy will always exist.

*You hold that fantasy yourself?*
Yeah, I think so. I like individuality. I think I enjoy people who are individuals.

*As history goes on, do you think people like that are going to triumph or be beaten?*
Who knows? It may become more of a fantasy as it succumbs to civilization and the mass amount of people. If you were in Orwell's 1984 and you looked at one of my pictures, you'd die of shock.

*There is an argument that the fantasy figure you represent teaches people that strength, force, and reductions like "Make my day" is a way of getting through life.*
Well, I think the appeal may be there. Everybody would like to do that, to come up with that kind of saying. But it's absurd—a person comes up and tells you how many bullets he might have fired and do you feel lucky? Everybody would like to be that cool at some point. How many times has someone said something smart to you and half an hour later you've thought of the perfect answer? "My God, I wish I could have nailed him." But you don't, so the fantasy character does that. He has the right saying. And the right act for the right moment. Sure it's a fantasy, and I think people need it. At the same time, he's advocating that there is hope for the individual.

*I'm not sure that all the audience sees the absurdity, and I think I prefer the greater doubt and vulnerability of, say,* Josey Wales.
Well, that happens to be one of my favorites. I have such feelings myself, obviously, or I would never have attacked something like *Tightrope*. I could have said it could be altered, we'll make him Dirty Harry, a little more confident, add a few "Make my days," or similar type squelches, and then you're off and running. That would be commercial. On *Honkytonk Man*, somebody said, "Why don't you make him live?" But self-destruct—that's the way that guy is, and you can't make a sudden change at the last frame. Hopefully, it's what the kid learns from it. *Bronco Billy*, it was suggested that I go back and get the sheriff (who humiliates him for standing by his man) and somehow one-up him *à la Superman II*, where the guy goes in and punches him out at the end. That isn't true to the story. That diminishes the scene where he takes the humiliation to get this guy off the hook. And that would be impure.

*These tags that become so important in some of your films, like "Make my day," do you think up some of those?*
That particular one came from the screenwriter, came from Joe Stinson. The only thing I did is I reprised it at the end—that's my contribution. I saw the line as a goodie, so I said let's throw it in right here. Much like we did with *Dirty Harry* and, Did he fire six shots or five...? "To tell you the truth I've forgotten in all this excitement. But seeing this is a .44 Magnum..." And so I thought, let's do it at the very end, let's close with it. Because it's obviously going to be something special. And I told Don [Siegel], I said I can play it looser, with humor, to begin with, so there's a certain irony, but at the end I can play it with a whole different attitude. With a certain, absolutely peak velocity. But that was written in there originally by Harry Julian Fink, in the screenplay. When I read the screenplay it jumped right out and I thought, "Oh, yeah, this'll be quite unusual." You can feel them. "Smith & Wesson and me," I made up. "Who's this 'we'? It's Smith & Wesson and me."

*Why did you move so much as a kid?*
Well, those were the Thirties, and jobs were hard to come by. My parents and my sister and myself just had to move around to get jobs. I remember we moved from Sacramento to Pacific Palisades just to be a gas station

attendant. It was the only job open. In fact, everybody was in a trailer, one with a single wheel on the end, and the car, and we were living in a real old place out in the sticks. People were actually living in chicken houses. And it was good: you saw a certain side of life that you don't see now unless you're ... The opportunities are so much more now. My dad was a hard-working guy, and he'd been brought up under the ethic, "Nothing comes from nothing." You get what you give. And you work for what you get. Old-fashioned ethics. Passed down through his family.

*Did your family settle eventually?*
Well, we just moved, but we were close. Then a good portion of the time I was in high school both my parents worked. We moved back to Oakland. My mother worked out at IBM. We should have bought the stock then! Then my dad worked at Bethlehem Steel and they'd go off in two old cars, '31 Chevy and a '32 Chevy, and they made ends meet that way. We lived in a fairly decent neighborhood in Oakland. That was during the Forties, war years, and there was a lot more work. That gas station still exists, on the corner of Highway 1 and Sunset Boulevard. There's a Spanish-style roof station there. I have pictures of my dad in that station.

*You admired him pretty much?*
Yeah, yeah. You look back as an adult and you see the struggles both of them went through and you think they put out a lot for us.

*You had real poverty.*
It wasn't like a lot of people suffer. I don't mean to make it sound Dust-bowl. There are people in that situation today, and let's hope they'll pull out of it. My father would have pulled his way out of it eventually because he was that sort of person. He would have been a winner eventually. And in the late Forties he got with a corporation and worked his way up and became well thought of. He played a little guitar and he sang, and he had a small group. And he liked theatrics. When I did *Rawhide,* he said, "It's very nice you've made a few dollars while you're young."

# Interview with Clint Eastwood

## MICHAEL HENRY/1984

*Let's begin with a "flashback" to your first steps in film production. Under what circumstances did you form the Malpaso Company at the end of the 60s?*
I had come back from Italy where I had just filmed *The Good, the Bad and the Ugly*. My agent was urging me to do *McKenna's Gold*, a big, spectacular Western, but this wasn't the kind of project I was looking for. I aspired to something more mature, more probing. That was when *Hang 'em High* came along, a much more modest project. I liked the idea of weighing the pros and cons of capital punishment in the setting of a Western. That gave me the idea of starting my own company to share in the production of this small film.

*Were you already thinking of directing films? Wasn't the formation of Malpaso a step towards directing yourself?*
Not really. Or maybe unconsciously. After *Hang 'em High*, I acted in several pictures without being actively involved in their production. Then I found myself making my directorial debut directing the second unit on a picture of Don Siegel's.

*Which one?*
*Dirty Harry.*[1] Don had the flu and I replaced him for the sequence where Harry tries to convince the would-be suicide not to jump into the void. That

Published as "Entretien avec Clint Eastwood" in *Positif*, no. 287 (January 1985): 48–57. Reprinted by permission; translated from the French by KC.

1. Eastwood had done second unit work on Siegel films before *Dirty Harry*, but *Play Misty for Me* wrapped before shooting on *Dirty Harry* began. — Translator's note.

turned out OK, because, for lack of space on the window ledge, the only place to perch me was on the crane. I shot this scene, then another one, and I began to think more seriously about directing. One of my friends, Jo Heims, had written a script I was fond of, *Play Misty for Me*. I'd even taken out an option on it. I had just been offered *Where Eagles Dare* when she called me to ask my advice. Universal was offering to buy her script and she had scruples about dealing with them although I wasn't in a position to renew the option. Of course, I encouraged her to sell it to them. And it was only some years later, after I'd signed a contract with Universal for three movies, that I could tell them, "By the way, you've got a project on your shelf I'd like to do. I also want to direct it." Because it wasn't a very costly production, I got the green light.

*Why choose this project in particular for your first movie?*
Because of the subject. I had lived through a similar experience, though it was less dramatic. The character played by Jessica Walter, which was suggested to Jo Heims by an acquaintance of hers, was also familiar to me. It's someone who fantasizes a love relationship. For the disc jockey, it's a one-night stand, but for her it's a devouring passion. This misunderstanding interested me: exactly when do you become involved in a love affair? To what extent are we responsible for the relationships we establish?

*Weren't the people you were talking to at Universal surprised that you chose a subject in which the dominant character is a woman?*
Yeah, sure. They kept asking me, "Why are you so eager to make a picture where the woman has the best part?" Their second argument was that the situation wouldn't be believable: "How could a big strong guy like you be threatened physically by a weak young woman?" I thought, on the contrary, that the obsessive dimension of this relationship would only come out the better. Besides, it's a type of behavior you can observe in either sex. I've known men who were just as possessive about the object of their passion.

*Was the story originally situated in Carmel and Monterey? Or was it your personal attachment to this region that dictated your choice of locations?*
In the script, the setting was Los Angeles. But a friend of mine, who had some features in common with my character, was a disc jockey for a Carmel radio station. And in a small town like Carmel a disc jockey has more

chances to become a celebrity than in Los Angeles. Besides, this region is spectacular, and it happens that I live there and I'm familiar with it.

*Did this first experience pose particular technical problems for you?*
No, none, except maybe for the one of directing yourself while you're taking charge of the entire production. The one who was most nervous was Don Siegel. I'd cast him in the bartender's role and he kept saying, "You're making a huge mistake. You should have gotten a real character actor. I'll never be up to it." To which I answered: "Don, you'll be sensational. And it will give you the chance to better appreciate what actors go through. Besides, if something goes wrong, I'll have a director on hand to get me out of it." In fact, in the evening of the first day of filming, Don confessed to me: "I had terrible stage fright. If you want to know the truth, I would have been completely incapable of helping you out!"

*How did you prepare? Did you draw storyboards before filming?*
No. *Firefox* is the only one of my pictures I used storyboards on. The last fifteen minutes required some special effects and I made a set of sketches, which I gave to a professional designer for retouching.

*Visually, some of your action shots imply a complex choreography. Even in this case, you don't draw your shots beforehand?*
I hate to be the prisoner of a diagram. The best ideas come to me when the camera is in place, ready to shoot. That's when I'm reinvigorated. Of course, I have a general idea of the sequence, but I try to remain as flexible as possible. I'll always leave the actor the latitude to modify one of his movements if he has a good reason. If I'm doing exterior shots, I always take into account the light and the way it evolves during the day, at the risk of having to change a camera position.

*What do you think you've learned from filmmakers you collaborated with before you became a director?*
I learned a lot, but I wouldn't be capable of distinguishing the contribution of each one. The films of Don Siegel, like those of Sergio Leone, were models of economy. They never went over their allotted budget. That was my school. I've made very few pictures where the money was spent without counting, and even when it was, the lesson was useful because I learned

what not to do. Each of the filmmakers I worked with taught me some-thing new, or at least helped me to define myself.

*Do you feel affinities with a Kurosawa?*
I like his films a lot, especially those of the first period, *Red Beard, The Seven Samurai,* and so on. It was *Yojimbo,* you know, that prompted me to make *A Fistful of Dollars.*

*When you were being directed by others, were you conscious of the directorial work that was going on around you?*
I don't think I was conscious of it, but I suppose my subconscious assimi-lated it all. I recall that since the time of *Rawhide,* I wanted to try my hand at directing. My contract with CBS even provided that I would direct sev-eral episodes of the series. But after they'd had some trouble on other series, where some actor-directors went over their budgets, CBS changed policies from one day to the next. It didn't do me any good to make a fuss—at the time I didn't have a choice—they never honored their contract. I did trail-ers and little things here and there, and I fumed, but I convinced myself to wait for a better chance.

*Visually and thematically* High Plains Drifter *evokes the Sergio Leone Westerns, but you appear to have wanted to exorcise this past while going even further in excess and cruelty.*
In the Leone films, the story was more fragmented. It was a series of vig-nettes that were rather loosely linked. In *High Plains Drifter,* all the elements overlap, even though there are several subplots. Everything is related to the protagonist's nightmare. And there's a moral perspective that only appeared episodically in the Leone films. I'm thinking of the scene in *A Fistful of Dollars* where the hero helps the family get away and pays for this rare mo-ment of compassion with a beating. After which he's got to return to take his revenge on the town.

High Plains Drifter *is a bizarre allegory that shatters all the rules of the classic Western.*
I decided to do it on the basis of a treatment of only nine pages. It's the only time that's happened to me. The starting point was: "What would have happened if the sheriff of *High Noon* had been killed? What would have

happened *afterwards*?" In the treatment by Ernest Tidyman, the sheriff's brother came back to avenge the sheriff and the villagers were as contemptible and selfish as in *High Noon*. But I opted eventually for an appreciably different approach: you would never know whether the brother in question is a diabolic being or a kind of archangel. It's up to the audience to draw their own conclusions. Tidyman wrote the script from this perspective, but he missed a certain number of elements and I rewrote it with the help of Dean Riesner who had collaborated several times with Siegel.

*You like characters who form part of the system, or at least appear to form part of it, but don't play by the rules of the game it has established and end up by revealing its corruption. The hero of* High Plains Drifter *is consequently a kind of Caligula of the West.*
I'm aware that that type of character attracts me. Why? Maybe because I've always hated corruption within the system, no matter what it is. In this respect, *High Plains Drifter* goes further than *High Noon*. When the hero helps them get organized, the townspeople believe they can control him, manipulate him. As soon as he leaves, they fall back into the error of their ways and their failure is obvious, their disgrace is unpardonable. They've learned nothing, but they're thoroughly traumatized. In *Pale Rider,* the Western I've just finished, the situation is similar, but this time the hero is really an archangel. He helps a small community of miners to organize themselves like a trust, he inspires them with the courage to resist and defend their rights.

*There is something of the infernal in the iconography of* High Plains Drifter, *a tonality of fire and scorched earth.*
That's due in part to the place where we filmed it, Mono Lake in California. The town in the script was situated in the middle of the desert, like in most Westerns, but this convention bothered me because even in the West a city couldn't develop without water. I discovered Mono Lake by chance, while I was out driving around, and I was immediately taken with the strangeness of the site. The saline content is so high that no vessel can risk going out on the waters of the lake. I spent two hours wandering around in the area. Not a boat, not a living soul, only the natural noises of the desert. From the nearest city I immediately called my art director and had him jump on the first plane. When he arrived, he blurted out, "You'd think you were on

the moon!" I told him, "It's a weird place, but that's exactly what I want this story to be!"

*The cinematography of Bruce Surtees was extremely elaborate, especially the chiaroscuro for the night scenes. How did he become your most faithful collaborator?*
He'd been the camera operator on several of Siegel's pictures, particularly *Coogan's Bluff*. When we were filming *Two Mules for Sister Sara* in Mexico, Don appealed to him because he had communication problems with Gabriel Figueroa. Figueroa's forte is lighting, Bruce's is composition. His help proved invaluable. So one evening, Don and I resolved that we would promote him to director of photography as soon as the opportunity came up.

*At what stage of the preparation do you discuss the style of the cinematography?*
In general, I only give Bruce the script when it's finished. Then I explain to him what I want. For instance, the light and the colors of autumn were the determining factors in *The Outlaw Josey Wales* and, once again, in *Pale Rider*. I have a predilection for exteriors, I feel more at ease there than in a studio. There's nothing like the atmosphere of an authentic place to inspire you, you and your crew. That's where we make most of our decisions.

*With* Breezy *you probably surprised a number of your fans. You couldn't conceive a film more remote from the type of movie the public at large here identifies you with. Is this a project that was hard to put across?*
No, not especially. It was a very inexpensive picture and shot on location [in Los Angeles]. I liked the script by Jo Heims a lot, her second I believe: the regeneration of a cynic, an older man, divorced, who's a success professionally but who doesn't have an emotional life any more. How he's rejuvenated thanks to a naive teenager who isn't so naive after all.

*You feel a particular sympathy, it seems, for those of your characters who learn something in the course of the narration.*
The audience follows a story by adopting the point of view of one of the protagonists, whether it's an adult or a child. And if this protagonist learns something, you'll identify with him all the better if you have the impression that you're maturing with him. In *Breezy*, I wanted to say that even a middle-class man of substance has something to learn from someone who

doesn't have anything. This girl hasn't got much of anything, but actually, she has a lot. She sees and feels what he's stopped seeing and feeling, all those things in life that he doesn't take the time to enjoy. It's a very simple fable, and it's true everywhere. All of us go past something and fail to appreciate all the colors of the prism.

*In* The Eiger Sanction, *friendship is stronger than the corruption of the System. Indeed, it's the only value that survives in a world of schemes and Machiavellian plots. Your character and George Kennedy's character make up in the end, foiling the Agency. In* The Outlaw Josey Wales, *the friendship that binds you to John Vernon appears in spite of everything to be a stronger feeling than partisan passion.*
Yes, it's an important value, friendship. Especially a friendship that doesn't have any other basis than friendship. In *The Eiger Sanction,* it's compromised by the pressures of the Agency, while in *Josey Wales* it succumbs to the psychoses of the war. Josey Wales is like a haunted man. He's beset by the ghosts of his past, even when he thinks he's starting a new life. Even the wounded soldier and the women of *The Beguiled* who are consigned to the periphery of the war don't escape from this corruption of feelings.

*Isn't the strangeness of* The Eiger Sanction *the result of the shape of the plot? It develops in three distinct stages, nearly independent of each other.*
There were, in fact, three stories in one and it was a very difficult picture to make. A good thing our gadgets were limited in number; we were running the risk of heading in the direction of the James Bond movies. And especially the mountaineering sequences posed enormous problems. We had to shoot with two crews, one crew of technicians and one crew of mountain climbers. Every morning, we had to decide, according to the weather report, which one to send up the mountain. The three actors and myself had to undergo intensive training. On the seventh day of filming, we lost one of our mountaineers, and, believe me, I asked myself repeatedly if it was worth it.

*Once again, in* The Eiger Sanction, *you short-circuit genre conventions by means of black humor.*
The humor was frankly sardonic, but I believe it was inherent in the story. I couldn't have considered handling it otherwise.

*But on the other hand, in* Firefox *this type of humor is nearly absent and the film would probably have benefited from a tongue-in-cheek treatment.*

Firefox was more "square," more traditional. It wasn't about bad guys with pink eyes, but ordinary characters faced with an impossible mission.

*By its naturalism,* Firefox *also contrasts with* The Eiger Sanction, *which like* High Plains Drifter *or* Josey Wales, *is a bizarre work.*

I'd have to place myself somewhere between the two. I don't believe you can label me, pigeonhole me in one style or another. My films all have a different "look." It depends on the story, on its progress, on the relationships that develop among the protagonists, and probably also on the way I feel about the subject.

*When Josey Wales says, "We all died a little in that damned war," you can't help thinking about a contemporary war, Vietnam.*

You can interpret it like that, but it's a feeling that isn't inherent in today's wars. In the case of the Civil War there had to be something particularly traumatic there: Americans fighting other Americans. One people tearing itself to pieces. And according to the state or the county where you were living, you were recruited to join one camp or the other. It was the same absurdity as today in Northern Ireland, where a single community is killing itself in the name of God and religion.

*You took over the direction from Phil Kaufman at the end of a few days. What happened?*

I was the one who'd hired him to rewrite the script and to direct it. His work as a writer was excellent, but when it came to shooting it, it turned out that our points of view were completely different. I had invested my own money to buy the rights to the book, I'd spent a lot of time developing this project, I'd conceived a precise vision of what the film had to be. Phil's approach was probably solid, maybe it was better, but it wasn't mine and I would have been angry at myself if the result hadn't corresponded to what I hoped for.

*Josey Wales, like the "archangel" of* High Plains Drifter, *only sympathizes with the marginal, or the humbled and the affronted.*

The irony is that Josey Wales *inherits* a family. After he's fled from everything he was tied to because everything he ever loved has been destroyed, he finds himself picking up these outcasts along his way: the Indian, the grandmother and her granddaughter, some Mexicans and even a dog. And soon this heterogeneous group becomes a kind of community.

*In* The Gauntlet *the reconciliation is even more unexpected. For the cop, the discovery of human solidarity happens by way of a woman, a prostitute moreover. Was it the impossibility of this romance that attracted you?*
This aspect, and the contrast with the *Dirty Harry* series. Inspector Callahan was always on top of the situation and he was in permanent conflict with the bureaucratic system. The cop of *The Gauntlet* is a guy who just follows routine, not very sharp, easy to manipulate. All he expects from life are simple things: to do his job well, find a wife, settle down. And when he confesses his longings, it happens that he's talking to a woman he would ordinarily have treated like a whore but who's much cleverer than he is. She's the one who opens his eyes, because he's too regimented to understand what's going on, he can't imagine that his superiors could deceive him deliberately.

*In* The Gauntlet, *which is a "film noir," the theme of betrayal recurs that was already at the heart of* High Plains Drifter, The Eiger Sanction *and* The Outlaw Josey Wales.
Betrayal is everywhere, isn't it? And it's universal. Since Judas, hasn't this been one of the great themes of literature and most kinds of drama?

*Is it possible to see in* Bronco Billy *a commentary on your activities and responsibilities as a filmmaker?*
I had a really good time. When I was sent the script by Dennis Hackin, at first I thought it was about Bronco Billy Anderson, the silent movie star. I devoured it at one sitting and I immediately thought it was the kind of film Capra would do today if he were still making movies. Once again, there was this micro-society you were speaking of, one composed of artists a little bit down-at-the-heels...

*Like the one that the outcasts of* Josey Wales *made up?*
Yes, but a contemporary version. More that in a certain way they belong to a bygone era. There aren't a lot of people who are interested in a "Wild West Show" today.

*Bronco Billy allows his fellow troupers to interpret the role of their choice in a world of illusions, to express their truth by becoming another. The circus tent is like a metaphor of filmmaking—or maybe even of Malpaso Productions?*

I hadn't ever thought of it from this angle, but maybe you're right: after all, it isn't so different from the movies! I'm always moving on, and I can't analyze what I do as consciously or objectively as an observer who's outside the project.

*You supervise the casting very closely. You often say that it's the key moment in the preparation.*

If the script is good and the casting is right, you've only got to stay on course. On the other hand, if the casting is wrong, you don't have a chance to achieve your goal. I don't mean that there's only one way to cast a role, or that only such-and-such an actor can fill such-and-such a role, but I have too much respect for actors, I'm too sensitive to the particular dimension they can give to a part, not to control the casting myself from beginning to end.

Bronco Billy *gives the impression of being a film of family and friends. You're celebrating a certain life style.*

The actors had almost all worked with me before, many times. They formed a very homogeneous group. The fact that we had this common experience meshed well with the story. The relationships of the characters with Bronco Billy were not very different from those the actors had with me. I think this helped the film. On the other hand, for *Escape from Alcatraz* we took the opposite approach, we only hired people who had never worked with us. On some films, I surround myself with my family, on others I search for new faces.

*In* Bronco Billy *as in* Honkytonk Man, *you offer us splendid scenes of provincial life, but the picture is often ambivalent: this rural America is far from being idyllic; it too is tainted by corruption. Let's take, for example, the episode with the appalling sheriff in* Bronco Billy.

When we were shooting this sequence, someone suggested, "Why not add a scene where Billy returns to town and takes vengeance on the sheriff?" I answered, "You can't do that. It would be another movie." Billy endures the sheriff's insults in order to get his young team member out of jail. This voluntary humiliation says everything about his character. Maybe it's even the message of the picture. If he returns to take vengeance, you're coming back to *Dirty Harry*.

*Do you participate directly in establishing the definitive script for your films?*
Formerly, I'd often make changes during the filming itself. Now, I try to make them beforehand in order to not to waste time and to be completely organized. If the original writer isn't available, I do the work myself. But for instance, on *Pale Rider,* the screenwriter wanted to be involved until the end and he was in charge of the modifications I asked for. For *Bronco Billy,* I added a number of scenes myself. For example, the one of the holdup at the bank. I'd attended a match with Muhammad Ali and after his victory, while reporters were bombarding him with questions like, "How did you place that lightning left hook in the last round?" all he would answer was, "I just want to say hello to my pals. And I'm eager to thank my father, my uncle, the reverend So-and-so, etc." That gave me the idea of the sequence where Billy is asked about the holdup, but his only thought is to promote his show. I also wanted to show that this anti-hero was still capable of accomplishing a brilliant action.

*In your selection of projects, you seem lately to be observing a rule of alternation: a little intimate, personal film, the reverse of your image, and a more important production, with an assured commercial potential. Thus, after* Bronco Billy *you fixed your choice on* Firefox *and after* Honkytonk Man *on* Sudden Impact.
Maybe that's only coincidence. I don't believe it's a conscious process. Even if I had been certain that they wouldn't be big successes, nothing would have stopped me from making *Bronco Billy* and *Honkytonk Man.*

*What attracted you to* Firefox? *It's the one of your films where the confusion of values and ideologies is the least marked.*
I liked the story and the script. It started out like a classic spy film, but then there were some pertinent reflections on the arms race and the imbalance of strengths caused by a new technological advance. What worried me a little was the special effects. Luckily, they only came up in the last part of the film. The problem, in particular, was that these special effects played out against a background of the atmosphere of our planet, and not some faraway galaxy off in the future sometime. I must confess I'm not crazy

about special effects. I'd prefer a thousand times over to have to deal with human beings and their problems.

*It's often been said that the film drew on the cold war climate that followed President Reagan's taking office.*
It was only a hypothesis: "What would happen if...?" I don't believe we manipulated the public's paranoia. We only noted that the cold war was there. And even if it hadn't been there, you need an antagonist or a certain kind of conflict. And as for conflicts, if it isn't the one that opposes the United States and the USSR, there are enough of them everywhere on the planet.

*The hero doesn't call into question either his mission, or the System. Not even when he discovers that the Russian dissidents must sacrifice their life for him.*
He's a professional, and he doesn't have any idea, before he goes over there, of what his mission implies for the dissidents. He doesn't know anything about the behind-the-scenes political machinations. And over there, he doesn't have a single moment when he's at ease. Except when he takes commands of the prototype, because there, at last, he's in his element.

*You suggest a possible friendship between the American pilot and the Soviet pilot. The friendship of two technicians as opposed to the infamous games of politicians.*
It's a little like *Josey Wales*: these two men could have been friends in other circumstances. If they hadn't belonged to two different types of society.

*On the logistical plane, was* Firefox *as difficult as* The Eiger Sanction*?*
Yes and no. We had to find a substitute for the Soviet city, Vienna as it turned out. The Russian base was set up in the Austrian Alps. The London scenes were shot here. And so forth. When I head toward a hangar, the shot was filmed in Austria, but the reverse angle was shot here, because we weren't about to transport the contraption from one continent to the other.

Honkytonk Man *is the only one of your movies, with* The Beguiled, *where you die at the end. Did you have difficulties imposing on Warners a project that contradicted your traditional image that decidedly?*

No, none at all. It was a small inexpensive picture, but since *The Beguiled,* exactly, I knew I was taking risks. I liked the story and I thought it deserved to be told. I hoped that the audience would sympathize enough with the young boy to be interested in it. There's one whole part of my public who expect heroic actions from me and I suppose they were disappointed by *Honkytonk Man.* I can't make all my pictures for a fixed stratum of society. No more than I can defend the same values constantly. A filmmaker worthy of the name can't keep remaking the same picture all the time. I need some new variations, or some completely new themes. Otherwise, it doesn't interest me, it's not a challenge anymore. If there's some advantage in being a "star," or rather in passing for a "star," it's being able to make projects happen that normally couldn't ever have seen the light of day. Pictures that can only be done because you are interested in them. Subjects that nobody else would have wanted to approach. As was the case for *The Beguiled, Bronco Billy* or *Honkytonk Man.* On the other hand, take the case of *Every Which Way but Loose.* No one wanted any part of it. The script had been refused 46 times! Finally, I shot it and it made a fortune. What the studio lost on one, it got back on the other, and so forth. Today, when you make a movie, you have to *want* to make it. You can't think about the box office. I never think about it. Even when the picture was one of my greater successes. I don't claim to believe that the public is going to rush to see one of my movies. Every time, I touch wood. Up to the last moment. Because you can't ever know.

*Your core public would probably have recognized itself in* Honkytonk Man, *but that public doesn't go to the movies to rediscover its day-to-day world.*
Unless it's a case of a pure fantasy. As in *Every Which Way . . .* exactly. But the story of someone like Red Stovall, that they don't want to see on the screen. But I do.

*Was Red Stovall inspired by an authentic singer?*
No. He's a collage. A mixture of Hank Williams, Red Foley, Bob Wills, all those country singers who drank their whiskey neat, burned up their life on the road and ended up by self-destructing.

*What are your own ties to country music?*
I discovered it at the age of nineteen when I was working as a lumberjack in Oregon. At that time, I only liked jazz, particularly West Coast jazz,

Dave Brubeck, Gerry Mulligan. I was looking for girls and I landed in the town's only nightclub. Bob Wills and his band were playing there. Since I didn't know anybody and I didn't know how to dance to this music, I spent hours listening to the band. While forgetting to try to pick up girls! After which I started listening regularly to the small local country radio stations.

*Were you recalling your childhood at the time of the Depression?*
Yes, a little. I was raised during those dark years, I had some contact with families like that during my wanderings from city to city, and I certainly did meet characters like Red Stovall. That probably helped me to recreate the atmosphere. But, you know, for me it was love at first sight for the book by Clancy Carlile and, although we pruned it a little, we remained very faithful to it.

*Since* Bronco Billy *and* Honkytonk Man *you seem more and more interested in family and community relationships.*
You can only do so much with the lone hero. If you give him some family ties, you give him a new dimension. The result is conflicts that enrich the story. In *Honkytonk Man,* he has a family but he's devoted to destroying himself. In *Tightrope* he seems determined to destroy himself and to drag his family with him. In *Pale Rider,* although he doesn't belong to the community, he gets close to two of its members in spite of himself because they become attached to him.

*Isn't it the fact that you've become your own director that has allowed you to change your image like this?*
That's right. It's allowed me to widen my register and to control my career better. I recall a picture I made in Yugoslavia: *Kelly's Heroes.* It was a very fine anti-militaristic script, one that said some important things about the war, about this propensity that man has to destroy himself. In the editing, the scenes that put the debate in philosophical terms were cut and they kept adding action scenes. When it was finished, the picture had lost its soul. If action and reflection had been better balanced, it would have reached a much broader audience. I don't know if the studio exercised pressure on the director or if it was the director who lost his vision along the way, but I know that the picture would have been far superior if there hadn't been this attempt to satisfy action fans at any cost. And it would have been just as

spectacular and attractive. It's not an accident that some action movies work and other don't. What makes the difference is the quality of the writing.

Honkytonk Man *is a picaresque journey through a forgotten America. Was it familiar ground?*
No, but I've had many opportunities to cross the country by car, observing the little back-country towns and storing these scenes in my memory. For *Bronco Billy,* I criss-crossed Ontario, Oregon, Washington, Idaho. In the first script, the setting was Oklahoma, but I made it the Boise area in Idaho because you can capture the "Mid-America" atmosphere that I was looking for there. For *Honkytonk Man,* I preferred central California to the flatness of Oklahoma, where the Dust Bowl has vanished anyway.

*Bruce Surtees's cinematography evokes the photographs of Walker Evans. During your research, did you consult photos and documents of the time?*
Sure. I browsed through piles of books on the 30s and the Depression. I was also inspired by photo albums of my family.

*This kind of "Americana" appears, unfortunately, to be vanishing and you are one of the few to remain faithful to it. Would like to continue along this route?*
Yes, I'd like to come back to it from time to time. Regularly, if I can. Today, the only thing Hollywood swears by is space adventures because that's what goes over well. For my part, I trust in my instinct and I make the films I believe in. If the public follows me, that's wonderful. If it doesn't follow, "c'est la vie" [in French in the conversation].

*Can one describe* Sudden Impact *as a "black" comedy?*
Sure. There are a lot of comic elements in all the Dirty Harry series. If only because Inspector Callahan's cynicism calls for a cynical kind of humor.

*The American critics blamed you for discrediting the judicial system, for recommending vigilantism and individual justice.*
If my sense of humor escapes some people, I can't help it. One of my favorite restaurants in Carmel is called the Hog's Breath Inn. When I asked the owner why he'd chosen such an ugly name, he told me, "We want to be sure we only serve customers who have a sense of humor." A few months before his death, I had lunch with Hitchcock and after we'd

speculated together about the movies, he suddenly concluded: "Don't ever forget one thing, it's only a bloody movie!" He was sure as hell right. No movie can change the world, or make it a more just place. Even if it contains an important message. *Dirty Harry* touched a nerve because the country was up to its ears in bureaucratic inefficiency. But it's only pure fiction. In today's society, no cop would be capable of assaulting the system while remaining as uncompromising as that. Even if some of them would like to have this power and if need be, to go beyond the law itself. Which, after all, Harry Callahan never did deliberately, but only under the pressure of time or when he was forced to by the urgency of the situation. To come back to your question: I can't worry about these kinds of problems. I do my best and I can only hope the audience will like the movie and the critics will be more sensitive to its positive aspects than to its negative aspects.

*You were unpleasantly surprised by the accusations of racism brought against* Dirty Harry.

When I hired blacks, I did it to give them work. Before filming the holdup sequence in *Dirty Harry,* a scene that had been written for whites, I told Don Siegel: "I'm tired of always seeing the same stuntmen in this kind of role. What if we got some new faces?" A group of black stuntmen had just been formed and they're the ones I suggested. That they were all blacks was logical: there are as many black gangs as white or Chinese gangs. It's absurd to conclude from this that only blacks commit crimes. Again, in *City Heat,* we changed all the casting and two-thirds of the roles written for whites have now been taken by blacks. Which conforms to the atmosphere of Kansas City, which in the 30s was dominated by jazz. Lord only knows what some critics are going to conclude from that!

*A number of your movies,* Sudden Impact *in particular, express the frustrations of today's America and the resurgence of populism.*

Maybe I can be accused of being old-fashioned, of dreaming of an era where things were simpler, more obvious, more honest. The power of bureaucracy is increasing in the proportion that the planet is shrinking and the problems of society are getting more complicated. I'm afraid that individual independence is becoming an outmoded dream. We're overwhelmed by paperwork, administrative formalities, committees and subcommittees. To such a point that in order to get themselves elected, from now on our politicians will have to promise they'll keep their intervention in citizens' lives to the minimum. That's the rhetoric that dominated the recent presidential campaign. What Dirty Harry says is, "If you have to fill out fifteen copies of every report, the criminal will have time to commit another crime before you've finished. There comes a time when you have to stop avoiding things." It's an extreme position, but that's where you get back to the irony: without it, the audience wouldn't go along. That's something I felt by instinct. For my part, I've succeeded in remaining pretty much independent, but to reach this stage, I've had to fight. And I continue to fight every day.

*In your movies, irony is most often tied to excess, whether it's a question of the improbability of a situation or the extremism of the hero.*
*The Gauntlet* is a good example. I had seen on television the barrage of gunfire that followed the abduction of Patty Hearst by the Symbionese Liberation Army. A tremendous barrage, in the middle of the city. Bullets flew in all directions and at least three buildings caught fire. I imagined what would occur in a city of middling importance like Las Vegas. A city where almost nothing happens, where the police don't have anything to do but arrest a drunk from time to time. If it were suddenly announced that Public Enemy No. 1 had seized a bus and taken a police officer hostage, all the cops in town would want to be in on the strike and it's predictable that their reaction would be excessive. Life offers you examples every day of the bizarre excesses you mention. The real is sometimes surreal. And anyway, as a filmmaker, excess is good dramatic material. What interests the public is the extraordinary, isn't it?

*Tightrope is based on a theme dear to Hitchcock, the transference of guilt. Was it this theme that attracted you to Richard Tuggle's script?*
What attracted me was that there's this cop who's been abandoned by his wife, that he's got custody of the children, that he's intrigued by Geneviève Bujold, but doesn't want to get involved with her because he's got enough problems in his life. He's perhaps more efficient than the hero of *The Gauntlet* but he's not a man to attack the system head-on like Dirty Harry. He just wants to do his job well. But as crime follows crime and the crimes get closer and closer to him, you begin to wonder: "Could it be him? What

is his connection with the criminal? Is he his alter ego?" And it does turn out that the criminal is also a police officer. The interaction of all these elements interested me.

*Why didn't you direct the picture yourself?*
Richard Tuggle was anxious to direct it. He had written the script, which was excellent. He's the one who wrote *Escape from Alcatraz*. Why not let him direct it? I have an enormous respect for anyone who can write a book or a script. Because that's where the real work of creation is. The rest is interpretation or illustration.

*Has it happened that you've written a first treatment and confided it to a professional screenwriter?*
Not a complete treatment, but it happens that I'll call a screenwriter and tell him: "There's the idea. It's up to you to develop it." That was the case with *Pale Rider*. The writers developed the story, then I added some scenes I wrote myself.

*It's to be hoped that* Pale Rider *will contribute to the resurrection of the genre, but isn't it a gamble to film a Western today?*
I don't know if the genre has really disappeared. There's a whole generation, the younger generation, that only knows Westerns from seeing them on television. And I notice that audience ratings for *High Plains Drifter* and *The Outlaw Josey Wales* continue to be excellent. When someone asks me, "Why a Western, today?" I'm tempted to answer, "Why not? My last Western went over very well." It's not possible that *The Outlaw Josey Wales* could be the last Western to have been a commercial success. Anyway, aren't the *Star Wars* movies Westerns transposed into space?

*Beyond the genre, are you interested in the West and its history?*
In a personal capacity, of course, but in my pictures it's mainly been a question of mythology. *Pale Rider* is no exception; it's got numerous biblical references. However, since it's about miners, I had to read a lot of works about the topic and the Gold Rush era. Again, we filmed it in Idaho, in the region of the Sawtooth Mountains. It's magnificent country, some of the most beautiful in the United States. As we did for *High Plains Drifter*, we constructed a whole town, from A to Z.

*Which of your films have given you the most satisfaction?*
*Josey Wales, Bronco Billy* and *Honkytonk Man,* because they were small films.

*More personal?*
More personal, better organized and more independent in proportion to their having been filmed in remote areas, far from Hollywood.

*What is the most exciting stage for you? Writing? Shooting? Editing?*
Editing. It's the time when you're subject to the fewest constraints. Because you're alone with your editor, putting together the pieces of the puzzle. While you're shooting, you have to deal with some sixty or eighty people who are bombarding you with questions and at every moment you have to find an appropriate answer. No chance to play for time. It's exhausting, but exciting of course, because it's there that everything is played out. You know that if the pieces aren't correctly shaped, you'll never be able to put them together. When I think about the number and the complexity of the elements that enter into play, I'm astounded that good movies exist.

*In the light of maturity and the experience you've acquired as a filmmaker, how do you feel you your character will evolve?*
I don't see him as an entity. Rather as a series of variations. It's true that on screen, from film to film, it's the same face, the same physique, but with the coming of maturity, you change your perspective. Especially in the selection of subjects. It's probable that now I'm choosing scripts that wouldn't have attracted me fifteen or twenty years ago, or that I wouldn't have had the audacity to make then. I can't imagine constantly re-doing what used to work for me. Maturity has to be an incitement to progress, to develop, and, you hope, to improve.

*In the course of your career, you've succeeded in altering your image profoundly. You risk it again in nearly every film. But isn't it difficult to live with this alter ego, who sustains a whole mythology, who has been the subject of innumerable commentaries and analyses, whom now they're even writing books about?*
I know it's not about me. I know that there's what I am as a person and what I represent as an actor. And this image only exists in the mind or the view of the audience. I'm very careful not to think about it. When I'm editing a picture, I don't think about protecting myself or favoring myself; I only

think about the character and his role in the story. Otherwise everything would be off-center. And I suppose it's the same thing in life. When people write about me, I don't take it personally. If the article is positive, I tell myself, "Perfect, he understood what I was trying to do." If it's negative, I accept the inevitable by telling myself that it takes all kinds to make a world.

*But when you approach a new project aren't you forced to take into account what your image was in previous films?*
You mean: how do I avoid repeating myself?

*Either repeating yourself or consciously embroidering variations on a pre-existing image. For example, Red Stovall, in* Honkytonk Man, *is a completely new character for you, whereas the policeman of* Tightrope *extends some of your previous roles.*
I don't think so. In the case of *Tightrope* I wasn't influenced either by *Dirty Harry* or by *The Gauntlet*. With this character, I started out again from square one. Even though some obscure character traits might appear similar, for example my professional behavior. Of course, it's still me. I can only disguise myself up to a certain point, I can't appear all of a sudden as Quasimodo. But internally, I approach every new character in a distinct way. That includes the case of the Dirty Harry series: when I was preparing one of the sequels, I forbade myself to watch the first one again. Even Dirty Harry has changed in fourteen years. He's changed as I've changed. I wouldn't want to reach the point where you're imitating yourself. You and I both know some filmmakers or actors who are reduced to that. I don't have this problem, but I sometimes wonder if the day will come when I'll tell myself: "Gee, I don't know what to do anymore. Maybe I should go back to doing the things that worked so well for me back then?" That would be sad. When I started work on *Pale Rider,* for a minute I was tempted to see *Josey Wales* again and my first Westerns. Then I told myself, "No, I can't do that. There isn't any connection. The only connection is that it's a Western and that there's a certain mythology associated with the genre. But I don't want to repeat myself, I don't want to be influenced by the past."

*The mythology that you elaborate in your pictures is regularly identified with that of deepest America. Your pictures are sometimes treated like sociological phenomena. Does that embarrass you?*

I don't think about it, I would be afraid to think about it. I don't like people who take themselves seriously and I especially wouldn't want to be categorized like that. If I started analyzing the impact my pictures produce, or what I represent in today's America, I would be paralyzed, incapable of functioning. It's is not for me to dissect myself. I could never have the requisite objectivity.

*What is the best antidote against the spirit of seriousness? Black humor?*
There isn't one!

*How do you see the future of Malpaso? Would you be able to consider developing and producing projects where are not you involved either as the director, or as an actor?*
That's not impossible. Maybe it's what I'll do later, but I'm anxious to keep Malpaso to its modest dimensions. I don't want to serve as a straw man. I'm anxious to put my personal touch on everything I do. The principle of Malpaso, originally, was: "Whether I succeed or fail, I don't want to owe it to anyone but myself." It remains my slogan.

# Clint Eastwood: The *Rolling Stone* Interview

TIM CAHILL/1985

PRECISELY TWO DECADES AGO, a friend of mine insisted I go see a movie about the American West, a film made in Italy and shot partially in Spain. At the time, it was intellectually acceptable to be passionate about Italian films that limned the sick soul of Europe; the idea of an Italian western was oxymoronic—at best, like, oh, a German romantic comedy. What's more, in America the western as a genre seemed bankrupt, and going to see *A Fistful of Dollars,* which featured an international no-star cast headed by Clint Eastwood, some second-banana cowboy on an American TV series called *Rawhide,* promised to be entertaining in a manner the director, another unknown named Sergio Leone, probably never intended. My friend was a graduate student in philosophy, and she'd seen the movie three times because she thought it was "existential." The Clint Eastwood character was called the Man with No Name, and he went around rescuing people for no stated reason and outdrawing ugly, sweating bad guys who insulted his mule.

A lot of the violence was stylized, tongue-in-cheek comic-book mayhem, and you couldn't take it very seriously, though several critics did just that, describing the film as "simple, noisy, brutish." This sort of abusive critical reaction didn't keep audiences away, but it did rather dampen the enthusiasm of philosophy majors who had seen smatterings of Sartre in the Man with No Name.

Clint Eastwood starred in two more of the movies that came to be called spaghetti westerns, then he went back to Hollywood in 1967 to make *Hang 'em High,* another popular success in spite of critical reactions like "emetic and intermitable."

By the early seventies, an interest in Clint Eastwood movies among film buffs was considered a shameful and secret vice, like masturbation.

In 1971, Don Siegel directed Eastwood in the enormously popular *Dirty Harry,* a movie that sent some critics into fits of apoplectic name-calling. "Fascist" was one of the kinder descriptions.

That same year, Eastwood directed his first movie, *Play Misty for Me.* The studio had warned him against the project. Universal was reluctant to even pay him for a film in which he would play an easygoing, soft-spoken, jazz-loving disc jockey who inadvertently gets involved with a psychotic young woman. The movie opened to lukewarm but favorable reviews. Pretty good directorial debut, was the consensus, for some damn cowboy.

Eastwood went on to star in three Dirty Harry sequels, all of which minted money at the box office. He directed nine more films, including the classic western *The Outlaw Josey Wales* (1976). And though Eastwood could count on box-office success simply by whispering, "Dirty Harry," he often made choices that confounded his studios, critics and fans.

The 1978 film *Every Which Way but Loose*—a PG-rated comedy featuring an orangutan named Clyde—was another film the studio foresaw as an instant flop. The studio was partially right: nobody liked the film but the public. Clearly, Clint Eastwood knew his audience better than anyone else, and his box-office success has allowed him to direct what he calls his "small films." *Bronco Billy* (1980) features Eastwood as a none-too-bright Easterner who runs an anachronistic Wild West show. In the pivotal scene, Bronco Billy allows himself to be humiliated by a gun-toting sheriff rather than betray a friend. The message might be that loyalty supersedes macho on the list of desirable modern virtues, a concept some critics interpreted as "punning on points of identity." Maybe, the critics seemed to be saying, Clint Eastwood isn't actually Dirty Harry after all. Another small film, *Honkytonk Man* (1982), is a character study, set in the Depression, of a self-destructive country singer. *Tightrope* (1984), Eastwood's depiction of a troubled cop in New Orleans, was both a critical and popular success.

By the mid-eighties, critics were having a difficult time defining Eastwood. *Sudden Impact* (1983), the fourth Dirty Harry movie, got strangely mixed notices. "The picture is like a slightly psychotic version of an old Saturday-afternoon serial, with Harry sneering at the scum and cursing them before he shoots them with his king-size custom-made '.44 Auto Mag,'" scoffed one reviewer, while another felt that "many who have long dismissed Eastwood's movies as crude cartoons now suddenly understand that the violence has always been in used with self-irony and moral intelligence."

The weight of opinion seems to be shifting toward the latter viewpoint. In an article in *Parade* magazine, Norman Mailer was adamant in his admiration: "Eastwood is an artist.... You can see the man in his work just as clearly as you see Hemingway in *A Farewell to Arms*.... Critics had been attacking him for years over how little he did onscreen, but Eastwood may have known something they did not." The *Los Angeles Times* noted that women in Eastwood's movies have always been strong, interesting as both heroes and villains, and that "Eastwood may be not only one of the best, but the most important and influential (because of the size of his audience) feminist filmmaker working in America today." The French film review *Cahiers du cinéma* noted the "self-parodying subtlety" in Eastwood's movies, while the London *Daily Mail* noted that Europe was discovering "hidden depths" in Dirty Harry. *The New York Times Magazine* ran a cover story on Eastwood the artist, appropriately titled "Clint Eastwood, Seriously."

It would be pleasantly ironic to report that this reassessment of East-wood's career has come on the heels of declining popularity at the box office, but the man who formerly had No Name is, by some accounts, the most popular movie star in the world. Theater owners named him the top moneymaking star of 1984 and 1985, a distinction he also won in 1972 and 1973. Since 1955, his forty films have grossed more than $1.5 *billion,* a figure that rivals the gross national product of some nations (Malta, Mauritania, the Netherlands Antilles, Rwanda, Tonga, Togo, Chad and Lesotho, among others). Moreover, a recent Roper poll found that Americans aged eighteen to twenty-four picked Clint Eastwood as their number-one hero. Ronald Reagan was a distant third (behind Eddie Murphy), which may account for the fact that the president of the United States has begun quoting from Clint Eastwood films when issuing challenges to Congress.

For all his renown, Clint Eastwood in person is affable, a gentle man who speaks in a whisper-soft voice. At six four and 190 pounds, he is physically imposing, but there is none of the coiled-spring tension one senses in Dirty Harry. Of all the roles he has played, Eastwood in person seems most like the mild-mannered California jazz DJ he portrayed in *Play Misty for Me*, a man happily out of step with the times and secure in his private enthusiasms. He lives alone in Monterey, California, where he jogs, works out with weights, plans his next projects and is sometimes seen in the company of actress Sondra Locke. He has two children by his former wife, Maggie: a daughter, Alison, 14, who appeared in *Tightrope*, and a son, Kyle, 17, who costarred in *Honkytonk Man*.

Eastwood is, as Norman Mailer noted, "a nice guy," a fifty-five-year-old man who has taken his chances and seems distantly amused by the sudden storm of critical acclaim after having weathered thirty years of dismissal and abuse.

This year, Eastwood was invited to the Cannes film festival to show his eleventh directorial effort, *Pale Rider*, a western in which he also stars. The movie was warmly received, and in the press conferences that followed, the questions sounded like something my philosophical friend might have asked twenty years ago:

One journalist wondered if, at the end of *Pale Rider*, Eastwood was really killing Sergio Leone, his artistic father.

The actor thought this one over — that is the kind of question you have to answer when people start taking you seriously — and said, finally, that he didn't think so: Leone and he were the same age.

Clint Eastwood understands that a good joke dies on the dissecting table, and like many of the characters he's portrayed on screen, he is often more interesting for the things he doesn't say than the things he does. Listen:

*You are, by some accounts, the world's most popular movie star. Do you sometimes wake up in the morning, look in the mirror and say, "Can that possibly be me?" I mean, does it surprise you?*
If I thought about it enough, it might. Yeah, I guess so. I guess you'd look back and say, "How did a kid from Oakland get this far?" I'm sure other people do that to some degree. It's like waking up with a hooker — how the hell did I get here?

*Let's start with* A Fistful of Dollars. *How did that come about?*
Well, at that time I'd done *Rawhide* for about five years. The agency called and asked if I was interested in doing a western in Italy and Spain. I said,

"Not particularly." I was pretty westerned out on the series. They said, "Why don't you give the script a quick look?" Well, I was kind of curious, so I read it, and I recognized it right away as *Yojimbo*, a Kurosawa film I had liked a lot. When I'd seen it years before, I thought, "Hey, this film is really a western." Nobody in the States had the nerve to make it, though, and when I saw that someone somewhere did have the nerve, I thought, "Great."

Sergio [Leone] had only directed one other picture, but they told me he had a good sense of humor, and I liked the way he interpreted the *Yojimbo* script. And I had nothing to lose, because I had the series to go back to as soon as the hiatus was over. So I felt, "Why not?" I'd never been to Europe. That was reason enough to go.

*You've said that in the original script, the Man with No Name shot off his mouth more than his gun.*
The script was very expository, yeah. It was an outrageous story, and I thought there should be much more mystery to the person. I kept telling Sergio, "In a real A picture, you let the audience think along with the movie; in a B picture, you explain everything." That was my way of selling my point. For instance, there was a scene where he decides to save the woman and the child. She says, "Why are you doing this?" In the script he just goes on forever. He talks about his mother, all kinds of subplots that come out of nowhere, and it goes on and on and on. I thought that was not essential, so I just rewrote the scene the night before we shot it.

*Okay, the woman asks, "Why are you doing this?" and he says . . .*
"Because I knew someone like you once and there was nobody there to help."

*So you managed to express ten pages of dialogue in a single sentence.*
We left it oblique and let the audience wonder: "Now wait a minute, what happened?" You try to let people reach into the story, find things in it, choice little items that they enjoy. It's like finding something you've worked and hunted for, and it's much more enjoyable than having some explanation slapped into your face like a wet fish.

*So you have a lot of faith in your audience.*
You have to. You don't play down to people, you don't say, "I'd better make this a little simpler, a little more expository." For instance, in *Josey Wales*,

when he rides off at the end of the picture, the editor and I had wanted to superimpose the girl's face over him. He said, "We want the audience to know that he's going back to her." Well, we all know he's going back. The audience wills him back. If he rides off on the other side of town, the audience will say, "Well, he's gonna turn left." It's really looking down on an audience to tell them something they already know. Or tell them something they can draw in because it arises out of the story. I try to make that part of their job.

*To . . .*
To think about it a little bit.

*You did two more of the Italian westerns with Leone:* For a Few Dollars More *and* The Good, the Bad and the Ugly.
Yeah. The other two, the productions were glossier, more refined. The stories didn't mean a whole lot. They were just a lot of vignettes all shuffled together. I enjoyed them, they were fun to do. Escapism. And the American western at that point was in a dull period. But when Sergio approached me about being in some of the subsequent westerns, I thought it would be going too far. So I came back to Hollywood and did *Hang 'em High*. Sergio was interested in expanding the size and scope of his films, and I was more interested in the people and the story line. I guess, selfishly, because I am an actor, I wanted to do something with more character study.

*You've described yourself as introverted. Do you think that's because you moved so much as a kid?*
Maybe, yes. We moved around California a lot We lived in Redding, Sacramento, Hayward. My parents were married around 1929, right at the beginning of the Depression. It was a tough period for everybody, and especially a young guy like my dad who was just starting out. In those days, people struggled for jobs. Sometimes jobs didn't pan out, or they couldn't afford to keep you. We drove around in an old Pontiac, or something like that, towing a one-wheel trailer. We weren't itinerant: it wasn't *The Grapes of Wrath*, but it wasn't uptown either.

It gives you a sort of conservative background, being raised in an era when everything was scarce. Once, I remember, we moved from Sacramento to Pacific Palisades because my father had gotten a gas-station attendant's job. It's still there, the station. It's at Highway 101 and Sunset Boulevard.

*Were you involved in any school activities?*
Yeah. I played a little basketball. Some football in junior high. I didn't really get involved in team sports, because we moved so much. I did some competitive swimming, and one of the schools I went to had a great gymnastics program, so I diddled with that for a while. I wasn't particularly suited for it, because I was so tall, but I liked it.

I suppose one of the biggest things when I was a kid—I always liked jazz. A wide spectrum of jazz. Back in the forties and fifties I listened to Brubeck and Mulligan. And I loved Ellington and Basie. I'd get books on everybody: Bix Beiderbecke, King Oliver, Buddy Bolden. I used to be very knowledgeable.

Then, up through the forties, I used to go to those Jazz at the Philharmonic things. One time, they had Coleman Hawkins, Lester Young, Charlie Parker and a whole group of classic players. In fact, nowadays, when I talk to composers that are maybe ten years younger than I am, they're all jealous about that concert: "You saw those guys live!"

*You play some jazz piano yourself.*
Yeah, when I was a kid, I played. Fooled around with some other instruments, but I was lazy. I didn't really go after it. I just started again in the last few years. I've been diddling around with composition. Five or six things. I used one as my daughter's theme in *Tightrope,* and I also did the theme for the young girl in *Pale Rider.*

I have some regrets that I didn't follow up on music, especially when I hear people who play decently. I played on one cut on the album for *City Heat.* After the session, Pete Jolly and Mike Lang and I were all talking about how we started out playing piano. We all started the exact same way, only those guys went on to really play. We began by playing blues: blues figures at parties. I was such a backward kid at that age, but I could sit down at a party and play the blues. And the gals would come around the piano, and all of a sudden you had a date.

*You had a country hit, "Barroom Buddies," a duet with Merle Haggard. When did you get interested in country music?*

Well, I think you can say that Merle Haggard had a hit and sort of dragged me along. I was never terribly knowledgeable about country music. The first real good taste of it I got was when I was eighteen or nineteen, working in a pulp mill in Springfield, Oregon. It was always wet, really depressing. Wintertime. Dank. I really didn't know anyone, and someone told me to go out to this place where there was a lot of country music. I wasn't very interested, but this guy told me there were a lot of girls there. So I went. I saw Bob Wills and his Texas Playboys. Unlike most country bands, they had brass and reeds and they played country swing. They were good. It surprised me a little bit, how good they were. Also, there were a lot of girls there, which didn't surprise me at all. So I guess you could say that lust expanded my musical horizons.

*Why didn't you follow up on the music?*
I was going to. I tried to enroll in Seattle University, where they had a good music program. I got my draft notice before I got in there, though, and ended up at Fort Ord [California]. And I guess I just failed away from music.

I served my two years and went down to L.A. City College, where I enrolled in business administration. In the service I had met some guys who were actors—Martin Milner, David Janssen—and when we got out, a cinematographer got me a screen test. I got an offer to go under contract with Universal, seventy-five bucks a week to start. They threw me out a year and half later. But it was a pretty good deal for a young guy. We had acting classes every day.

*Is that when you realized that being introverted could be an asset for an actor? That you could play on it?*
I don't know if I played on it consciously. I know that for many years before I became known for the way I act now, I played characters that were not terribly talkative. Economical characters. Some books—even Stanislavsky's people—discuss the fact that sometimes less can be best. Sometimes you can tell more with economy than you can with excess gyration.

The *Rawhide* series was a great training ground. All of a sudden, everything you ever studied about being an actor you could put into play every day. It's one thing to work for a week in a Francis the Talking Mule picture—which was how it had been going for me—and another thing to be doing it all day for eight years.

It's like the story of the great classical trumpet player they found one day playing in a baseball orchestra at Wrigley Field. Somebody recognized him and said, "My God, Maestro, what is the greatest classical trumpet player in the world doing playing in a baseball band?" He said, "You must play every day."

In *Rawhide*, I got to play every day. It taught me how to pick up and run, how to make things up, wing things in there.

The New York Review of Books *recently ran an article about you that said, "What is most distinctive about Eastwood . . . is how effectively he struggles against absorption into mere genre, mere style, even while appearing, with his long-boned casualness and hypnotic presence, to be nothing but style." Do you want to comment on that?*
Well, yeah, style. Take guys like Kirk Douglas and Burt Lancaster. They're terrific actors, but their style is more aggressive. Both of them did some marvelous things and some films that weren't big hits but were great all the same: Douglas in *Lonely Are the Brave* and *Paths of Glory*; Lancaster in *Trapeze*. But their style was a little different than, say, Gary Cooper's or Henry Fonda's, because those guys were more laid-back, more introverted, and you were always leaning forward, wondering what they were thinking. With the Lancaster-Douglas school, there was never any doubt. Fonda or Cooper: you were never quite sure with them. They had a mysterioso quality.

*Which is something you strive for: that little taste of ambiguity.*
Exactly.

*Let's go over a few of your films.* Dirty Harry.
There was something there I felt some people missed. One critic said Dirty Harry shot the guy at the end with such glee that he enjoyed it. There was no glee in it at all, there was a sadness about it. Watch the film again and you'll see that.

Every Which Way but Loose.
All of a sudden Norman Mailer comes out and says he likes this film, and because he's such a well-thought-of writer, people think, "Wait a second, maybe that wasn't such a bad movie after all." I thought it was kind of a

hip script myself when I read it. Here's a guy pouring his heart out to an ape, and losing the girl. I like the correlation with some of my westerns, too. The guy purposely loses the big fight at the end because he doesn't want to go around being the fastest gun in the West.

Bronco Billy.
It's about the American Dream, and Billy's dream that he fought so hard for. And it's all in the context of this outdated Wild West show that has absolutely no chance of being a hit. But it's sweet. It's pure.

*In the pivotal scene, Billy allows himself to be humiliated by the sheriff rather than allow his friend to be arrested. That played so against your established image: it must have been fun to do.*
Really fun. It was suggested that Billy come back at the end and punch this guy out. That would have ruined the picture, the whole theme of loyalty. Billy doesn't approve of this kid being a deserter, and he doesn't know enough to intellectualize what his friend's feelings were about the war in Vietnam. He just knows he doesn't approve but he's going to stick by his friend. Now if Billy had come back and kicked the crap out of the sheriff at the end, it would have wrecked all that.

There's no real excuse for being successful enough as an actor to do what you want and then selling out. You do it pure. You don't try to adapt it, make it commercial. It's not *Dirty Bronco Billy.*

Honkytonk Man.
Red Stovall is based a bit on some self-destructive people I've known. He's wild and funny, but he's been a coward in his time. He won't face up to his ambitions. He's not that great a singer, but he writes some interesting things. When he gets his moment, he's already destroyed himself.

*And the studio suggested that it might be a good idea if Red didn't die in the end?*
I resisted that.

*Your new one,* Pale Rider.
It's a western. One of the earliest films in America was a western: *The Great Train Robbery.* If you consider film an art form, as some people do, then

the western would be a truly American art form, much as jazz is. In the sixties, American westerns were stale, probably because the great directors—Anthony Mann, Raoul Walsh, John Ford—were no longer working a lot. Then the Italian western came along, and we did very well with those; they died of natural causes. Now I think it's time to analyze the classic western. You can still talk about sweat and hard work, about the spirit, about love for the land and ecology. And I think you can say all these things in the western, in the classic mythological form.

*You're not generally credited with having any sense of humor, yet certain of your films get big laughs in all the right places. The first half of* Honkytonk Man, *for instance, was very funny.*
That's the way it was designed: a humorous story that becomes a tragedy. A lot of the humor is not in what you say but in how you react. Comedians are expert at that. Jackie Gleason in *The Honeymooners*: Alice zaps him, and his reaction—just the look on his face cracks you up. Jack Benny could do that. Comedy isn't necessarily all dialogue. Think of Buster Keaton: the poker face and all this chaos going on all around him. Sometimes it's a question of timing, of the proper rhythm.

*Does it amuse you that the president is quoting from* Sudden Impact?
Yeah, it was kind of amusing. I knew that "Make my day" would have a certain amount of impact in the film, but I didn't realize it would become a sort of "Play it again, Sam."

*I've read that you occasionally speak with Reagan on the phone.*
Well, I don't know where that came from. I think some secretary or someone mentioned it. I've talked to him a couple of times, but they make it sound like I'm some great adviser.

*I want you to meet my secretary of state, Dirty Harry...*
Yeah, right [*laughing*].

*You're not going to tell me what you talk about with the president?*
I haven't really said that much. I was in Washington not too long ago, and I walked to the White House for lunch. We didn't discuss much of anything except the National Endowment for the Arts medal we were passing

out. There were some former members of the NEA there, of which I was one. It was a small luncheon, a few laughs.

I mean, he doesn't ask me for advice. I could suggest some better places to go than that cemetery in Germany.

*And you're not going to run for political office.*
That's something nobody has to worry about.

*You have a reputation for shooting your films quickly and bringing them in under budget. Do you think that has anything to do with having grown up in the Depression?*
I would like to say it's just good business, but it may be that. It may be a background of not wanting to see waste.

*There's a rumor that people work quickly on your sets because you don't provide chairs.*
That rumor derived from a comment I made. Someone asked why I liked shooting on location as opposed to in the studio. I said, "In the studio, everyone's looking around for a chair. On location, everyone's working." But there are chairs on the set and on location.

*You also have a reputation for bringing in young or underappreciated talent.* Thunderbolt and Lightfoot, *for instance, was Michael Cimino's first film. Some people might say that you do that because you get these folks cheap.*
Nothing's cheap, and I don't think I'd cut off my nose to spite my face. I don't think I'd get somebody cheap just because I thought he was cheap. I think I'd want the film to be the best possible. Otherwise you're selling yourself short. An awful lot of directors are expensive, but you don't know how they got to be that way. Sometimes it's just a matter of salesmanship and agenting.

I haven't worked with a lot of big-name directors, but I came up during an era when they were all beginning to retire: I never worked with Hitchcock or Wyler or Stevens or Capra or Hawks or Walsh. I missed all that.

I suppose the most expensive director I've worked with is Don Siegel. I think I learned more about directing from him than from anybody else. He taught me to put myself on the line. He shoots lean, and he shoots what he wants. He knew when he had it, and he didn't need to cover his ass with a dozen different angles.

I learned that you have to trust your instincts. There's a moment when an actor has it, and he knows it. Behind the camera you can feel that moment even more clearly. And once you've got it, once you feel it, you can't second-guess yourself. If I would go around and ask everyone on the set how it looked, eventually someone would say, "Well, gee, I don't know, there was a fly 600 feet back." Somebody's always going to find a flaw, and pretty soon that flaw gets magnified and you're all back to another take. Meanwhile, everyone's forgotten that there's a certain focus on things, and no one's going to see that fly, because you're using a 100-mm lens. But that's what you can do. You can talk yourself in or out of anything. You can find a million reasons why something didn't work. But if it feels right, and it looks right, it works.

Without sounding like a pseudointellectual dipshit, it's my responsibility to be true to myself. If it works for me, it's right. When I start choosing wrong, I'll step back and let someone else do it for me.

*The critics are beginning to say that you've made some pretty good choices.*
Some of them. But it's luck. It's instinctive. It comes from the animal part of the brain: the instinctive, intuitive pact. The analytical brain can kill you as an artist. You want to stay in touch on a deeper level.

*Why do you think the critics have begun to reassess your career?*
I think it just finally got to the point where people said, "Well, he does quite a few different things. Maybe it isn't all some cowboy or cop who happened to click." It's easy to dismiss those kinds of films unless you're consciously looking for the best in them. Then again, I've changed. I've done films, like *Bronco Billy,* that were unusual for me, unusual for anyone. At a Museum of Modern Art retrospective in New York, they liked *Bronco Billy* and worked back from there. The French worked back from *Honkytonk Man,* which was one of the best-reviewed English-language films of the year there. In Montreal, at the film festival there, they liked *Tightrope.* All those films accumulate, and after thirty years, people are beginning to look at a body of work.

*But how do you feel about it, this critical reassessment?*
It's gratifying.

# Eastwood on Eastwood

## CHRISTOPHER FRAYLING / 1985

FRAYLING: *Could we talk about the origins of the "Eastwood style," in the Spaghetti Westerns of the mid-1960s? In retrospect, they changed both the look and the feel of the traditional Western.*

EASTWOOD: Yeah, I think they changed the style, the approach to Westerns. They "operacised" them, if there's such a word. They made the violence and the shooting aspect a little more larger than life, and they had great music and new types of scores. I wasn't involved in the music, but we used the same composer, Ennio Morricone, in *Sister Sara* and I worked with him a bit there...They were scores that hadn't been used in other Westerns. They just had a look and a style that was a little different at the time: I don't think the stories were any better, maybe they were less good. I don't think any of them was a classic story—like *The Searchers*, or something like that—they were more fragmented, episodic, following this central character through various little episodes.

FRAYLING: *Someone once wrote that Leone's films are "operas in which the arias aren't sung, they are stared" [laughter]. But when you say "a look and a style," do you mean that their main contribution was a technical one?*

EASTWOOD: Uh-huh. I think the technical effect is the biggest—the look and the sound. A film has to have a sound of its own, and the Italians—who don't record sound while they're shooting—are very con-

---

Published as chapter 6 in Christopher Frayling, *Clint Eastwood* (London: Virgin, 1992), 61–67. Reprinted by permission of the Peters Fraser & Dunlop Group Ltd.

scious of this. Sergio Leone felt that sound was very important, that a film has to have its own sound as well as its own look. And I agree...Leone'll get a very operatic score, a lot of trumpets, and then all of a sudden "ka-pow!" He'll shut it off and let the horses snort and all that sort of thing. It's very effective. So, yes, I think you've hit on it when you say "technical"—that was the star—technical changes. The lighting was different, too. It wasn't flat lit. A little more...style.

FRAYLING:  *I've read somewhere that, when you were preparing for the role of The Man With No Name, just before you left the Universal Studios set on* Rawhide *for Rome and Almería, you bought the costume at a Santa Monica wardrobe store, and borrowed the leather gunbelt, pistol and suede boots from* Rawhide. *Yet Sergio Leone has told me that the transformation of Rowdy Yates into The Man With No Name—the basic change of "look and style" from which everything else followed—was mostly* his *idea.*

EASTWOOD  *(eyes narrowing momentarily):* He didn't accept that...? Well—I guess I heard that too, and I heard stories where people would say that he would lay a rope down the line on the ground where I should walk—and all that stuff—and I thought "Funny, he's the only one who ever had to do that." But I guess it's normal for him—all of a sudden I go off back to America, and he does several films in the same vein and then drops out for a while, and he sees me going on to do other things and maybe that affected him. Who knows why a person says different things?

FRAYLING  *(not feeling lucky, not pushing it): Whoever it was, the character's sense of visual style—the poncho in* Fistful of Dollars *(1964), the long-waisted coat in* The Good, the Bad and the Ugly *(1966)—was a world away from the fringed buckskins of Alan Ladd in* Shane, *or all those well-scrubbed army scouts in 1950s Westerns.*

EASTWOOD  *(visibly relaxing again):* Yeah, that was accepted at the time—sixties—and yeah, that buckskin does look a little drugstoreish now. But we did similar things in *High Plains Drifter* and *Pale Rider*, where he's kind of a stylised character, with a little bit of a different look—the hats, the long coats, and various other things. But it was mostly the people who were *in* the clothes. Gian Maria Volonté had a good face, and all those Spanish, gypsy faces—that was just general...everything kind of tied together and made an interesting-looking film. You ask most people what the films were about and they can't tell you. But they tell you "the look" [*he mimes throwing the poncho over his shoulder*] and the "da-da-da-da-dum" [*he hums the opening bars of* The Good, the Bad and the Ugly *theme*], and the cigar and the gun and those little flash images that hit you, and we get back to "technical" again, technical changes. Maybe I had some contribution in there, and er, maybe not . . . I remember we cut out quite a bit of dialogue together, on *Fistful*, before and during.

FRAYLING: *I don't know if you recall, but in the Italian press of 1964 you were billed as "Western consultant" on* A Fistful of Dollars.
EASTWOOD: Uh-huh? *(laughter, and quizzical look.)*

FRAYLING: *A lot of the technical lessons of the Italian films seem to me to have been carried over into your first Western as a director,* High Plains Drifter: *the sound effects, the heavy framing, the way in which the hero is presented . . .*
EASTWOOD: Yeah. I don't really associate *High Plains Drifter* as closely with those films as maybe some do—other than the same actor and this mysterious drifting character who comes in, which is like the character in *A Fistful of Dollars*. But then that's sort of the classic Western—that's been done so many times before—with *Shane*, with William S. Hart, with . . . [*pause*] there's nothing really new under the sun there, it's just a question of styling. And it was the same actor playing it. Some elements that come with that character are going to come into other characters that I play, too, along the line. You adapt it to yourself, you know . . . The *Fistful of Dollars* character, also—it was fun for me to do everything that was against the rules. For years in Hollywood there was a thing called the Hays Office, there were certain taboos that were put on the Western, even more so than other things. One was that you never could tie up a person shooting with a person being hit. You had to shoot separately, and then show the person fall—and that was always thought sort of stupid, but on television we always did it that way . . . We did it that way on *Rawhide*—and everybody talked about it, and it was sort of a thing that hung over there. And then, you see, Sergio never knew that, and so he was tying it up and that was great—that's terrific, tie up the shots. You see the bullet go off, you see the gun fire, you see the guy fall, and it had never been done this way before. Those things seemed to me very bad for television. Where everybody was shooting sort of standard things, the typical television filming would be where the per-

son is in the door CUT. CUT around to other person who says some lines. CUT walks up to him. Two head closeups. You never do see the two people together. So that was part of it.

FRAYLING: *Turning to* The Outlaw Josey Wales *(1976, or twelve years after* Fistful*), which I think is one of your finest films as a director so far, there's much less emphasis on "style," on the detached, comic-strip aspects of the Spaghetti Westerns, and much more on the kinds of things that might be on Americans' minds after the Vietnam war. It's about the rebuilding of a small community after the bloody dislocation of the American Civil War—but it could just as well be about post-Vietnam America. How conscious was that?*
EASTWOOD: Right. It was inherent in the story, but I guess it made it attractive to me, but I didn't sit there and say, "Well, I'm doing this now because this parallels some situation in history, then and now, like Vietnam." But I think the dislocation could be the same after every war... is the same.

FRAYLING: *In a way,* Josey Wales *puts the morality—the American morality—back into the character of "The Man With No Name." Josey is determined to get his revenge on the Kansas Redlegs—"I don't want nobody belonging to me," he says—yet he's constantly being deflected from his quest by various drifters who refuse to take his macho image seriously. Even the hound-dog he picks up along the way isn't taken in by the image. The punch line is that we should choose—whatever the odds against—"the word of life" rather than "the word of death." It's the gentle option, rather than the violent one...*
EASTWOOD: Well, the thing that I liked about it was that it was a Western with a very good story and a central character, and the effects on this character and what life had done to this guy, and his search for something it would be easier to run away from—and by accident things always happen to him, which make him a better person. He starts out as a farmer, becomes a killer, and in the end, I think, becomes a farmer again—although the audience decides that. Because, like I said, the films that I did with Sergio, if they'd been done with less style, they would have been very poor shows because they weren't really good strong stories, and I like stories. It's not that we drifted apart, but I think we just became philosophically different.

I was drifting—naturally, being an actor—towards more personal, more real stories. And he wanted more production values as a director, so he was always going towards vaster and vaster scenes, with trains blowing up, and more Indians over the hill, or whatever—I'm just using examples, nothing specific...and I wanted more personal stories. He got into larger, epic pictures and I got into smaller pictures. In *Josey Wales,* there was a personal story that also had a large landscape to it, and that was ideal for me.

FRAYLING: *It must be unique for an entire cinematic genre to depend on the fortunes of one individual, but, through the 1970s and 1980s, the future of the Western has to a large extent hinged on the boxoffice performance of your work. Why do you think that the Western virtually collapsed in the 1970s? Why, for example, did an Arthur Penn Western with Jack Nicholson and Marlon Brando—which must have seemed gilt-edged to those in the know—why did it go down so badly?*

EASTWOOD: I don't blame all that on the Western as much as on the material...that Nicholson and Brando thing, *The Missouri Breaks,* for instance, was ridiculous. It wasn't a good script and they obviously felt so, too—why else would a guy dress up like his own grandmother? Brando obviously thought there's nothing here, I might as well enjoy myself. So he's going to go off and screw off somewhere. I think that if he'd truly believed it was a great piece of material and that he was going to contribute to something that might be a fine film, he might have thought otherwise. I like to think that, anyway.

FRAYLING: *So what d'you think your particular contribution has been to the American Western of the 1970s and 1980s?*

EASTWOOD: Well, the answer maybe is just what you said. Maybe that I was lucky enough to make a few of the most successful ones of that period. I don't have any great bolt of lightning from the sky about that one. I just feel the Western is part of the American heritage; the earliest American film, as you'll know, was *The Great Train Robbery.* Americans don't have many art forms that are truly American. Most of them come from Europe or wherever. Westerns and jazz are the only two I can think of which are American art forms. But *High Plains Drifter* was great fun because I liked the irony of it, I liked the irony of doing a stylised version of what happens if the sheriff in *High Noon* is killed, and symbolically comes back as some avenging angel or something—and I think that's far more hip than doing just a straight Western, the straight old conflicts we've all seen. *Josey Wales* just had a much stronger story as far as the personal, the individual was concerned, and a good character. *Bronco Billy* wasn't really a Western at all . . . More Frank Capra than Western.

*Pale Rider* is kind of allegorical, more in the *High Plains Drifter* mode: like that, though he isn't a reincarnation or anything, but he does ride a pale horse like the four horsemen of the apocalypse, and he could maybe be one of those guys. It's a classic story of the big guys against the little guys, little guys versus big guys, the corporate mining which ends up in hydraulic mining, they just literally mow the mountains away, you know, the trees and everything . . . all that was outlawed in California some years ago, and they still do it in Montana and a few places. It was outlawed way back, even before ecological concerns were as prevalent as they are today. So we play on that in the film. It's kind of an ecological statement — the fact that this corporation is moving fast because they're afraid laws against it will come along. And so they rabble-rouse these other people and shoot 'em up — ruin their property — and a little girl prays for this figure that comes out of the mountains. He comes down, and there's a series of incidents, and he helps them . . . ! I like stories you can't guess the endings of. Most Westerns, you can guess the ending.

FRAYLING: *So you think Westerns still have an audience, can still carry themes which are about today as well?*

EASTWOOD: I think there's a market there, if somebody can make a good one — because in America, on television, Westerns do extremely well. Some of mine have been run many times — and, like the chairman of Warner Brothers, Bob Daly, said, he'll be selling *Josey Wales* for ten years. So if they do well on television, maybe that means there is a more adult audience. Maybe if these people could come out to the cinema, plus maybe find a group of people who haven't seen a Western recently . . . ! I mean if I was taking a poll — like those studios have to do, throwing the thing in hoppers and computers, which I wouldn't — I think it would come out positive. But I'm not sure . . .

FRAYLING: *Certainly, country and western music, "new" and "old," has never been more popular — and Willie Nelson, and Kenny Rogers have both made Westerns* (Barbarosa, The Gambler) *on the strength of their success as singers. So maybe the way forward might be in modern Westerns. Urban cowboys. Electric horsemen . . .*

EASTWOOD:  Well, I think the Western *has* to be period. I don't think it can be modern. I don't think anybody's interested in a Western set today necessarily—or maybe they might be, depending on the film—I hate to say that definitely. Perhaps a picture about rodeo riding or something like that *might* help to excite somebody. Maybe. But I think a period Western is always that kind of escape—another time, times when things were more simplified . . .

# Clint Eastwood Interviewed by Milan Pavlović

## MILAN PAVLOVIĆ/1988

STEADYCAM: *What attracted you to the idea of filming the life of Charlie Parker?*

CLINT EASTWOOD: Parker was an exceptional human being, his story had never been told, and I've been interested in jazz since I was a boy. My mother had a collection of Fats Waller records; when I was growing up, there was a Dixieland revival in the San Francisco area, and that was when I saw Bird for the first time.

*When and where?*
In 1946, at "Jazz at the Philharmonic" in Oakland, along with Lester Young, who was my first idol. I saw then that Parker was one of the greats of jazz, a forerunner, a trendsetter, a giant of jazz. He brought a whole new expressiveness of feeling into the music.

*Did Bertrand Tavernier's jazz film* Round Midnight *help you to realize* Bird?
Yes and no. We would surely have been able to do *Bird* without Tavernier's film, it didn't open any closed doors for us. On the contrary, I even helped make it possible for *Round Midnight* to get made, by going to the head of Warners to make him agreeable to doing the film. And then we found out how a jazz movie shouldn't be marketed. It's a shame that a film as wonderful as *Round Midnight* didn't find an audience.

Published in part as " 'Kein Popcorn-Film' " (" 'Not a Popcorn Movie' ") in *steadycam*, no. 10 (Fall 1988): 18–20. Reprinted by permission of the author; translated from the German by KC.

*But there is one movie that really helped you: the picture that Warner Bros. owned
the rights to that was traded to Columbia in 1980 for the rights to* Bird. *What
picture was that?*
It was a property called *Revenge.*

*That's the film that's just now being shot by Columbia under the direction of
Tony Scott with Kevin Costner in the leading role, isn't it?*
Yes, but it still hasn't been made *(laughs).* It was a property Warners owned
for a while. Ray Stark absolutely had to have it. When I found out about it,
I spoke to Robert Daly and Terry Semel and asked them if they wouldn't
trade it for the Charlie Parker project.

*Are you always so well informed about such studio matters?*
No, we were just having a meeting about another project. Occasionally,
somebody mentioned *Revenge,* which was a script I knew, and during the
discussion that grew out of that, it occurred to me that Columbia had the
Parker project, and then I started to exert some pressure. Which I had to
do, because even so it took two years before the trade was settled.

*Did you work on a script of your own during this wait?*
No. I had read Oliansky's script and thought it was perfect. Ironically, some
years before, when John Calley was still production chief, Warners had a
Charlie Parker project in development. But that never got made. But I liked
Oliansky's script immediately.

*Then why did you have to wait so long until you could shoot it?*
It wasn't so long as all that, I only took a great deal of time for the preparation: first in my head, and then planning the art direction, because there
were a whole lot of elements and places that had to be researched. Today
nothing is the way it was then. Fifty-Second Street is unrecognizable, Kansas
City and all the rest has changed. I didn't have to use a whole crew for
that, however, because I have a wonderful "production designer," as they
call them today, Edward C. Carfagno, who carefully researched it all.

*Was it your idea to keep Parker's original music?*
Yes. The way Columbia planned the picture, they were going to hire a
musician who would re-record Parker's music *(smiles),* because they wanted

to have the sound in stereo and so forth. There are some very good alto sax players, but I was of the opinion that Charlie Parker was an unique musician and that it would have been a shame not to use his music. I found some outstanding recordings Chan had made. In some cases, she had recorded almost nothing but Charlie's solos, so that we "only" had to add the rest. Lennie Niehaus retreated to the studio to undertake it, and he electronically isolated Charlie's solos. Then we hired musicians like Ray Brown, Walter Davis, Buddy Alexander, Ron Carter, and Barry Harris, and Red Rodney came back to re-record the solos he had played 40 years ago. We got Jon Faddis to do Dizzy Gillespie, because Dizzy was on tour, and Faddis plays a lot like Dizzy, very strong, just like Dizzy 40 years ago.

*Did you see any friends of Charlie Parker's before you began shooting?*
I talked a lot with Chan Parker in Paris, where I went to get as much background information as I possibly could. Then there's a bass player, Buddy Jones, who lives in Carmel; he played in the 40s, and told me a number of stories from the period. Red Rodney filled us in on a whole lot of details, and I've spoken with Dizzy Gillespie several times, with Leonard Feather and all those musicians. They were very cooperative, they wanted to see the picture get made, especially the musicians. Charlie Parker is very much admired by all the jazz players who live in and around L.A., also by younger musicians who never saw him. They were enthusiastic about the project.

Parker has an incredible aura. I recall that when I was shooting *Dirty Harry,* which Lalo Schifrin composed the music for, Lalo and I spoke the whole time about Charlie Parker. I told him about how I'd seen Charlie for the first time, and he got ecstatic and asked me incredulously: "You saw Charlie Parker?" It had been one of his greatest wishes to see Parker live, but he never had the chance.

*Have any of these musicians seen the film?*
So far only Chan and Leonard Feather have seen the film.

*How did Chan Parker react?*
She was speechless, couldn't say anything, so I told her to take her time to make up her mind. And after a few hours, she came and let me know that she likes the picture very much.

*Did you put something of your own memories into the film?*
Yes, I'll never forget how Parker moved, how he walked and how he stood; and of course the sound. This stirring, joyous music, which didn't hint at all at the player's tragic fate. It's a tragedy—Charlie Parker could be among us today, and he would be only 67 years old. He could still be making music, maybe together with Red Rodney, who as recently as two weeks ago appeared on stage in a club in L.A. He could still be alive, but on the other hand who knows how he would be doing. And just look at what he managed to achieve in his short lifetime, how greatly he influenced music and musicians. Everyone who plays alto saxophone today has been influenced by him. And he left his mark on audiences, he introduced people like me to a completely new music.

*You've just spoken to Leonard Feather. He once said there are two great jazz musicians whose life stories ought to be seen on the screen, but that they would never be filmed by Hollywood: on the one hand Duke Ellington, because nothing dramatic happened in his life, and on the other hand Charlie Parker, because his end was too tragic. How did he react to* Bird?
He liked the picture very much. He started out as a journalist, and he knew Charlie and Chan and the others. It was an exciting trip into the past for him, and he had nothing to criticize. Ellington was an extremely disciplined musician; he was, just as Dizzy says in *Bird*, the exact opposite of Charlie Parker: a very quiet, precise, disciplined man with a long and apparently happy life. I didn't know about this statement by Feather.

*I have it from a Belgian documentary,* Bird Now.
From Belgium? I haven't seen the film. Is it new?

*Yes.*
And I thought I'd seen everything there is to see about Parker.

*Which recordings of Parker's do you like particularly?*
I like some early sessions with Dizzy a lot. I would have liked to have used a few things in the picture, "Little Suede Shoes" for example, but there weren't any usable recordings. As a kid, I had all his "strings" records.

*Do you also listen to new jazz records?*
I've heard so much jazz from the 40s and 50s recently... *(he thinks it over and nibbles olives)* There's a marvelous trombonist by the name of Bill Watrous,

also I hired Jon Faddis myself, for *The Gauntlet* and *The Enforcer,* and in *Bird* he played the solos of Dizzy Gillespie. He also imitates Howard McGhee perfectly, on his new record, I don't know if you know it, he has a ball imitating all the greats: Roy Eldridge, Dizzy Gillespie, Howard McGhee, there he has the same sound, very raspy.

*Is it true that Malpaso is producing a music film?*
Not a feature film, no, but we're financing a documentary...

*...about Thelonious Monk?*
Yes, and it's turned out that in the case of Monk, in contrast for instance to Bird, there's a whole lot of black-and-white footage around that can be used as is in a film. So it will be a lot easier than if you wanted to do a documentary about Bird. There're only a few usable shots of him, and not many photos.

*In* Bird, *you can briefly glimpse one of the rare photographs, where he's accepting a prize. Did you film more than only the one shot?*
No, it's really a photo of a photo. It's strange: although Bird was respected so greatly and was honored by music magazines like *Metronome* and *Downbeat,* he was never "in." When *Time* magazine decided to do a jazz cover story, they chose Dave Brubeck.

*As you so often do, you've taken a risk again with* Bird, *a bigger one than ever before.*
*Bird* is different. But that's exactly what's fun for me about filmmaking. I was always a big jazz fan and an even bigger Charlie Parker fan, so I thought, here's a wonderful opportunity to give that expression.

*As a director you're known for doing only a few takes of a shot. According to what we've heard from the* Bird *actors, that was somewhat different this time.*
I'm satisfied with a few takes when I've seen what I want. If not, then I keep shooting.

*Wasn't there anything special about* Bird?
Yes, we tried out a few things. The actors sometimes had their own ideas, which we discussed and often shot as well. And occasionally we combined their ideas with what was planned.

*How did you find Forest Whitaker?*
I'd always hoped that somebody could play Bird. And I didn't want a famous actor in this role in any case, because that would have only caused problems. There are so many good actors out there that I was always convinced I'd find the right one. When Columbia still had the rights to the screenplay, Richard Pryor was very interested in playing Bird. That would not have been my film. But as time passed, Pryor lost interest, and I've heard he had a falling out with the Columbia administration. At the latest, that was when I became convinced that *Bird* would not star Richard Pryor and would not be produced by Columbia. Who knows, if I hadn't taken so much trouble then about getting this picture made, it would never have been done, the project, like so many others in Hollywood, would be gathering dust on a shelf. Often it's the case that if a project's been passed around for ten years and doesn't get made by anyone, it won't ever be touched again.

*And when did you decide in favor of Whitaker?*
I'd liked him for a long time, I'd enjoyed him in his supporting roles, particularly in *The Color of Money*. He always conveyed a truthfulness. I looked at a few other actors, but I decided in favor of him very early. That was the second decision. The first was Diane Venora as Chan. I'd seen her on a videotape in New York, and I just said, "Get her!"

*You began the shoot with scenes that were emotionally difficult for the actors: Whitaker in the hospital, and Diane Venora's first scene was the one after the death of the child. Why did you do that?*
Normally I don't begin with such scenes, but in this case, it seemed important to me to start very deep, with scenes where the actors could and had to plunge deep into the characters. Both actors are young talents with a whole lot of energy and good instincts, and it helped them that they were challenged like that right from the beginning.

*Your pictures are a classic example of the principle that each film requires its own visual style.*
That's how it has to be. For example, every film must be lit in accordance with the subject, the optical expression of the film must reproduce what you think about it as a director. Because *Bird* is a movie about musicians,

who often play at night, there are a lot of night scenes, a lot of blackness. After all, the greatest part of their life takes place at night. And I like the hard contrasts that arise through the extreme darkness.

*You make no compromises at all in that regard. Hasn't Warner Bros. ever expressed the wish that you would shoot your films more brightly?*
No, not so far. With *Bird,* a representative only told me beforehand that he was worried because of the length of the picture *(Bird is 163 minutes long— Interviewer's note).* But after he'd seen the picture, even that wasn't an issue for him any longer. I simply had the feeling that the film had to be like that, and also that long, in order not to waste the genius of Charlie Parker.

*Why did you prefer Jack N. Green to your long-time cameraman Bruce Surtees once again?*
Jack had been a camera operator for a long time, also on films Bruce photographed, *Bronco Billy* for example.[1] Like Bruce, he has a good eye, and he was a good assistant, a good complement for Bruce. Bruce became ill when we were shooting *Tightrope,* and Jack took over the camera for some weeks already back then. I thought he did such a good job with it that I should promote him someday. He comes from the same direction as Bruce, he subscribes to the same camera philosophy, regarding the lighting. And that's also my philosophy. Besides, Jack is the hardest worker I've ever met.

*With your preference for dark lighting, you ignore the Hollywood trend to light films in such a way that their transfer to video won't cause any problems of visibility.*
That's a side effect I didn't take into account. All I'm ever doing is trying to find the true light for a scene. There are also bright scenes in my pictures, even in the darkest like *Tightrope* and *The Gauntlet.* But I detest making compromises, not only as to the lighting but also as to the composition of shots and the format of the film. If somebody wants to do a television movie, let him go ahead and do one. But theatrical films shouldn't be shot with the television format and good visibility in mind. Of course, good lighting

---

1. Green was the camera operator on *Bronco Billy,* but the d.p. was not Surtees but David Worth. The first time both Surtees and Green worked in these capacities on an Eastwood shoot was *Firefox* (1982)—Translator's note.

on a theatrical film can also come across on the television screen. You only have to look at some of the black-and-white pictures from the forties, if Ted Turner hasn't already colorized them. But lighting has always preoccupied me. Already on *Rawhide,* I had heated discussions with the producers. They wanted to put around 900 lights on you, and they were also convinced that you needed that much light. But on the contrary, if you look at those wonderful old pictures, *The Third Man* for example, with their hard contrasts, then you know that isn't true.

*Did* Bird *turn out just as you imagined it at the beginning?*
Yes, pretty much exactly. Of course there were a few question marks, but they involved things like the mix of the soundtrack.

*Was the complicated structure, with all the flashbacks and flash-forwards, already present in the script, or did it only develop with the editing?*
It was already designed like that. It also wasn't anything entirely new for me, I've done pictures with flashbacks before.

*But none with flashbacks within flashbacks, right?*
That was the complication, because I absolutely wanted to do it in such a way that the spectator gets it from the visuals, I didn't want to be constantly inserting titles: "Los Angeles, April 8, 11:50 PM." We have voiceovers a few times, but the voices never explain the leaps in time. It's certainly not a movie where you can keep running out to get popcorn.

*You also never have the feeling that the movie is that long.*
I hope not. You have to bring along a little time and patience and understand the film as a saga. But I also believe that the time passes more quickly than you think. It's like with underground recordings of Charlie Parker concerts, some of his solos there last over ten minutes and you don't have the feeling that they're lasting so long.

*Did you have to make some cuts in the screenplay?*
Yes, a few scenes, and since Oliansky was working on another project, I did it myself and kept him informed about the changes.

*You shot* Bird *before* The Dead Pool, *the fifth Dirty Harry picture. The Dead Pool is being released earlier in America: as a typical summer entertainment?*

The summer is more suitable for *The Dead Pool* and the fall for *Bird*. That's why we also worked really fast to get *The Dead Pool* ready for a July start. *Bird* was prepared more carefully, that was always planned that way, and as you can imagine, we won't be releasing the picture with 1500 prints in the States.

*When exactly will Warners release* Bird *and how?*
*Bird* will be released at end of September in a few theaters, so that the picture hopefully will have enough time to find its audience.

*So the film will be marketed more conscientiously than* Honkytonk Man? *(That picture was released in 667 cinemas with disastrous results, and it never had a chance to find an audience that would take it to heart.)*
Yes, in the case of *Bird* initially no more than 20 prints will be released. *Honkytonk Man* was a painful experience, and the chief blame for the failure lies with me. I simply misgauged the reaction of the public at the time.

*When you were in Cannes in 1985 with Pale Rider, you said that there would be no new Dirty Harry picture, as long as no good script was available. Was there one available now?*
Three years is a long time. Three years ago, I had different views on some things than today. The script turned up, and I thought it was fun. I think of Harry as an old friend: You check in again from time to time to see how he's doing.

*Does he change?*
Always, hopefully. He's calmed down a little, he's not so angry any more, but he still manages to get into trouble.

*Will you stick with the title* The Dead Pool?
Yes.

*Reminds you a little of* The Drowning Pool.
That wasn't intended. The title comes from the game "The pool."

*What kind of a game is that?*
A pretty simple game, in which bets are placed on celebrities—sports stars, politicians and others, who are in a big list: who's going to die when. That's

based on an actual event. The people have to die a natural death. In the story that's built from that, a murder soon takes place, and when Harry investigates he finds out he's way up on top of the list.

*Is this the last visit of Dirty Harry?*
I can't say. Every time, whenever I do a Dirty Harry picture, I say that's enough. But as I said, Harry's become an old friend to me, and I like to look in on him now and then.

*Probably there will be discussions about violence once again.*
I've gotten used to it. There was always violence, in the movies and in literature. But if tragic cases occur in reality, that isn't so much because of the movies but rather the tolerance of violence in our society. Because when violence occurs in everyday life, many Americans say to themselves, "So what!?" But in the movies they condemn it.

*You're now in Cannes for the second time. In 1985 you were here with a Western, now it's a film about jazz. You once said that the Western and jazz are the only two means of expression that were capable of defining America and the American way of life and culture. Do you still believe that today?*
It wasn't deliberate that the films I've come to Cannes with would be *Pale Rider* and *Bird*, but it's a marvelous and significant coincidence. I'm confident that jazz is one of the true art forms of America, and translated to film, nothing comes as close to it as the Western.

*Are you looking for a third art form? You've now tried out politics.*
Yes *(laughs)*, I've got that behind me.

*Would you be interested in shooting a Western again?*
Yes, very much, and I've got a script on hand that I'd like to shoot in a year or two.

*Why is it that the Western has no chance nowadays, despite films like* Silverado?
The American public seems to be fixated on formula pictures at the moment, and the American studios are reluctant to take risks. But I'm convinced that there also can and will be Westerns that are hits once again. You've got to do the best you can. Pale Rider did well, after all.

*But it wasn't as big a success as* Sudden Impact, *not even as big a draw as* Tightrope, *which was more complex.*
That's right, but we still made a considerable profit with *Pale Rider,* and I'm not at all disinclined to make another Western.

*Weren't you supposed to direct an episode of the* Rawhide *series at the beginning of your career?*
I was, but it didn't happen, because an actor colleague on another series exceeded the budget and the schedule with his directorial debut.

*That taught you a lesson.*
Yes, that made it very clear to me how you can make yourself unpopular. So at that time I could only prepare a few trailers.

*Is it difficult for you not to intervene in the direction when someone else is directing you?*
No, it's not a problem, there are many ways to achieve something, and my own idea about how to do something isn't the only one. Maybe I would have seen that differently some years ago.

*Buddy van Horn directed* The Dead Pool. *How do you choose your directors?*
I look at the production figures and the shooting schedule. For *The Dead Pool,* we had very little time, and I knew Buddy was capable of working that quickly. Sometimes I can only shake my head when I see how other pictures go over their limits. I've never been willing to indulge in that, certainly not at this stage of my life. But I have to note that the director isn't always to blame if a picture goes over schedule. Often, it's because of miscalculations, or management, or illnesses. Just think of Dustin Hoffman, who became allergic to body makeup while working on *Tootsie.* In that case the production had to be interrupted for a week. Or it's simply just because of the weather. When we came to Utah to shoot scenes for *The Outlaw Josey Wales,* people there told us that the year before a film crew had to suspend operations for seventeen days, because it rained continuously. I still remember how we examined the sky every day.

*The budgets of your pictures are always much lower than on an average Hollywood film. The standard budget there is up around 30 million dollars these days. How high was your budget for* Bird?

We required less money than we had calculated. We had estimated the budget at 11 million dollars, because it's a period film we had to build sets for, and because it's almost three hours long. Without the expenses for advertising and prints, *Bird* finally cost 9.1 million dollars.

*There are also films that devour 63 million dollars.*
I've also heard about such numbers. *(smiles)* That's a hell of a lot of money. If you can see it on the screen, that makes up for it a little, but I tell you, if it only looks like 62 million dollars... *(laughs)*

*Are you withdrawing from acting?*
No, I'm only taking a little break because of my official duties as mayor of Carmel. Like always, everything depends on the project, on the script. I think if I had three or four projects that would give me a directorial challenge, without a role for the actor Clint Eastwood, then I would concentrate completely on directing for these projects. If on the other hand three or four interesting roles were available, I would concentrate on acting. But I don't plan so far in advance at all.

*So the stories aren't true that claim you only want to direct in the future?*
No, that's only one of the many rumors I only know about from the newspapers.

*Do such stories still annoy you?*
You get used to it. Lee Marvin once said, "I'll know my career is coming to an end when they begin to quote me right."

*(A green spider is creeping up on Eastwood, Eastwood takes it in his hand like a ladybug and lets it crawl around. A press agent exclaims rapturously, "Hollywood's 'tough guy' coddles a spider.")*
I admire living creatures. There's a sweet critter. Only it mustn't get on my T-shirt, or I won't see it any more. *(To the spider:)* You like my shirt, eh?

*When you saw* Fatal Attraction, *didn't you think: Now they've done a remake of* Play Misty for Me?
Absolutely *(laughs)*. No, I'd already heard about it before I saw the movie. Universal has the rights to *Play Misty for Me,* and the people there didn't

complain, so it doesn't matter to me. Except that I'm flattered if somebody notices the relationship, which means they've seen *Play Misty For Me.*

*You've given a lot of writers and directors their starts: Michael Cimino, Richard Tuggle, Buddy van Horn. You've just made another movie with Buddy van Horn. Can you imagine working with other people? Michael Cimino perhaps?*
Who knows, the only time I worked with Cimino, he was very disciplined and worked well. He kept within the schedule and under the budget. Maybe for the last time *(smiles).*

*What has become of Bruce Surtees and Fritz Manes?*
Bruce is working on other projects, Fritz also.

*Do you have plans with them?*
Not at the moment.

*Are you still in contact with Don Siegel?*
Yes, quite often.

*Is he better?*
Yes, he has gotten over his illness. I spoke with him just a few weeks ago. He's finished writing a book I've contributed the foreword to. And if the book sells well, I believe he will also be able to do a film again.

*I've read that you've known Lennie Niehaus for a long time.*
I knew him in the army. He was drafted from the Stan Kenton Orchestra, and afterwards he worked for Jerry Fielding. Later, he worked on the sound-tracks for *The Outlaw Josey Wales* and *The Gauntlet.* Then Jerry Fielding died, I tried out some other people, but I was always thinking: who do I know who could produce the sound I want. Then I thought of Lennie, called him, and we got going.

*You have many friends who appear again and again in supporting roles in your movies: Woodrow Parfrey, Geoffrey Lewis, Gregory Walcott, Dan Vadis, Matt Clark and several others. Besides you, only John Ford had such a stock company. (smiles, gratified)* Thanks for the comparison.

*Do you feel comfortable among friends?*
Yes, very much so. I'm very happy to have them around me. Preferably as a big group, like in *Bronco Billy*, they were all in that one. It's almost like a home movie then.

*In* Bird, *you didn't have any of your old friends.*
Yes, one. The man who plays the doctor was in *Heartbreak Ridge*: Arlen Dean Snyder. Didn't you recognize him?

*You've said you don't know why you do a certain film at a certain time. Looking back on it, can you perhaps say why you did* Heartbreak Ridge?
*Heartbreak Ridge* . . . well, what warriors do when they haven't got a war has always interested me. And I thought: Here's a character, let's see how he interacts with people, especially with women. It was an interesting story, also about a soldier who hasn't ever done anything but fight wars, and he discovers that he's reached the end of his career, and he has nothing to look back on and nothing at all he can concentrate on now.

*Did* Heartbreak Ridge *turn out the way you wanted it to?*
Not completely, but I was satisfied.

*You lowered your voice into the vocal range of Ronald Reagan.*
*(laughs)* No, the voice in *Heartbreak Ridge* was my uncle's. He had damaged his vocal cords and always had to talk rather slowly and deeply. So he always had an embittered expression. As a kid, I imitated him when I played gangsters. He was a nice guy, and he didn't like that at all. But I recall it well, so that wasn't hard at all. I spoke with this voice for days, and I didn't notice it at all.

*Until a few years ago you were treated rather disdainfully by the press. An American reduced it to these words: "Eastwood is somebody who deals with murderers, monkeys and mayhem." That has changed somewhat at least* (at that time I couldn't suspect what Schütte[2] & Co. would be guilty of).

---

2. Several German critics, among them Wolfram Schütte, disliked *Bird*; Schütte declared that he "preferred" to leave the Cannes screening of *Bird* before the film's conclusion— Translator's note.

Everyone changes. The critics change, and so do I. *Honkytonk Man* had its premiere in Germany only the year before last, I heard yesterday. So there is a movie (an Eastwood movie) without violence, and it takes four years for it to be shown. Elsewhere in Europe, the picture still hasn't been released. But better late than never. I've been lucky enough to be able to do all the things I've planned. I would hate it if I leaned back one day and would have to say: *"I've done 30 Westerns, 40 police films and two films with a monkey and they've made me a good living."* That wouldn't be especially satisfying.

*You were also often accused of making fascistic films. Now that's often seen differently by the same people.*
Well, I find that amusing. Incidentally, it happened in America and in Europe at the same time. At the beginning of the 70s some people spoke of a fascistic attitude if you showed the way things were in the streets. Violence couldn't be shown without the director being accused of glorifying violence. That was immediately declared to be the director's attitude. Since then, thank goodness, something has changed. And these days films like *Dirty Harry* almost look like documentaries.

*Have you brought Kyle along?*
No, he's just finished with school, and he's devoted a whole lot of time to music lately. He plays bass and guitar, and for that he takes as much time as possible. But I did invite him to come along.

*What kind of music does he play?*
He likes jazz a lot, but also a fusion in the direction of rock.

*Do you have plans to do another film with him or with your daughter Alison, who acted with you in* Tightrope?
No, not at the moment. When we shot *Honkytonk Man* with Kyle and *Tightrope* with Alison, it was just their summer vacation. Now they're finished with school, and if they want to become actors, then they should go ahead and try it.

*Does Sondra Locke have a new project?*
Yes, several. The one she's working on now she will probably only direct.

*To what extent were you involved in* Ratboy?
All I did was to encourage the participants. I liked the film, I like mythical stories like that.

*How is your golf handicap these days?*
Fifteen.

*Are you improving? Do you manage a birdie on the 13th hole lately?*
Yes, but the professional golf scene doesn't need to be afraid of me.

*Success hasn't especially changed you. Do you still live quite normally in Carmel, with billiards and beer in the . . . ?*
Yes, and I enjoy eating there. Admittedly it wouldn't get any Michelin stars, but I like it.

*Has your involvement as mayor brought you closer to politics?*
I enjoyed the time. There were some things that had to be done, and I put the necessary plans into action. But I'd planned in advance to run only once. The term of office is two years, and in that time, I got some things moving, but I never intended to go into politics permanently.

*You didn't want to become President anyway.*
No, *(laughs)* that's not in my horoscope.

*The motto of* Bird *is a literary quotation: "There are no second acts in American lives."*
It's a quotation from F. Scott Fitzgerald's *The Last Tycoon,* and it's exactly right for Bird. He had a meteoric rise to the top without a pause, without a chance to enjoy the second act.

*You're not exactly that type.*
No, I hope not. After all, I'm already older than 34. I'm trying now to live my second act.

# Flight of Fancy

## NAT HENTOFF/1988

CLINT EASTWOOD, I HAD heard, is somewhat of a jazz buff—
otherwise, why would he take the director's seat for *Bird,* the film biography
of jazz great Charlie "Bird" Parker? As it turns out, Eastwood is more than
a buff, he's a downright enthusiast. When he talks about jazz, or Parker in
particular, Eastwood's voice noticeably brightens. Like most moviegoers, I
figured the off-screen Eastwood would be a taciturn man. But when he dis-
cusses his new film, there is nothing of the "star" about him. Jazz is a subject
that opens him up. A pianist who used to play clubs in Oakland, California,
Eastwood still writes music and has collaborated on the themes for many
of his films including *Tightrope* and *Pale Rider.* Since listening to jazz is an
integral part of Eastwood's life, *Bird* is a particularly personal film. For the
moment, Eastwood has put aside the guns and car crashes in favor of a
character study. He clearly wants *Bird* to be a portrait of that explosive
musician and the sounds he made. Eastwood's pride in this project is not
likely to be affected even if reaction to the film is tepid. He told me, that if
*Bird* doesn't fly, another jazz film eventually will.

AMERICAN FILM: *At what point did you decide to do a movie about jazz,
and particularly about Charlie "Bird" Parker?*
CLINT EASTWOOD: I've done a lot of pictures with jazz scores, from
*Play Misty for Me* to *The Enforcer.* But I had never done a picture about a

Published in *American Film,* September 1988, 24–31. Reprinted by permission of the
author.

jazz personality per se. Why Charlie Parker? When I was fifteen or sixteen, I'd seen him on two or three occasions, and I'd always been fascinated by him. There was something special about the way he played, a very confident sound. His presence was overwhelming. It was like Gary Cooper or Clark Gable standing next to John Doe. There was a big magnetism there.

Another reason for doing the picture is that I'm fascinated by the forties and fifties. And I wanted the music to really be of that era. So often, when people do period films, they start deciding, "Well, we'll update this a little bit." And it loses its purity.

AMERICAN FILM: *So, in the movie* Bird, *you extracted Parker's solos from original recordings for the soundtrack?*
EASTWOOD: Yeah, we used Bird's own recordings. No sound-alikes. On those original recordings, his solos are always up front, and it seems like everybody else kind of disappears. So we built around those solos by bringing in as many of the original sidemen as we could and then added equivalent players of today. From then and from now, we got Walter Davis, Barry Harris, Ray Brown, Jon Faddis, Ron Carter, and Red Rodney. Red knew Bird well.

AMERICAN FILM: *As you know, there are people who try to figure out where you are politically by the movies you do.* Dirty Harry *might indicate that you and Ed Meese could be members of the same law-and-order club. Yet films like* Bronco Billy *celebrate a gentler kind of independence. Is* Bird *going to further confuse your audience?*
EASTWOOD: I don't know why anybody would want to look for political ramifications in any film. After all, if you love making pictures, if you like doing the whole spectrum, no particular picture has any bearing on what you feel in your own life.

I've always said, for instance, that Adolf Hitler must be a fascinating character to play in a movie. The role is probably an actor's dream. That doesn't mean the actor is a fascist.

I'm just a filmmaker. *Bird* does have roots in my own experience though. I was raised in Oakland, California, around this kind of music. A lot of it is out of the black experience, and I feel I know it as well as any white person around.

AMERICAN FILM: *You're one of the few director/producers with stature—both artistic and box office—to try to make a serious film about jazz. Why has there been such avoidance of jazz in film and on television?*

EASTWOOD: It's a crime, in a way. Hollywood has largely avoided treating the music and the players seriously because we're trendy here. We think of culture in European terms—European music, European art. But when it comes to jazz—which is an innovation from the guts of American cities and is so revered around the world by really sophisticated audiences—we don't spend enough time on it. And most of the time, when we do make something about jazz, we go for the commercial angle.

AMERICAN FILM: *When you direct, you do something that reminds me of Duke Ellington—a distinctly noncommercial jazzman. He used to say that if he had to do more than two takes on a recording he'd worry, because, if it sounded perfect, it was dead. And you're known for preferring one take whenever it can work out that way.*

EASTWOOD: Well, sometimes the imperfection of things is what makes them real. Many times, I've seen movies that are beautifully composed, beautifully laid out, but there's something dead there. And the deadness comes out of it's having been overworked. The actors have been kind of beaten to death.

What I try to do—and it's just a matter of technique—is to get my performers in the mood before we ever start rehearsing. I'll say, "Would you like to rehearse one on film?" Because many times you do a rehearsal and you say, "Gee, that's beautiful. I wish we'd shot it."

So I tell everybody to just rehearse quietly, and I'll have the camera running. You get some marvelous little pieces because everybody's just doing it, they're not just sitting there thinking about acting in front of the camera. They're doing it for real.

AMERICAN FILM: *A character in the film that struck me as quite real was Chan Parker, probably the most important woman in Bird's life. Many of the women in your movies have been strong, whether in leading or supporting roles, and Chan is in that tradition. Has this approach to women's roles been conscious on your part?*

EASTWOOD: No, I think I just gravitated toward that approach. Although it's true that the first film I directed was *Play Misty*, which had a compelling woman's role. It came right after *The Beguiled*. That film had seven major parts for women—Geraldine Page, Elizabeth Hartman, along with other wonderful actresses. But that was in the early days of feminism, and some feminists stood up at some functions saying, "Why are you oppressive to women?" I told them that I'd been reading all the time that there's not enough good roles for women. I was just trying to help out. It's ironic that a half decade later, people are calling me a feminist director.

Actually, my preferences for strong roles for women in my films stems from when I was a kid. I grew up on pictures in which the women always played very important roles. Barbara Stanwyck, Bette Davis. And Clark Gable's role in *It Happened One Night* was only good because he had Claudette Colbert's to play off of. Those movies are more true to life than many films now where you have the guys sort of motivating most of the stories and the women in secondary positions.

AMERICAN FILM: *You haven't tried to make this film in a commercial way. Nonetheless, could it be commercial?*

EASTWOOD: I can't tell. If you judge the history of movies about jazz, they have not turned out to be very commercial. But I still wanted to make this, and I'm appreciative of Warner Bros. for allowing me to make it.

I told Warner Bros. that we weren't going to use a name actor, and they went along with me. Columbia had the script first, and they were talking about using Richard Pryor, which I think would have been wrong. He's done some wonderful things, but you'd see Richard Pryor, not Bird. People would be expecting a lot of gags. I wanted very good actors whom people could see as the characters.

AMERICAN FILM: *Was it much of a search to find the leads?*

EASTWOOD: No. I'd always liked Forest Whitaker in other films. He'd been in smaller roles, but he'd stood out. He did a test on film that was also very good, so I said, "Let's go for it!" As for the role of Chan, I hadn't met her but, having talked to people about her and read about her, I saw the right look and the right quality in Diane Venora. She was the very first girl I looked at. I saw her on tape and she just jumped out as Chan. I said, "That's it!"

AMERICAN FILM: *The Dirty Harry series is popular with black audiences. Why do you think that is?*

EASTWOOD: First, audiences, regardless of race or ethnic background, have the same feelings, the same frustrations. And blacks have just as much to worry about concerning crime as anybody else. Moreover, Harry is a loner out there, and blacks have the same feelings about the strengths of individuals, and the rights of individuals, as white people do.

Dirty Harry has a broad appeal because he's fighting the bureaucracy. He's trying to get things done. And it's hard to get things done. You're not only fighting the criminal element, you're also fighting the bureaucracy of society.

AMERICAN FILM: *In various ways, most of your pictures are like an extension of the Frank Capra films with Jimmy Stewart and Gary Cooper. The loner trying to fight the system. It's like an eternal theme.*

EASTWOOD: It's the eternal theme of being different. Whether it's Mr. Deeds going to town and wanting to give money away so that people think he's a screwball, or Mr. Smith going to Washington and wanting to be different from what is perceived as a normal politician. Whatever the political philosophy involved, the basic point is that because a person is different doesn't mean he is necessarily wrong. And in the Capra films, the different person was always the one who was right.

AMERICAN FILM: *Is it fair to say that the basic theme — with variations — in your pictures is the Capra theme: the individual against the system? Bird would be part of that.*

EASTWOOD: I guess that is the basic theme. Yeah. Nobody understood what I was doing at the beginning and some of them still don't understand me now. Some people, for instance, still cling to the idea that the Dirty Harry films are some kind of right-wing statement. You can look at those pictures that way if you're looking to pigeonhole somebody. But you can interpret them as other things too. If you want to take the time to think about it. You can certainly interpret Dirty Harry as an individual going against the system.

AMERICAN FILM: *What do you have planned, now that* Bird *is done?*

EASTWOOD: I've got a few projects. Some of them are adventure films, some of them are different. Every once in a while, I like to do the unusual. A Bronco Billy kind of character. He is a favorite of mine. Because of the idealism. The guy is simply out of touch with the world as it is today. But he has a dream of the world he wants—traveling around with a little, broken-down, carnival/Western act, which is totally obsolete.

AMERICAN FILM: *You've said, "The more I branch out, the more audiences branch out with me, which I like." Have there been no exceptions?*

EASTWOOD: They go with you to some degree, sometimes not wholeheartedly. But you hope they'll travel with you on some of your journeys and enjoy characters different than the more commercial ones you've done. But sometimes they don't go with you at all.

Certain parts of *Honkytonk Man*, for instance, were well received in France and other places, and some critics like it a lot. But the audiences didn't go with me. They don't like me to go on a self-destruct, and that was sort of a self-destruct movie. *The Beguiled* was also sort of total self-destruct, and the audience didn't enjoy that either. But I thought they were enjoyable films to do, and have no regrets about doing them.

AMERICAN FILM: *When you make a picture, do you have any sense of your audience?*

EASTWOOD: No, I don't. I just see the project. I don't like to think in those terms. I don't see the audience. I make the film, and that's it. And they like it, or they don't. That's up to them. You're always hoping they're going to see in the story what you saw, but you have to make it, then let it go. You have to make it for yourself, otherwise you're not true to what you're doing. If you make it with an audience in mind or a reviewer in mind, you'll get fooled every time.

AMERICAN FILM: *T. S. Eliot said that you're likely to get fooled whatever you do, that once work is out there, people are going to interpret it in ways you never intended, and there's nothing you can do about it.*

EASTWOOD: That's true. I've conducted cinema classes around the world, and people will sometimes put the wildest interpretations on something you've done. Whatever they say, I say, "that's right." It's their participation that I want. What counts is what gives them the best enjoyment.

AMERICAN FILM: *And has* Bird *given that enjoyment to you?*

EASTWOOD: Yeah, jazz has been with me since I was a kid. I remember once going to work in Springfield, Oregon, when I was nineteen. I'd been

Jessica Walter as Evelyn Draper and Eastwood as Dave Garver in
*Play Misty for Me,* 1971

Eastwood as "Dirty" Harry Callahan and Buddy Van Horn in Don Siegel's
*Dirty Harry*, 1971 (in a scene directed by Eastwood)

Eastwood directs Kay Lenz as Breezy and William Holden as
Frank Harmon in *Breezy*, 1973

Eastwood as Josey Wales in *The Outlaw Josey Wales*, 1976

Scatman Crothers as Doc Lynch and director Eastwood as Bronco Billy,
*Bronco Billy*, 1980

Eastwood as Red Stovall in *Honkytonk Man*, 1982

Eastwood directs Samuel E. Wright as Dizzy Gillespie and Forest Whitaker as Charlie Parker, *Bird*, 1988

Eastwood as William Munny in *Unforgiven*, 1992

Kevin Costner as Butch Haynes and T. J. Lowther as Phillip
Perry in *A Perfect World*, 1993

Director Eastwood with John Cusack as John Kelso and Alison Eastwood
as Mandy Nicholls, *Midnight in the Garden of Good and Evil*, 1997

used to living in the Bay Area where we had a lot of jazz. In Oregon, there is nothing but country music, except for one jazz program out of San Francisco late at night. Hell, just to hear a taste of it, I used to stay up late even though I had to get up early and go to work. I'd hear one or two numbers and I'd feel, wow, just fine.

That's what jazz does to you, and I hope people are going to feel that about *Bird*. Already, I've been getting some amazing reactions from musicians across the country. They come up—they're all young people, jazz people—and they say, "Thank you for doing a jazz movie, thank you for doing this story." Even though they don't know what the story is. That makes me feel just fine.

AMERICAN FILM: *As a director—and this is only the second film you've directed in which you didn't also appear—you seem to agree with jazz musicians who say that their playing is simply a matter of telling a story.*
EASTWOOD: Exactly. Create a mood, then tell a story, and leave people with some feeling, some thought about the persons in the picture, about that era, and maybe some understanding of what made people tick in that particular era. And with *Bird* hopefully they'll enjoy the music of that era—those who knew it at the time and those who didn't know it. And maybe those who didn't know it will go away realizing how much fun it was to make and to listen to that music.

Nowadays, a lot of people take jazz more seriously—as an American art form. But in Bird's days, they weren't thinking about that sort of thing. They just enjoyed playing what they wanted to play and they were happy coming up with new things. And they had a hot sound. You know, nobody's really shown how hot bebop could be. That's really what we tried to do in *Bird*. We tried to bring back how it really was.

# Interview with Clint Eastwood

## MICHEL CIMENT/1990

*What was the origin of* White Hunter, Black Heart*?*
A fellow by the name of Stanley Rubin, who I'd met a long time ago at the beginning of the fifties when he was a producer at Universal, was working for Ray Stark, and he asked me whether I'd be interested in reading a script that had been hanging around in Columbia's offices for quite a while along with some others. I think I read it in the plane coming back from France where I had shown *Bird* and the subject fascinated me. Then I read some later scripts that had been touched up, and finally the original book. It turned out that Columbia was going through a period of transition, being sold to Sony, and it was finally with Warners that I made the deal. Then I met Peter Viertel and found out the whole story of the novel, how he began to write it and the adventures of the pre-production period for *The African Queen*. It fascinated me, as obsessive behavior always does. Here was a personality that offered a real dichotomy. He could be full of charm and generosity, concerned with the down-and-out, and at the same time cruel to people in his entourage, if that was his mood. It was a very interesting character to explore.

*Did the script evolve once you had made the decision to film it?*
I took the last script of Peter Viertel, Burt Kennedy, and James Bridges, cut out a few things and added a few, but in the main it was a work of adjust-

Published as "Entretien avec Clint Eastwood" in *Positif,* no. 351 (May 1990): 5–11.
Reprinted by permission; translated from the French by KC.

ment. What I liked about this script is that it was faithful to the book, contrary to some previous versions, which had eliminated elements that in my opinion had to be preserved.

*Among the films you've directed, the ones that are about men of action have a very tight narrative structure and a fast rhythm, while your films on artists—* Honkytonk Man, Bird *or* White Hunter, Black Heart, *all about self-destructive characters—, offer a suppler shape, a more relaxed tempo.*
I don't sit down to try to make connections among the films I've directed. What I know, as I've said, is that I'm interested in obsessive behavior. The behavior of the *White Hunter* character is very different from that of the character in *Honkytonk Man,* who was a singer who hadn't known success, who even resisted it and was afraid of it. Bird, on the other hand, was very successful from a certain point of view but, from another, he was self-destructive. I don't think that Wilson's character, as he is portrayed in this picture, is completely self-destructive, but he's capable of being diverted from his goal. The irony is that he can still accomplish some very interesting things, while straying from his objective like that.

*Dozens of films have been made that evoke the world of Hollywood. Since you've now made one as well, what do you see as their limitations and in what sense do some of them seem to you to be faithful to the spirit of the place?*
What guided me is not so much what I've seen in other pictures as what I've felt in my own professional life. I've often been the witness of conflicts between producers and directors. More than once I've heard the same arguments about budgets and watched people doing stupid things, although I never knew someone like Wilson, who's an amalgam of several people. I never knew Huston either, so I don't know what he was really like. According to testimonies of people who knew him, I suspect that Wilson is very close to him in many areas. I admire Huston's work a lot and I think he directed some marvelous films. Sometimes it's preferable not to know someone, in order to have more distance with regard to the topic you're dealing with. I spoke to numerous people who knew him: Peter Viertel, his daughter Anjelica, and so forth. When I began the movie he was already dead. If I had sat down with him and we had chatted together, maybe it would have given me some insights or, on the contrary, I might have listened to the reflections of a man talking about his past experiences, while I was more interested in the drama of the present moment.

*Did you do research in order to comprehend the character?*
Yes. I screened some documentaries that had been made about him, listened to several narrations that he did for films, and of course I had seen him as an actor on the screen.

*Did Peter Viertel tell you about the reasons that motivated him to write his novel?*
He told me that during the filming Huston became hostile to Sam Spiegel, though he'd worked with him before. In his autobiography Huston says he was searching for a period of three weeks he could use to go on safari while he was in Africa. That's what gave Peter Viertel the impetus to write his novel. He was in the presence of someone, surrounded by all his technical crew, who was supposed to be scouting locations and getting ready to direct a film and who left in search of elephants to kill! What happens when this tragedy takes place and how does it affect a certain group of people?

*You avoided two dangers in portraying Huston: on the one hand, not to be capable of suggesting his presence, and on the other, to attempt an imitation.*
The main trap would definitely have been to do a sort of imitation like the kind you see in nightclubs. What I tried to do was to think like him, to seize on the very particular development that was his, sometimes a little condescending but deliberately so. He had a way all his own of asking people to listen to him. I wanted to recreate this kind of attitude. Being tall myself, pretty much Huston's height, observing his behavior and his diction in the movies, striving to reconstruct his turns of thought, after that things came very naturally. I wanted to seize the interior feeling, the philosophy, to share the same attitude with respect to the world. I didn't really try to imitate his gestures, though I often acted with a cigarette in my hand because he was a chain smoker. But also, because the character is called John Wilson, there is a fictional side, and I didn't want the spectator to be overwhelmed by the resemblances.

*The character is close to Huston, apart from the fact that the latter didn't film documentaries in London during the war, but in the Pacific and in Italy.*
When I was drafted into the army, at the time, in fact, when Huston was shooting *The African Queen,* one of my auxiliary jobs, besides swimming instructor, was to project training films for the soldiers. I kept showing *The*

*Battle of San Pietro*, one of my favorites, which I must have seen around fifty times during my two years in the service! To have listened to the commentary spoken by Huston in this film very early in my life made me familiar with his voice.

*Did you think about another actor to play the role?*
No. I liked the role and as soon as I read the script I immediately thought of playing it. It was afterwards that I considered directing it.

*Obviously you're attracted by artists—folk singers, jazz musicians, film directors—and by the relationships between art and life.*
Whenever you want to film a story, it's always interesting to grapple with the unusual, and Huston was a thoroughly unusual personality, the same as Charlie Parker.

*The film isn't about the making of a film—that's also unusual. Even the characters of Humphrey Bogart and Katharine Hepburn are seen as silhouettes in the background.*
Because that isn't the story I want to tell. People have already seen *The African Queen. White Hunter, Black Heart* is another movie. It tells how someone came to film *The African Queen* and how this character becomes obsessed by things that don't have anything to do with filmmaking and nevertheless succeeds in making his movie. It's like someone who takes a fall and yet lands on his feet.

*Outside of the two scenes on racism you share the points of view of all your characters by turns. You give each his chance, like in the conversation about simplicity in art.*
Absolutely. The screenwriter in the film is playing a little bit the role of a conscience, he has his own philosophy and sticks to it even though the director, Wilson, sweeps everyone away in his wake inasmuch as he's the commander-in-chief of the project. That's what I liked about this story, that it didn't confine itself to one character expressing his ideas. Everyone has his reasons. Paul Landers—inspired by Sam Spiegel—says some true things also. He's not the "bad guy." He has his own responsibilities. The movie and the novel are about the interaction of several individual philosophies. The only "bad guy" in the story is Wilson's obsession. What attracted

me to this story is not only the dramatic aspect but also the exchange of ideas. I *also* believe in simplicity in art, but I believe just as much that there aren't any rules.

*Do you think that artists, as they grow older, tend towards simplicity? Are you sensible of a similar evolution in your work since* Play Misty for Me *and* High Plains Drifter?

It all depends on the project. But I do think that when an artist feels more confident in his capacities and when he has more experience, it's easier for him to be simple. When you've asserted yourself, people know your work better and you can draw some simpler lines instead of putting down blotches here and there. A lot of young directors who come from television believe that they have to make their presence felt onscreen, that they need to constantly move the camera. Being an actor frees me from to having to impose my presence as a director, so that the public can remain inside the story without being distracted by the "interesting" angles of the man behind the camera.

*There is also a discussion on art in relation to the audience where Wilson claims that one must not think about the spectators whereas Peter opposes movies that have unhappy endings.*

Again I consider that they both have very solid viewpoints. Wilson is at a stage of his life as an artist where he believes he must be completely honest with regard to the subject he's dealing with and to know whether or not people will want to see his film is not his department. I agree with this position. If, as a filmmaker, you believe that a car has to go through a shop window because the public will like it, you're going to make a movie that won't have a lot of substance. Once you believe in a project, it's necessary to go ahead, and with luck the public will follow you. A lot of people advised me not to make *White Hunter, Black Heart* because it didn't correspond to marketing studies on public tastes, and, although I didn't use the same terms as Wilson, I told them that you couldn't worry about the supposed desires of audiences. I'm like a guide: I lead the tour, and if people don't like it they can leave along the way. In the movies, spectators always have the possibility of walking out. That leaves the final decision on what they want to watch to them! I've felt that since the time of *The Beguiled.* Albert Maltz had written a script with a happy ending: the hero who had lost his leg went off into the sunset with the girl. Don Siegel and I thought that the conclusion of the novel had much more strength as an anti-war statement. We adopted John Wilson's point of view back then: we decided to go ahead and to be faithful to our convictions.

On the other hand I can understand the screenwriter in our movie when he says that there are enough misfortunes in the world and that the project they're working on gives them the opportunity to bring a little happiness. And in fact on this particular film, *The African Queen*, that's what happened. But it was strictly due to the Hays Office of the time. The conclusion of the script was pessimistic, as Huston had wanted it.

*There's one strong idea in the book: the one that life (here the elephant hunt), for an artist, can take precedence over his art. It was typical of Huston, the opposite of Hitchcock for whom the cinema was everything.*
It's another aspect of the character that pleased me: he was interested in other things besides his art. He liked women, gambling, living the high life, traveling. He could have a life parallel to his work. I could identify with this type of behavior. But, because of this very fact, he became attracted more and more by other things, so that what interested him in life moved away him from his art to the point that he nearly lived a tragedy. And the tragedy brings back him to reality.

If you study Huston's life, you realize that at the age of nineteen he thought he didn't have long to live because of a heart defect a doctor had notified him of as a result of a misdiagnosis. It drove him to elaborate a personal philosophy according to which he would profit from life to the maximum. He didn't take care of himself—he was a confirmed smoker, a heavy drinker—, and yet he lived to be more than eighty. Paul Newman spoke to me about him when we were acting at the same time, each in a different movie, in Tucson, Arizona. He was starring in *The Life and Times of Judge Roy Bean* and I was doing *Joe Kidd* with John Sturges. Huston drank martinis and smoked cigars all night long, slept from one o'clock to four o'clock in the morning because he was an insomniac, did everything he shouldn't do to live to be old, and yet he died at a very great age! It was the same thing with John Wayne, who was first of all the opposite of a health fanatic.

*The style of your last two films is very bound to their topic.* Bird *was an extremely free conception like a jazz improvisation.* White Hunter, Black Heart, *on the*

*contrary, has a linear narration like, precisely, a movie by Huston or Hawks, the odyssey of a man who, at the end, finds himself.*
I've always thought that every film imposes its own life, its own rhythm. I suppose that also had to be the case for Huston because he shot some very different kinds of movies. Hawks, too, could direct *Red River* on the one hand and *His Girl Friday* on the other with almost opposite rhythms and points of view. My philosophy of filmmaking always seemed to me to be similar. Every film takes control of its director, not necessarily intellectually and sometimes even on a purely emotional level. You find yourself directing and doing the editing in a way that's maybe different from everything you've done up to that day. But maybe there are directors who make all their films the same way...

*You have, of course, added quite a lot of elements to the script: the habit, for example, that John Wilson has of sketching while he speaks to people.*
While I was discussing Huston's particular characteristics with Peter Viertel he disclosed to me that he was a very good draftsman and that he liked to sketch as a pastime. I thought I could use this detail and that it would be interesting to see him represent the woman as Hitler. It's the kind of idea that occurs to you during the filming.

*How did you conceive the color scheme of the movie with Jack Green?*
Africa and its skies have a very particular look. England too. I don't recall precisely what concept we elaborated for the cinematography, except that I wanted to maintain a certain rhythm in the film and to oppose England to Africa, although this isn't a big African adventure picture but a very personal story that takes place in Africa. But Africa has skies like Montana and I didn't want to overlook this dimension. I wanted to achieve a happy marriage between the intimate story and the dimension of the landscape. The cinematography would not be dark like in a nocturnal movie such as *Bird* but on the contrary rather luminous.

*For the opening of the film you create a very dynamic movement by means of camera movements and the editing, which sweeps the spectator off toward Wilson's house. Was it planned like that in the script?*
Yes, and the scenes were filmed consequently to create this kind of impetus. I wanted to enter very quickly in the film and give the public a foretaste of the characters without wanting to explain too much: this is how they are,

this is what they do, here's an idea of their philosophy and let's pass on to what comes next . . .

*How did you find Jeff Fahey, who plays Peter?*
He's an actor I had considered two or three years ago for another picture, but he wasn't free at the time. I regarded him as a very talented young actor. Then I realized he would be great for *White Hunter, Black Heart.*

*Playing a part yourself and directing must change your relationship with the other actors?*
It's definitely difficult but, on the other hand, I've done it so often that I know I'm capable of it. Once I'm in the scene myself, I play it with all possible concentration. It's true that during rehearsals I'm maybe only 50% in what I'm doing, the rest of my attention is devoted to setting up the shot. The first time I gave myself up to this kind of exercise in 1970 for *Play Misty for Me,* it seemed a little schizophrenic to me, but after the first two or three days of filming I got used to it. As for the other actors, I can devote more time to them because I know my own character very well, since I've already worked a lot on the script and thought about the direction. If you really care about the project as a whole, it shows, and the whole crew will be very aware of it. On the other hand, if you're only interested in your own character, everyone will realize that too . . .

*The movie has for a theme a metaphysical quest like* Moby Dick, *which Huston would shoot some years after* The African Queen.
That's a reflection of Huston's personality. He had such varied interests that they could conflict with his practice of filmmaking. In certain pictures he made, you can see the part he liked best. For example in *Reflections in a Golden Eye* there's a sequence with a horse in the woods and you are aware that Huston very definitely liked filming that. On the other hand, in other sequences, you don't find his soul as much. From this point of view he was impulsive. In his autobiography he speaks of his obsession with elephants and it may be that Peter Viertel felt a certain emotion in the face of their extermination. This was probably not his main preoccupation in 1953 but in my view it's become an important topic for our time. At any rate for me. And it's probably one of the subtexts that attracted me to this project. This animal, the elephant, is a tie between the prehistoric era and today.

*Isn't there a contradiction between his very violent attack on the anti-Semitic woman and his tirade directed at Paul, the producer, whom he calls a Balkan rug peddler and to whom he declares: "It's way too difficult a subject for your small little brain to grasp . . . Why, I'd have to explain to you the sound of the wind and the smell of the woods. I'd have to create you all over again, and stamp out all these years you spent on the dirty pavement in cramped shoes." Apparently for him, the Jew cannot understand the WASP ethic of the Hawkses and the Hemingways.*

I don't think that by calling him a Balkan rug peddler he was necessarily referring to the fact that he was Jewish. He's alluding to the attitude of an individual who was a hustler during the greatest part of his life. It's one of the interesting aspects of the script. On the one hand John Wilson admits that he was also a hustler, and probably also in cramped shoes, and on the other he's going to persecute Paul for similar behavior. I think he's cruel in general with respect to Paul Landers, judging that he lacks sensitivity, and it doesn't make any difference whether he's Jewish or not. With regard to the irony of the scene with the anti-Semitic Englishwoman, Peter Viertel told me that he didn't have to write it: it actually took place at the time. Viertel witnessed the conversation between Huston and this woman and it piqued his curiosity to the point that he immediately went up to his room and noted the exchange word for word.

*His attitude with respect to blacks is much more coherent than towards Paul. He fights to defend the honor of a black, he loves Kivu and feels guilty for his death.*

With Wilson—like with Huston—there was a very strong feeling for the victims of society; he felt drawn to them. On the other hand he could appear very brutal towards people who worked closely with him. During the filming of *The African Queen* there really was an antagonism between him and Spiegel. I've witnessed this in my own life, I've seen directors who would oppose producers simply because they were in front of them. Don Siegel is a very good example of this type of behavior. Don completely lacked respect for producers, it was part of his character. When we were filming *Dirty Harry* I told him, "Don, this time you're producer and director at once. You won't have anyone to hate on the set anymore!" He would always say, "I don't know what a producer does." It's true that some producers don't do anything, but others are great workers. Sam Spiegel was one of them and he produced some remarkable movies. For a reason I'm unaware of there was a conflict between Huston and him on *The African Queen.*

*The script of* The African Queen *is by James Agee. What was Peter Viertel's involvement?*
He was hired to rewrite certain scenes and adjust the script in the direction Huston wanted. But in fact he was more of a buddy. As Wilson says: "Don't worry about the script. We're going to Africa to have a good time!" He took his pal along with him to do some retouching and go hunting.

*Women are especially badly treated in the movie, from the secretary to the mistress with her little dog and of course, the anti-Semitic woman.*
The picture is less flattering towards the character of Wilson and the way he treats them than with respect to women in general! He's cruel to a secretary who is very efficient! Once again, it's because he feels close to her.

*Do you consider it easier to film action scenes than confrontations between characters?*
To a certain extent, yes. For example it was difficult to film the sequence where they go downriver on a boat because there were crocodiles in the water and we needed helicopters to shoot it. Technically that posed problems, but you can solve them if you're prepared to take the time. But when you have two people in a room you have to bring out all the constituent elements of the scene, otherwise you won't manage to hold the attention of the audience. The sequence can crumble because of bad performances by the actors or an inadequate rhythm and then you will lose the public more easily than in an action scene.

*Wilson declares that Africa revealed to him aspects of his personality. What were your own reactions on encountering this continent?*
Before shooting this picture I had never been to Africa, and I must say I adored it. There's something special about feeling so far from home, and even with today's means of communication, it's still very far. But when you think that Huston and his team had to travel to locations in a DC3, that must have been a real expedition! I liked the Africans a lot, particularly those of Zimbabwe. The landscape has a particular tranquillity and it makes you think about the world in different terms. We filmed on Lake

Kariba, then at Tiger Bay and at last in Hwange, where we shot the elephant hunt. Then we went back to Victoria Falls. We filmed for seven weeks in Africa and two and half in London.

*The music is very unobtrusive.*
I didn't want a typical African score, and I didn't want the music to take over the picture. When I was filming the soccer game, the extras were so great that they got carried away and began to sing and dance. I decided to keep on shooting. After editing this sequence I thought it would be nice to repeat it at the end. I asked Lennie Niehaus for a very sparse score. He had the idea of contacting Emil Richards, who's an expert in percussion instruments and a jazz drummer. His passion is collecting percussion instruments from all over the world. He brought us into a big room full of thousands of drums and we spent the whole night there gathering all the audio materials we needed for the score. The only other instrument we used is an alto flute for certain sequences, and that's all. Lennie Niehaus was the arranger for Jerry Fielding, who I'd worked with, and after Jerry's death I was looking for someone who would be creative in the same direction. In the case of *Bird* it was more complicated than for *White Hunter, Black Heart,* where we were only looking for different sounds. For *Bird* I asked Charles McPherson to follow the filming. I asked him to use the musical themes that corresponded to the states of Parker's soul and to play them as if they were in his head.

*The editing on the other hand is quite complex.*
I have a concept and I see the film edited in my mind. Sometimes a sequence is longer than you think it needs to be. For example the airplane scenes in this picture. Generally I also have an idea about the editing when I begin to film a sequence, so that I know the material I need. When the picture is finished, I don't sit down at the editing table for an eternity. I assemble the elements as I'd conceived it at the beginning, I give my chief editor some ideas and he does the editing. If, for any reason, it doesn't look like what you wanted, you retouch it, you make adjustments. Sometimes everything falls into place and it's marvelous.

*The film itself looks like a sketchbook like the one Wilson carries with him. It's a series of drawings whose strokes are not heavily drawn.*

I don't shy away from dramatic pronouncements, but for this film in particular it seemed to me that it was rather a fragment of someone's life. He had a life before this, he'll have a life after it, but he's going through an experience at this moment that will influence the rest of his existence. I have a project for this spring that will be full of action. It's another cop picture, very different from this one. It has its own character and if it's done well it can turn out to be something good. It's an original script titled *The Rookie*. Charlie Sheen will play the rookie and I'll play the mature cop *(laughs)*.

*What is your debt to Don Siegel, who was in a way your mentor and whom you were able to observe at work when you acted in his films?*
I've been asked that before and I can never give a satisfactory answer. I know that he had an influence on me, but I can't say precisely what, except that he had a personality close to that of his predecessors Walsh, Ford, Hawks or Wellman (for whom, incidentally, I played a small role), a personality like you don't find anymore today in the world of film. They were men who were direct in many ways. Don had a lot of audacity and the reason we got along so well is that we encouraged each other to prove our daring, like with *The Beguiled*, for example. I used my influence on the studio to go ahead with it and to be as faithful to the book as we were able to.

*Did you meet with difficulties in getting* White Hunter, Black Heart *produced?*
I think that Warners really liked the material and the script but that they probably would have been happier if I had come up with another action picture. And although *Bird* was not a success comparable to *Roger Rabbit*, Warners realized, because of the very good reactions the picture got in a lot of places, that they could be proud of it. It's another aspect of filmmaking. I've always tried to convince the studio that it's nice to make movies that rake in a lot of money and make the shareholders happy, but that it's also possible to be proud in retrospect to have produced some pictures. There are many pictures produced by studios in the past that were probably not commercial successes, but they're happy today to have them carry their logo.

# Clint Eastwood: Dirty Harry Is No Rookie When It Comes To Directing

## DENISE ABBOTT/1991

FOR 25 YEARS NOW, Clint Eastwood has reigned as one of the world's top box-office stars. Few people outside of the industry think of him as a director, yet he has directed 15 of his 30-something films. He's arguably been responsible for more box office mint as a director than any other active filmmaker, except for Steven Spielberg and George Lucas.

His list of credits are varied—from his 1970 directorial debut with *Play Misty for Me* (the original *Fatal Attraction*) to the string of westerns—*High Plains Drifter, Bronco Billy,* and *The Outlaw Josey Wales*—all of which have achieved near cult status, to *Sudden Impact,* the *Dirty Harry* film that introduced "Make my day!" into the language, and *Bird,* a stylistic homage to genius saxman Charlie Parker. Last year, he gave us *White Hunter, Black Heart* (loosely based on John Huston and the making of *The African Queen)* and, most recently, *The Rookie,* an action thriller in which he co-starred with Charlie Sheen.

Whatever the project, Eastwood, the filmmaker, is known for a tight budget and scheduling, brisk pace, location shooting, and working with a crew of experienced professionals. "I like to work fast," he says, lounging on a corner sofa in his Malpaso Company offices at Burbank Studios. "I prepare myself, and I expect the people I work with to be equally prepared. I know what I'm looking for in most situations, and I don't think a lot of takes will help bail you out of something that might be unclear to begin

Published in *American Cinemeditor* 41, no. 1 (winter 1991): 14–15. Reprinted by permission.

with. I think it's important to know where the film is going while you work, to edit while you shoot. I like to establish a rhythm and keep it moving."

Interestingly, post-production is his favorite part of filmmaking. "After months of having to be responsible for 75 or 100 crew people all day long, it's nice to go off with your editor, clear your head and fine-tune the film."

Eastwood's editor, more often than not, is Joel Cox. And like many directors and editors who work together frequently, the two have developed a symbiotic relationship. "Joel reads me pretty well by now," says Eastwood, whose manner is direct and serene. "He knows just by the nature of the material what I'm going to want. We go over how I see the film, and we discuss specific scenes. We'll put it together and later on look at it on the Kem."

He rarely storyboards, so there's no need for Cox to come in early on pre-production. Neither does Eastwood ask Cox to spend time with him on the set. "There would be nothing for him to do. It's my responsibility to get him the material, if I don't, it's my problem."

Eastwood involves himself in the entire dubbing process, from predub to ADR, although he walks away from it occasionally so he can keep a clear ear. "If the crew is doing predubs or dialogue dubbing, as opposed to effects dubbing, I'll split and come back later. I've seen directors go in and sit through Foley and every other thing, and after a while they get brainwashed and don't know what they're watching. I try to save myself since I'm the last word on the print. I've got to be as fresh as I can."

He works rapidly in post and has been known to have a final cut ready within two weeks of finishing shooting. He relies on instinct and his own sense of what works more than input from outsiders. He sees no need to preview before audiences. "In the early days, I had more people looking at a film because I was less decisive. Now, I'll get the film to where I like it and then maybe bring a few people in to take a look. Generally, if it works for me, it's right. But if enough people say a scene is long or something doesn't work, you can't deny it."

He prefers to edit with a concept in mind and doesn't believe in defensive editing. However, he says he's had many experiences where editorial shuffling gives the film more life or speed. "The creative process begins with the written word, but post is the final stage where you have an opportunity to make a film work or not. Post brings the disparate pieces together. Without all those elements, the film is just an empty shell."

Although he makes pictures all over the world, Eastwood frequently edits up north in Carmel, his home base for many years. "I like to get away from the ringing phones. Studios have the habit of calling constantly, wanting this or that, sometimes pertaining to a film you did several projects back. Once I get out into the country, I can do the work in half the time."

Unlike some directors who stamp their films with a trademark style, Eastwood believes each movie should dictate its own style. "All my films are very different from one another," he says softly. "Each looks like it could have been directed by someone else. *Bird* was my most stylized film," he continues. "Instead of a straight-on approach, it had flashbacks and a lot of jockeying around because the story was woven, much like a musician playing a solo."

Eastwood credits Don Siegel, his director in the first of the *Dirty Harry* films, with teaching him some of the directing ropes. "Don taught me to put myself on the line. He shoots lean, and he shoots what he wants. Don knows when he has it, and he doesn't need to cover himself with a dozen different angles." Before Eastwood had ever directed a feature, he tried his hand at directing several sequences for Siegel when they worked together on *Dirty Harry*. He remembers one instance, in particular, when Siegel was too ill to come out for a night shoot of a guy jumping off a building crane. "The shoot was scheduled for three days, but I shot it in one because I got halfway through the night and realized I was on a roll," he says with a sly smile. "I called Don the next morning and said, 'Well, we're done with that.' He said, 'So, what are you going to do for an encore tonight, Clint?'"

Eastwood's instincts on the *Dirty Harry* films propelled the phrases "Do you feel lucky?" and "Make my day!" smack into the heart of American pop culture. Everyone from former President Reagan to rap artists has been heard quoting from the *Dirty Harry* movies. Eastwood recalls how the original *Dirty Harry* script called for him to ask, "Do you feel lucky?" just once in the beginning of the film. "I told Don we should reprise it at the end because it's going to be a key saying in the picture." It was also his idea to reprise the tag line "Make my day!" at the end of *Sudden Impact* when Harry's chasing the bad guy down in the amusement park. "And the phrase is still buzzing," he says with a bemused grin.

Eastwood seems to alternate his personal projects with more commercial films, but insists that what a film will or won't do at the box office doesn't affect his choices. "I just go with my instincts and how I feel about the story," he notes. "I constantly quote John Wilson, my character in *White Hunter, Black Heart,* who says 'You can't let eight million popcorn eaters pull you this way or that.' I have no idea what makes a film commercial. I don't think anybody does. Just when you think you're an expert, someone comes along with something out of the blue, and you have no idea why it works, but it does."

When asked to recall his best directing experience, he expresses a fondness for many of his films. Eastwood mentioned *Play Misty* because it was his first as a director and "the anxieties were much more intense than they are today." *Bird* was a pleasure because it dealt with a subject matter close to his heart. He found *Bronco Billy* rewarding because he loved the script. *White Hunter* was also special. "I gravitated to the literate writing, and I shared many of the philosophies of the lead character. Even though he was obsessed with shooting elephants, I related to his 'onward and upward' attitude and his refusal to be dictated to by audiences."

Even though Eastwood works steadily, he manages to find time for numerous other interests. He's an avid golfer, jazz aficionado, and fitness buff, who's as trim today as he was in his *Rawhide* days. He's the owner of the Hog's Breath Inn in Carmel and even squeezed a two-year term as mayor of Carmel into his filmmaking schedule. "I became mayor simply because I was interested in my community," he flatly states. "Everyone speculated I'd run for office on the state or federal level, but that's not the case at all. I'm not interested in politics," he concludes, "I'm interested in making films."

# Interview with Clint Eastwood

THIERRY JOUSSE AND
CAMILLE NEVERS/1992

AFTER THE VISION OF *Unforgiven,* it seemed to us to be indispensable to meet with Clint Eastwood. We did so at the end of this past August, in the course of an intensive publicity tour. Reserved, humorous, perceptive: Clint Eastwood, the man as he is.

*Unforgiven is a Western relatively different from the ones you have directed or acted in before. Why the desire to take up this genre again, and what would you say is the difference between this one and the others?*
I couldn't tell you exactly why I wanted to make a Western again, because I didn't have any reason to make one or not to make one; it wasn't a decision that came out of a particular trend, there wasn't any prior reason in fact, and that's what made the project all the more exciting to me: I prefer to do things without giving myself a starting direction. So why a Western? That seemed to be the only possible genre the story was calling for, because in fact everything grew out of the story. In any case, I've never thought of doing anything because it's *in fashion,* on the contrary I've always felt a need to go against it. And anyway, I probably feel a little guilty for always having tried to go against success like that, against the fashion.

As for what makes this Western different from the others, it seems to me that the film deals with violence and its consequences a lot more than those I've done before. In the past, there were a lot of people killed gratuitously

Published as "Entretien avec Clint Eastwood" in *Cahiers du cinéma,* no. 460 (October 1992): 67–71. Reprinted by permission; translated from the French by KC.

in my pictures, and what I liked about this story was that people aren't killed, and acts of violence aren't perpetrated, without there being certain consequences. That's a problem I thought it was important to talk about today, it takes on proportions it didn't have in the past, even if it's always been present through the ages.

Unforgiven *is dedicated to Sergio Leone and to Don Siegel. What relationship does your film have with their cinema?*
In my mind, the film doesn't have much to do with Sergio and Don. But it's equally true that we never know to what extent the things of our life, the people we've worked with or haven't worked with, will come to play a role in what we do—whether it's John Ford, for instance, or others. They're two people I'd worked with at important moments in my life, and both of them, ironically, died in the course of the last couple of years; that's why I wanted to pay homage to those two men who had influenced me so much, whether they had anything to do with the film or not. I like to think they would have liked the story. Maybe not, but I think Don would have liked it a lot.

*Did you change the screenplay, for instance regarding the theme of violence?*
The theme of violence was already present in the screenplay, as well as its repercussions on the characters, whether they're the victims or the perpetrators. This theme is interesting in a Western because Western stories have always been built around violent behavior, a frontier of violence in man. And this one called certain things into question, notably concerning the theme of justice. You could think that if the Little Bill character [*Gene Hackman*] had granted justice to those women in the beginning, that would have changed the whole story. And his lack of concern in the face of an act of violence, or even his indifference to it, actually sets the story in motion—straight towards his own death.

*Is there a connection between the political situation in the United States today and your film?*
I think you could make some comparisons, yes. But that wasn't the original intention. Deep down, it's a matter of eternal concerns, not just those of a given era, but considering the present situation in the United States, it seemed to me this was the right time to make this picture. Even though

the screenplay of *Unforgiven* was written a long time ago, I was quite influenced at the time of making the picture by a number of recent events.

*Such as the Gulf War, for instance?*
No, I wasn't thinking any more of the Gulf War than of other international conflicts, but rather of domestic conflicts America is prey to at present.

*You were directly engaged in American politics when you became mayor of Carmel...*
Yes. I was mayor of Carmel, but only for two years. And during those two years I even made two films, *Bird* and *Heartbreak Ridge*...I've been a Republican because I chose that party at the time of my military service at the beginning of the fifties, and I voted for Eisenhower, but I have a tendency to consider myself more of a "free thinker." My political choices don't really fit in with any of the camps, and actually I feel myself to be something of a libertarian, in the sense that I think you have to let people live in peace, respect individual freedoms.

*Do you think it would be possible to reconstruct your personal trajectory through all your films, which all to a certain extent tell a human story, your story?*
Well, I'd rather say that from one point of view there's a little bit of me in all my characters, and from another point of view there's nothing at all of me in all the characters I've had to interpret. After all, I don't have to be in agreement with any of the characters I've played. Some of them absolutely don't correspond to my philosophy, others undoubtedly do more. I've played a few good characters that were "losers," like the fellow in *Honkytonk Man* for instance, men who self-destruct. But I chose to play them because I know a lot of people who are like them, and I'm somewhat fascinated by them. So, even though I don't resemble them deep down, I've seen so many of those men given up to self-destruction, who didn't make use of their talent— when they had a talent...I don't know. Some of my pictures, more than others, get a message across that I agree with. And finally, I always see an implicit message there that corresponds to what I am.

*Is it true that* Unforgiven *will be the last of your films where you will also appear as an actor, and that in the future you will only act for other directors?*

I began to direct my own films in 1970. At that time, the only means I had to be able to direct was to act in the films... It was a practical question at the time. Afterwards, I grew to like it. There was one of my pictures, the second or third, that I didn't act in [*Editors' note: his third film,* Breezy, *with William Holden, which was a financial disaster...*]. Then I continued doing both things when I was especially involved with a project. But in the future I don't think I'll do it so continually. It's a lot of work to act in a film you're directing. So from now on, I think it will be easier for me to let someone else have the job of directing when I'm acting, or of acting when I'm directing.

*You're a producer too...*
Yes. But it's easier to be an actor and a producer, than an actor and a director.

*Do you differentiate between films like* Pink Cadillac *and* The Rookie *on the one hand, and films like* Bird, White Hunter, Black Heart *and* Unforgiven *on the other hand, or in your opinion do they all come from the same development?*
I consider them all to be different, because none of them is really connected to the others, it seems to me... There could be similarities between some of the characters, in the problems they try to confront, but I don't think there's a real relationship. And if there had been one, I probably wouldn't have done it in such a repetitive way.

*Do you consider the films in the first group to be commercial films, and the others to be less accessible films?*
I don't make my films with regard to the commercial aspect. In that respect I'm entirely in agreement with the phrase of John Wilson in *White Hunter, Black Heart: "I won't let eight million popcorn eaters pull me this way and that."* ... If you're constantly thinking about what the audience's reaction is going to be, you stop thinking in terms of how the film should look, because the film will end up by being made around preconceived notions, on a hypothetical expectation of what the audience will do. It's impossible to tell a story with ideas like that. And most of the time your work will be degraded by the contact with this kind of compromise. The essential thing is to stick to what you want to say, to the impressions you want to express in a picture. Then afterwards, it's up to the audience to accept it or not. Having had both sorts of experiences, it finally seems to

me that all you can do is resign yourself to fate. The audience seems to know what it wants to see and what it doesn't want to see, it seems to sense whether such and such a picture will agree with them or not.

*For years your production company, Malpaso, has collaborated with Warners, which is distributing your latest film. Are you completely independent?*
Yes, I am independent. Warners has distributed most of my films and shared in their financing. But I work in complete freedom. The people at Warners have been very supportive for more personal projects, like *Bird*, without forcing a commercial obligation onto it that would have changed the nature of the film. It wasn't *Batman Returns*...And I think in the long run they thought the film was good. Not every picture can be a great financial success. But you have to try, or else production companies wouldn't be able to take the liberty of working with proper means. Of course, it's not always the best pictures that are the most successful. Sometimes you get lucky, the film hits home, and people are knocking each other over to see it. It's like a "home run," to use a baseball term...

*You've worked with two cinematographers in particular, Bruce Surtees and Jack Green, and you seem to attach great importance to the lighting in your films. As time goes by this lighting gets darker and darker. Why?*
Jack Green was camera operator on *Tightrope*, and he replaced Bruce Surtees as cinematographer when Bruce fell ill. He did a good job, and I decided to give him a chance by continuing with him. There are some of my films that I conceive more as brightly lit films, and so you have the lighting I asked Jack for in *White Hunter, Black Heart*, which isn't a particularly dark film. *Unforgiven* is quite simply a "stormy" film...What you have to remember is that it takes place at a time when people didn't have much to use for lighting, and the only artificial light came from oil lamps. So if in shooting a night scene we had decided to flood the action with light, people would have done right to ask us where all that light was coming from...

*In several respects,* Unforgiven *reminds me of* My Darling Clementine *by John Ford, a film that already had this very dark lighting scheme, and your acting is not without a connection to Henry Fonda's. Have you seen this film?*
Yes, and even if I'm not sure that *Unforgiven* is much like *My Darling Clementine,* I know what you're trying to say. Ford's picture has a number of

nocturnal scenes, all right. Maybe I was unconsciously motivated by an idea close to Ford's. I tried to light my film—or rather I asked Jack Green to light it—like a black and white film. The costumes and the scenery were likewise conceived as a function of this particular lighting scheme, like one in black and white.

*It seems you like to remain loyal to the people you've worked with, like Bruce Surtees, then Jack Green, who turn up in the credits for most of your films, or Joel Cox, your editor since* Sudden Impact. *Is this a desire to have a "film family," with people you can trust in completely?*
Some of the people I've worked with have seemed trustworthy to me, sure. Of course, it's certainly easier, when you're working with someone, to be able to communicate, to be able to explain to him in a few words how you see things. And that's possible for me with the people you mentioned. I don't have any trouble making Jack Green understand how I envision a scene and how it ought to be lighted. So if I were to find myself with a new cinematographer for every picture, someone I didn't know, I'd have to start all over again. It's the same with Joel Cox, my editor, I can call him up on the phone because I know he'll understand very quickly and very accurately what I expect from the editing of a scene.

*Your films appear to be very detached from all that is going on in American cinema at present, and to only depend on yourself. Do you have the feeling that you're playing the "lone rider" in the cinema as you conceive it?*
In the American cinema I've always felt I was a little bit "somewhere else" (*Laughs*) . . . There certainly has to be room for a great variety of movies in any country. But it's true that in America today, everything is subject to the sway of statistics and information science to such a degree, in the form of data that tell you who is going to see what, where and when, that people impose it on you to make a certain type of picture under the pretext that the age of the audience is exclusively between sixteen and twenty-one . . . I would especially hate to have to work that way, it would seem incredible to me to have to make a picture entirely for people between sixteen and twenty-one. With a little luck, a sixteen-year-old could like my film, in the same way a person of forty or more could. Why force adults to stay home by insisting on producing only films that aren't meant for them? I recall the last time I was in France, the *Cahiers du cinéma,* I think,

asked me why the United States was no longer producing anything but children's pictures... And it's a question that bothers me: why must important themes be treated on an infantile level? If it's really difficult to get people to leave home to go to the movies, you have to want to take up the challenge. Instead of which, the types of pictures that get made are more and more limited.

*Then what do you think of Hollywood today and those who reproaches it for its violence?*
I suppose there's room for what they call program pictures, the films that draw crowds with action, according to a certain mentality that says that if there's not an action scene every five minutes, the picture will seem boring and the audience will get up and leave.... But I'd rather think—maybe I'm wrong—that audiences are more intelligent than people believe, and that it's enough to tell them a good story for them to want to keep their seats, to see how a character is going to evolve, how a story is going to take place, instead of saying, "I'm going to keep my seat because in five seconds an armored car is going to crash into the wall"...

*Do you attach importance to your recognition as an* auteur *in Europe?*
Yes, very much. This time, the US has been very appreciative of *Unforgiven,* and they've begun to recognize that I might be a director. But it all started here, a number of years ago. Actually, the Europeans encouraged me much more from my first film as director, *Play Misty for Me,* than the Americans, who had a hard time convincing themselves I could be a director because they already had a hard time recognizing me as an actor. They were asking, "Why is he doing that? Who does this guy think he is?," that sort of thing. The Europeans, on the other hand, supported me a lot in the beginning and tried to find some value in what I was doing. But that's an historical process, it's far from concerning only me; quite a few other directors have had this sort of reaction in the past. Especially here in France, there are those you call "cinéphiles"—is that the word?—who are interested in movies not only as an entertaining spectacle to eat popcorn by. Now the rest of the world is beginning to come to an agreement around this way of thinking. The coming of film schools in the universities and other places causes people to begin to think of film in terms of artistic merit. France

was a pioneer, with the creation of cinémathèques, for instance, but I believe
that today this influence is felt all over.

One of my favorite pictures is a film by William Wellman from the forties, *The Oxbow Incident* [1943]. I worked with him once, I had a small role
in one of his pictures, not one of his best [*editors' note:* Lafayette Escadrille,
*which Wellman directed in* 1958]. And I asked him quite a few questions about
*The Oxbow Incident,* which I thought was a great film. He told me that at
the time, the wife of one of the studio bosses had hated the film at its first
screening — she thought it was the worst crap a studio had ever financed —
and then the producers had more or less gotten rid of it by distributing it as
a B film. But when it was released in France, the critics were very appreciative of the film, they emphasized the value of its point of view, of what it
had to say about capital punishment, about mob violence, about justice:
Wellman's picture had a right to excellent reviews. Then it came back to
New York by way of France, and the Americans began to see its qualities
too, but it was already too late, the film was at the end of its run and was
taken out of distribution. It was a terrible fiasco — and totally unmerited.
Today, people see it again with a different eye, and, I hope, in the US as
well as elsewhere . . .

*Can you explain to us the choice of the title* Unforgiven, *which has no equivalent in the French language. Moreover, there is already a film by John Huston
that bears the same title.*
Yes, I think I was given to understand that there is no French translation
for "*Unforgiven,*" and that the film is being called "*Eem* . . . Impitoyable,"
that's it. Huston did make a picture by the same title, in the fifties I think
[*editors' note:* The Unforgiven, 1960]. Well, it's a good title, it seemed to me
to suit the film perfectly, and since I think the film by Huston isn't one of
his best, like *The Treasure of the Sierra Madre* or other classics, I didn't see
anything wrong in using it for mine.

*What do you concentrate on above all at the moment of beginning a film?*
I try to concentrate above all on the story, because it's there that it's all
tied up, it's the "kernel," so to speak. Then I try to see how the image can
best agree with the story, what form I want the story to appear in, with what
emotions, what sonorities. In *Unforgiven,* there is this storm that becomes

almost a character itself, a determining factor: the three protagonists, as they approach, seem to be bringing the storm along with them. This sort of thing isn't written in the screenplay, it gets inserted later on. But the basis of the drama, the question of justice and violence, all that was already present in the screenplay.

*In your films, art is frequently connected to destruction and self-destruction, as in* Bird, Honkytonk Man *and* White Hunter, Black Heart . . . *Is this a subject that fascinates you?*
Bird *and* White Hunter, Black Heart *are in fact two pictures that deal with this subject, like* Honkytonk Man *with its character who has a real talent and "kills himself" before this talent has really had time to express itself. I find it hard to explain what fascinates me about this subject, they're things you so often encounter in real life, probably that's what attracts me to it. Take Charlie Parker, for example, it's such a great loss, such a waste when someone very creative, gifted, the bearer of new ideas, self-destructs as he did. No one can ever properly understand how a person could have so much talent, so much enjoyment in playing, and at the same time set in motion his own destruction. That remains a mystery, and undoubtedly I've always been fascinated by mysteries.*

*Several months ago, we interviewed Jodie Foster for her first film as director, and according to her, actors probably possess more aptitude for directing a film, because they succeed in functioning naturally at the emotional and intellectual level at the same time. What do you think of that idea?*
There are indeed quite a few precedents, actors who directed their own films. You can go back to William S. Hart or Charlie Chaplin, Welles, and so on. Directing seems to be a natural extension of the actor's performance. When you find yourself involved in a story in front of the camera, you're not so far from being able to find yourself behind the same camera. If you've come from editing, or from screenwriting, the gap is greater, because you're used to working alone and you haven't had any experience with a film crew. And then an actor undoubtedly has a greater understanding of the language of filmmaking, its difficulties, its insecurity, things that are inherent in the production of a film. But at the same time, I can't say that there's a rule. It's an individual question. An actor might have the aptitude

I'm describing for directing a film, but that depends heavily on the capabilities of each one. There are editors and cinematographers who also make wonderful directors...

*What do you think of the behavior of Little Bill Daggett (Gene Hackman) in your film? Do you consider him to be a sort of dictator?*
I think he's a good sort, at least in appearance. He has a certain charm...I believe he thinks he's doing the right thing, just a man who's doing his job. He probably has a violent past, the same as William Munny, my character, but he hides it behind a rational appearance. He's the representative of the law, and so he's on the side of the Good...But he isn't prey to guilty feelings like Munny with regard to his past deeds. He's deeply convinced he's doing right with his decision to have total gun control, and he believes that the acts of violence he commits for the sake of setting an example are a lesson that will discourage everyone else from coming to town to make trouble. He's a sadist at heart, and whether this sadism is innate or whether he's developed it in the course of the acts he's committed all his life is something that can't be known. But in encouraging violence as he does, violence giving rise to violence, it's also his responsibility that comes into play. Deep down, he considers himself to be a worthy human being, he's building a house so he can sit on the porch and watch the sunset, he'd like to live a good life, a quiet life...But he has no way of stopping the wheel of destiny.

*With* Unforgiven, *did you intend to tell the truth about what the West was like, or is it a fable?*
I think it's more of a fable, but a fable that would demythify the West, in a certain way, by appealing to other elements than the classical Western. As, for example, the fact that it's not so easy to do things, that people's aim isn't so precise, that guns don't always work every time they're fired the way they're supposed to. I don't know if that's the truth about the West, but the film probably does approach it. Oddly, it contains two stories that coexist in parallel, the one of the journalist who wants to print the legend of the West, and the one that runs through the film and contradicts it completely. The meeting of these two stories was what I liked about the script. Everyone changes in the course of the story, everyone starts out from one place and finishes somewhere else, just as in real life we learn some-

thing every day that transforms our way of looking at things. All these characters are taught a lesson in a tragic way, at least for most of them. And from the tragedy everybody can learn something.

*Do you think you have related the story of a vengeance?*
I don't know that it's a question of vengeance, even if there is a connection to vengeance in the film, because of Morgan Freeman's character who gets killed. You could see the triumph of vengeance there, but, deep down, no one wins anything at all in this story; everyone suffers some sort of a loss, whether it's a part of themselves or... their life. And that's what happens when people indulge in violence in order to obtain justice.

*A last ritual question: What are your next projects?*
I'm getting ready to make a picture in which I'll just be an actor, and where I won't have a hand in the production this time: I'll be a humble employee. This film will be directed by Wolfgang Petersen, produced by Castle Rock-Columbia, and John Malkovich and Rene Russo, among others, will be in the cast, which isn't complete yet. As director, I'm working on a project I may do next year. But it's only at the planning stage at present... On the other hand, I'm planning to do this other part as an actor and only as an actor, for the first time in quite a while, and it has a good chance of being well received, I think, I hope. In any case, this time I'm letting someone else have all the responsibilities and the headaches *(Laughs)* ...

# Portrait of the Gunslinger as a Wise Old Man: Encounter with Clint Eastwood

## HENRI BÉHAR/1992

DESPITE HIS SUCCESS AS an actor, Clint Eastwood the film-maker has never drawn the crowds in America. Not until *Unforgiven,* his sixteenth directorial effort, which has been a popular and critical triumph. This time, even the most reserved are speaking of an Oscar nomination for Best Director. Neither the actor Clint nor the director Eastwood had attained such recognition before, in a country where directors' names are not even printed in the television programs when their works are telecast.

His skin bronzed, his face deeply lined, Clint Eastwood in *Unforgiven* portrays William Munny, a Kansas farmer at the end of the last century. A former thief and hired killer, he has married a woman who got him to hang up his guns and gave him two children. With Claudia dead, Munny is lost, and his farm is on the verge of ruin... In a small town in Wyoming where the sheriff Little Bill (Gene Hackman) makes the law ("No guns in town unless they're mine") a young prostitute has had her face slashed by a big brute whose virility is microscopic; her friends, led by Strawberry Alice (Frances Fisher) put a price on his head... Accompanied by a young hot-blooded bounty hunter (Jaimz Woolvett), Munny sets out to execute the contract. Along the way he picks up his old colleague Ned (Morgan Freeman), who likewise has retired from the business, and crosses paths with English Bob (Richard Harris), another bounty hunter, of British ori-

Published as "Portrait du flingueur en vieux sage: rencontre avec Clint Eastwood" in *Le Monde,* 3 September 1992, 28. Reprinted by permission; translated from the French by KC.

gin, flanked by a journalist-biographer (Saul Rubinek)... Everything is now in place for the final showdown.

Written by film editor David Webb Peoples, *Unforgiven* is an enterprise of demystification. It is not a question of justice, but of cash. Virility? Male vanity. The code of honor? An illusion. Heroism? A false myth. Women, children, "I've killed just about everything that walks or crawls at one time or another." The merciless killer, was he ever scared in the old days? asks the young bounty hunter. "I can't remember. I was drunk, most of the time."

Sparing with words, soft-spoken to the point of whispering, his blue eyes sparkling or observant, in much better shape than William Munny, and taller, if possible, in real life than on the screen, Clint Eastwood, at sixty-two years of age, exudes a total confidence in himself. He says calmly, comfortably, but firmly, what he has to say, and so much the worse if some people don't like it.

*After the John Wilson (inspired by John Huston) of* White Hunter, Black Heart, *who was a regular chatterbox, you've gone back to the men of few words.*
By nature, I'm rather introverted. Sometimes it's an advantage, sometimes it's not.

*You've had* Unforgiven *among your projects for almost seven years. Why did you take so long to do it?*
It called for a lot of preparation. I wanted to do it right.

*Wasn't it because you were waiting until you were the right age?*
(Smiles.) If you say so...

*Isn't it, among other things, a film about aging, the courage to grow old and the fear of growing old, which concerns you personally?*
I'm not doing penance for all the characters in action films I've portrayed up till now. But I've reached a stage of my life, we've reached a stage of our history where I said to myself that violence shouldn't be a source of humor or attraction.

When I asked Gene Hackman to be in the film, he answered, before reading it, that he didn't want to make any more violent pictures. He thought there was too much violence around us, and he had been taken in by a number of films where the sole concern was to outdo the competition, or find unheard of ways of killing. I insisted he read the script all the same, and I told him maybe we had a chance here to deal with the moral implications of violence. The consequences of a violent act affect the one who commits it as well as the one who is the victim of it. All the better if we could deal with this subject in a Western.

*The reporter in the film claims to be telling the story of the West, but above all he's trying to produce a heroic portrait...*
...whereas in reality what's going on isn't heroic at all.

*Those who accuse movies of making violence attractive forget that a hundred years ago the dime novels did about the same thing.*
Right, it was the same thing. Literature has always found violence attractive, as long as there's been literature — the Old Testament is the best example. But today I'm disturbed by the more and more widespread use of violence for dramatic purposes — I'm not talking about Harold Lloyd bumping into a wall or Chaplin slipping on a banana peel, that kind of violence doesn't bother me. But the other... To wipe out, erase, eliminate a life... The only difference between William Munny and the sheriff Little Bill is that Little Bill has as his excuse, pretext or justification the fact that he's on the side of law and order. But Munny has only his demons to be accountable to...

*Little Bill's zeal in enforcing the law borders on sadism. When he bullwhips the black actor Morgan Freeman, his deputies look on, horrified but passive. It makes you think of the videotape of the beating of Rodney King by the Los Angeles police.*
To show the deputies' horror was deliberate, to make an allusion to Rodney King wasn't. But the association isn't wrong. Everyone could ask himself how he would have reacted that night, as a young rookie cop, faced with the violence practiced by his superiors.

*During the final showdown, after you've killed the sheriff (Gene Hackman), you walk by a dying man and finish him off with a careless gesture, without even looking at him.*
Which, if I've succeeded in what I was trying to do, ought to be even more terrifying. Because at that moment Munny is almost on a suicide mission.

Except for the sheriff, he doesn't give a damn about anything: his friend Ned has been killed, he feels guilty about having dragged him along on this job, and he's gone back to being what he was—a killing machine.

*Have you become more and more of a moralist?*
I don't know what you mean, except that I've grown older and wiser. There are things you don't discover until they happen to you. And they can reinforce your misgivings. I'm not speaking only of violence in the movies or on television, which belongs to fiction and entertainment, but of violence in society, of the habituation to it, of the tolerance we give it. That society gives it.

*Habituation and tolerance to which the movies contribute? That was said of* Dirty Harry, *it was said more recently of* New Jack City *and of a whole group of black films . . .*
I refuse to accept that statement. We grew up with *White Heat* and *The Public Enemy,* we watched Robert Mitchum or James Cagney pick off a man locked in the trunk of a car. That didn't make us become criminals. You were always aware that it was only a movie.

*Are people less aware of that today?*
You would have to be seriously deranged not to know the difference between reality and fiction. But the film industry and especially the television industry have always been targets of choice in the matter of violence, because they always react out of fear. While the problem is even worse in other sectors of the communications industry. In television news, because of the competition, the winner is the one who films the most blood on the freeway. We ought to try to understand the results of this situation.

*Female characters have always been very strong in your films.*
A male character loses a lot of his interest if all he has opposite him is a decorative partner . . .

*It's the women's rebellion that unleashes the action of* Unforgiven.
Because at that time women were treated like second class citizens, and even more so, I suppose, the prostitutes, they were treated like an underclass within this disadvantaged group. In the film, their revolt (against the

violence one of them has been the victim of, but also against the exploita-
tion they've always been subjected to) is justified. And yet that's what
provokes the tragedy.

*There is also Claudia, your character's wife, who died after having put him back
on the straight and narrow—which he concedes, not without bitterness.*
He resents her for abandoning him with two children he's having a hard
time bringing up. He resents her for dying and daring to deprive him of
his moral support.

*The director Eastwood is hardly sparing of the actor Eastwood.*
I always make a separation between the two. I only see the actor who's
playing a role. If the character has to be beaten up or crawl in the mud,
there's no place for vanity, you do what the role requires.

*With Jack Green, your camera operator since* Bronco Billy *and your director of
photography since* Bird[1], *you have given the film a very somber tonality.*
It's always a delicate business to try to give the impression that a scene is
lit by oil lamps, while still allowing everything to be seen. When I see
some of the old Technicolor Westerns today, I find them atrocious, far too
brightly lit. On the other hand, a Western in black and white like *My
Darling Clementine* strikes the right tone visually, if I can put it like that.
For *Unforgiven,* as for *Bird,* I chose to light the film as if we were shooting
in black and white.

*You almost always work with the same technical crew.*
Because I know that with them the filming will go well. I like to work, but
I'm at a stage of my life where if there's a chance the experience will be
disagreeable, I'll decline it. An actor needs to have a feeling of security—
even the most experienced actors will lose their footing if they're
surrounded by people who give them the impression of being adrift. And
if I'm not ready, for my part, no one will be, and the result onscreen will
be a disaster. I simply manage to be sure of what I'm doing. And I sleep
more than anybody else...

---

1. Green's first film for Eastwood as operator was *Every Which Way but Loose* (1978); his
first as DP was *Heartbreak Ridge* (1986), not *Bird* (1988)—Translator's note.

*Why do you keep coming back to the Western?*
That's due to my tastes, my past, my career. The Western brought me a certain notoriety, it's also a film genre that leaves you room for an original analysis of certain subjects or certain moral principles. Regularly, some expert will proclaim that the Western is dead—that goes in cycles—until another Western comes out that does well. And another expert will proclaim the rebirth of the Western. Hollywood, which is a little bit silly on that level, follows the fashion like sheep. Somebody declares, "That genre is dead." Hollywood follows suit. Without even saying to itself, "Just a minute! Every time one of our films of that sort is on television, it tops all the ratings."

*Unforgiven is dedicated "To Sergio (Leone) and Don (Siegel)."*
You're always reweaving the skein of the projects you've been involved with, in an almost automatic, unconscious way. I spent some time in Rome with Sergio Leone, just before he died. When I came back, Don Siegel was already ill. I'd written the preface to his memoirs and I encouraged him to finish them. It's sad that he died, it's also sad that he couldn't go out with a great film. Very few people have had that chance. John Huston was one of the rare ones in that situation . . .

*And, uh . . .*
(*Smiles.*) If *Unforgiven* was to be my last Western, it would seem to me to be a very good sign-off.

# Any Which Way He Can

## PETER BISKIND/1993

You're Clint Eastwood, huge box office star and iconic leading man. In four decades, you haven't won an Oscar. So you try directing a great movie — and not giving a damn.

It is 6 p.m. on a Saturday night in Alberta, Canada, on the set of *Unforgiven*. Clint Eastwood likes to shoot westerns in the autumn, so the production descended on the town of Longview just as the leaves were beginning to turn. But now it's four weeks later. The trees are bare, and the production is bumping up against winter.

The cast and crew are expecting to break for their day off, Sunday. But there's a storm coming in. The weather service in Calgary says it's supposed to snow twelve inches on Monday, with freezing weather the rest of the week — meaning the snow won't melt.

They still have half a day's shooting in the town. Then, on Monday and Tuesday, they're scheduled to do a pivotal exterior scene, the one under the pine tree where the whore rides in, tells Eastwood's character, William Munny, that Little Bill Daggett has beaten his partner Ned to death, and Munny takes his first, long pull from the bottle of whiskey that will send him on a rampage of killing. There are eight and a half pages of dialogue. Eastwood wants to see the town in the distance — with no snow on the ground.

Executive producer David Valdes comes up with a nutty idea: shoot into the wee hours of Sunday morning; wrap at 2 A.M.; go back to the hotel, an

---

Published in *Premiere*, April 1993, 52–60. Reprinted by permission of the author.

hour away; let the crew grab four hours of sleep; on Sunday, go up to the hill, without breaking for meals, and do the Monday and Tuesday sequence till the sun goes down; then film the scene where Munny emerges from the bar in the rain, through the night into Monday morning. Had Valdes called the studio, they would have gone ballistic—Eastwood and Co. were about to break every rule in the book: double time for working the crew on Sunday and a hailstorm of penalties for not feeding the crew when they're supposed to be fed. The weather report has been wrong before. Valdes is not going to be a popular guy in Longview (or in Burbank, for that matter) if the storm passes a little to the east or a little to the west of them. But the alternative is to risk having to shoot the scene in California later, which would cost hundreds of thousands of dollars more and forfeit the tie-in to the town.

They complete the eight and a half pages on Sunday and continue on into the night, 21 hours straight. It's so cold, the water from the rain machines is freezing, making for a treacherous purchase on the muddy ground. The horses are slipping and sliding all over the ice, and the people aren't doing too well either. It's so cold, Eastwood's teeth are chattering. At about 2 A.M., pissed-off crew members are demanding pizza. "We're in Bumfuck, Alberta," Valdes screams back, "and there's no Domino's around the corner."

At 5:30 or so Monday morning, Jack Green, the cinematographer, turns to Eastwood and tells him there's time for only one more shot before dawn. Fifteen minutes later, they're finished. The first snowflakes begin to fall— and don't stop until the following evening. A foot of snow arrives on schedule. Winter in Alberta has begun.

Clint Eastwood hasn't been to the Oscars since 1973, when he was asked to present the Best Picture award and ended up subbing for host Charlton Heston, who was stuck on the freeway. "Howard Koch said, 'Here's the script,'" recalls Eastwood. "It was a parody of Moses, *The Ten Commandments*, thou shalt not be this and that, all relating to movies. Bad material, even for Moses. I said, 'You gotta be kidding. Never invite me again.' 'Will you come back if you're nominated?' 'Yeah, I'll do that.' Koch says, 'Then I don't have to worry.'"

Well, Eastwood might have come back with *The Outlaw Josey Wales*, and most certainly with *Bird*, but as it turned out, he stayed away for nineteen years. In the twentieth year, the Man With No Name finally rode into town with a clutch of nominations for *Unforgiven* in his saddlebag: Best Picture, Best Director, Best Supporting Actor, Best Original Screenplay. Not bad for a guy who used to be dismissed as a cowboy, one of whose films was derided by Rex Reed as a "demented exercise in Hollywood hackery."

It's been a long and twisted trail from *A Fistful of Dollars,* the first spaghetti western Eastwood did for Sergio Leone, in 1964, when Lyndon Johnson occupied the White House, to the Dorothy Chandler Pavilion in this, the spring of the Clinton presidency—39 pictures, with another, *In the Line of Fire,* in the can and scheduled for a summer release, and still another, *A Perfect World,* which he directs and costars in with Kevin Costner, set to begin shortly. Sixteen of them he directed himself. Eastwood, always philosophical about the Oscars, once said, "I figure that by the time I'm really old, somebody at the Academy Awards will get the bright idea to give me some sort of plaque. I'll be so old, they'll have to carry me up there.... 'Thank you all for this honorary award' and SPLAT. Good-bye, Dirty Harry."

Standing around the Westin Bonaventure hotel, in downtown Los Angeles, watching director Wolfgang Petersen shoot inserts for *Line of Fire,* Eastwood is uncomfortable talking about his Oscar prospects. *Unforgiven* is the frontrunner, after grabbing a slew of critics' awards, and it makes him nervous. Or maybe it's the inserts, pickups, bits of business, whatever, that make him impatient. He is legendary for working quickly, coming in ahead of schedule and under budget. It's a matter of pride to him—more, a way of life. Recalls Frank Wells, who was president of Warner Bros. during the '70s, "His favorite time was the last day of a picture. He would call me, and I would guess how much under budget he was." Eastwood is fond of saying things like, "The more time you have to think things through, the more you have to screw it up."

*In the Line of Fire* boasts a very good script, by Jeff Maguire, a bit along the lines of *Tightrope,* or even *Unforgiven*—films in which the character Eastwood plays is less a superhero than an ordinary guy with a Past, a guy who's been damaged by life, a guy who has to live with something he'd rather forget. Here he's an aging Secret Service agent who is convinced he let John F. Kennedy die, those many years ago in Dealey Plaza, by not moving fast enough, perhaps paralyzed by a flaw in his character. It is a story of Conradian dimensions—whether the execution matches the ambition remains to be seen. Like *A Perfect World, Line of Fire* represents a more commercial, less personal choice for him than *Unforgiven.*

Eastwood, who had director approval, selected Petersen, best known for *Das Boot*. People in advanced stages of megastardom often hire flunkies for the express purpose of second-guessing them and making their lives miserable. But Eastwood, it is said, does not operate that way. When he decides his employees can perform the jobs they've been hired for, he leaves them alone, relies on their judgment, and if they come through, he hires them again—and again. Glenn Wright, his costume designer, has been with him since the *Rawhide* days. Eddie Aiona has been his prop master for some 25 years. Joel Cox, his editor, started working for him eighteen years ago. Valdes began as a second assistant director thirteen years ago,

Listening to the people who work for him saves Eastwood enormous amounts of time. He doesn't audition actors; he looks at tapes supplied by his casting director. When Valdes or the production designer chooses a location, he often won't see it until the day before the shooting begins. The look-of-show meeting is usually over in ten minutes because he can count on cinematographer Jack Green (22 years) to react to a script the way he does. Eastwood lets Cox put the first cut together himself, from rushes of Cox's selection. Five to six weeks after the film wraps, the editing is finished.

Eastwood's people have a refreshingly casual approach to making movies. "It's fun," says Valdes, "and everyone realizes we're not curing brain cancer." Cinematographer Bruce Surtees, who worked on a number of Eastwood's pictures, once said, "There's no trick to lighting. You turn on a light, and if it looks good, you use it. If it doesn't, you turn it off and put it some other place."

No one sits around waiting for the sun to go in or out of the clouds on an Eastwood set. His luck with weather is a legend in the business. If he needs snow in the Mojave Desert in July, it will snow. But it's not all luck. He moves so fast, he doesn't have to worry about matching one part of a scene with another. "Once you get that kind of velocity, suddenly weather doesn't matter," says gaffer Tom Stern, the baby of the group, who's been with Eastwood for a mere eight years. "Instead of calling it adversity, you call it serendipity."

Eastwood hates overlighting, which he associates with television, especially in his thrillers. He prefers a noir-ish, chiaroscuro effect. Pauline Kael once wrote, apropos of *Bird*, "The picture looks as if [Eastwood] hasn't paid his Con Edison bill." On *Firefox*, which is a bit on the murky side, there is a shot that is so dark, only Eastwood's elbow is visible. The cameraman wanted to do another take. Eastwood said, "Am I in the frame?"

"Yeah." "Can you hear my voice?" "Yeah." "They know who I am. Let's print it and move on."

In an industry where first takes are virtually always rehearsals and actors don't get serious until the fourth or fifth, where it is not unheard-of to shoot 30, 40, 50 takes of the same scene, Eastwood is famous for shooting rehearsals—and not just rehearsals, but first rehearsals. He walks the stand-ins through the scenes, to get a rough sense of blocking, light placement, and so on. Then, says Green, he brings in the actors. "They're working with the words for the first time, and we're rolling. They have to paraphrase or deal with props in a naturally awkward way. If they do hit the light, we're lucky; if they stay in the frame, we're really grateful." On the other hand, says Jeff Fahey, who played the writer in *White Hunter, Black Heart,* "he'll never walk away from something until he has what he wants."

Usually Eastwood will do no more than three to five takes, and print two. On *Bronco Billy,* Scatman Crothers had just come off *The Shining,* where Stanley Kubrick had put him through something like 50 takes on one scene, and he was almost paralyzed with fear. Eastwood did one take and printed it; Crothers nearly burst into tears.

Eastwood's method works. It lends his pictures a fresh, improvisatory, realistic flavor. The extraordinary first scene of *Unforgiven,* in the whore-house when the woman is cut, is a first rehearsal. It has the impact of real violence; it's over in an instant, and we're not really sure what has happened. We feel like voyeurs, as if we walked down the hall, passed an open door, looked in, and saw something unspeakable.

Eastwood has never believed, as Sam Peckinpah did, in drawing out violence, aestheticizing it, and indeed, these two masters of the western never worked together. "One time I was talking to a class at USC and somebody said, 'How come you never worked with Peckinpah?'" recalls Eastwood. "I said, 'Well, he's never asked me.' And all of a sudden some guy got up in the back and said, 'I'm asking you now!' I look up and it's Peckinpah sitting in the class. He was so wild; he'd go off and live in whorehouses. Some of those guys were amazing—John Huston, staying up to all hours doing whiskey and then directing the next day. I can't do that. I always have to train up, run, like it's an event."

The Bonaventure, where the endangered president makes a campaign stop, has a cold, inhospitable lobby consisting of a cavernous atrium punctuated by concrete columns. Someone has spent a good deal of money to create a series of small concrete pools filled with stagnant-looking water covered with a dull gray film. One finds oneself looking in vain for floating condoms. Watching Petersen do take after take of his insert, it's clear what Eastwood is thinking, but he would never say anything. Nor will Petersen, a short, lively man with shaggy blond hair and an engaging smile, admit to being intimidated by his star, who could get an Oscar for directing. And maybe he isn't. "Clint knows if I'm directing the film, to let me alone," says Petersen. "He's not a guy to step up and say, 'Shoot it this way.' Still, sometimes, when I say, 'Clint, this was great, but please, let's do it again,' he says, 'If it's great, why do it again?'"

Despite the fact that *Dirty Harry* was made more than twenty years ago, Eastwood is constantly beset by fans asking him to make their day. Once a cop lurked about the Eastwood-owned Hog's Breath Inn in Carmel, California, for a week, waiting for the actor. Eastwood finally showed up; the guy entered and in one sudden sweeping movement pulled an enormous .357 magnum from the small of his back. The customers hit the floor. But he only wanted Eastwood's autograph on the barrel—he'd brought along his etching tool. Eastwood signed it, thought for a moment, and said, "Don't go leaving this around anywhere," like the guy might do a liquor store and drop the gun on the floor.

Now a large, buxom woman pushes her way through the crowd of onlookers and tourists surrounding Eastwood on the *Line of Fire* shoot. She is yelling "Clint, Clint, let me at 'im." She heaves up in front of him and bellows, "East Clintwood! I got all your records!"

Eastwood was born on May 31, 1930, in San Francisco, right in time for the depression. His father scratched out a living at odd jobs before ending up in Oakland at Bethlehem Steel. After high school, Eastwood traveled around, mostly in the Northwest, working at Boeing, Bethlehem, fighting fires for the Forest Service, hauling lumber at a Weyerhaeuser pulp mill, baling hay, and so on. He once described himself as a "bum and a drifter," but he later attributed his sure feel for the blue-collar audience to these experiences.

After a stint at Fort Ord as a lifeguard during the Korean War, he went down to Los Angeles to find work as an actor. Every day, he said, was like getting slapped in the face with a wet towel.

In 1954, he got a job driving a truck around the Universal Studios lot and eventually hired on as a contract player for $75 a week, acting in a couple of cheapies that later became shlock classics, *Tarantula* and *Revenge of the Creature* (from the Black Lagoon). Eventually, Universal let him go (because his Adam's apple was too big, his buddy Burt Reynolds once joked).

For two years, he scrambled, digging swimming pools, pumping gas. Then, in 1958, through a chance encounter, he got the part of Rowdy Yates, the sidekick of Eric Fleming's Gil Favor in *Rawhide*, a TV western that ran on CBS for seven years. In 1965, Fleming left the show (a year later, he was killed by a crocodile while on location in South America, according to director Ted Post), and Eastwood had the series to himself.

In 1964, his agent asked him if he was interested in starting in a western to be shot in Spain by an Italian named Sergio Leone. "I had questions, normal questions, like who is Sergio Leone? It wasn't like Fellini was offering to do it." For $15,000, he agreed to go over to Spain during his hiatus from *Rawhide*. He even brought his own cigars, which he found at a tobacco shop in Beverly Hills. "They were about that long," says Eastwood, placing his hands about a foot apart. "I said, 'I'll chop 'em in threes.' Boy, they tasted ugly. Put you right in the mood for killing.

"Leone knew 'good-bye,' and I knew '*arrivederci,*'" says Eastwood, and they communicated through gestures and intermediaries. The script was wordy, and Eastwood cut out dialogue by the mouthful. "Whenever I had a problem, I'd use my street psychology, Psych 1-A. I'd just say, 'Well, Sergio, in a B western, you'd have to explain. But in an A western, you just let the audience fill in the holes.' He'd say, 'Okay.'"

Eastwood did two sequels to *A Fistful of Dollars*. When the first of his spaghetti westerns arrived in America, in 1967, the critical reaction was mixed. The films were acclaimed—and disdained—for their hip, surreal cynicism.

The trilogy established the formula for the Eastwood western: the Man With No Name squinting in the fierce midday sun, laconic, cool, and laid-back but remorseless and vengeful at the same time, coming from nowhere, going nowhere, without a past, without a future. He was the antithesis of the liberal Freudian western hero of the '50s—Paul Newman's Billy the Kid, say, in Arthur Penn's *The Left-Handed Gun*. "I was the king of cool," says Eastwood.

The western was *the* American genre, as critic J. Hoberman has said, the one in which America stared itself in the face and asked the big questions:

What is good? What is bad? What is law? What is order? Eastwood's westerns were no exception. The pasta pictures were the cultural Muzak for the post-Kennedy era; the Man With No Name became the big-screen version of J.F.K., who forced Khrushchev to back down over the Berlin Wall and the Cuban Missile Crisis, launched the Bay of Pigs, and cultivated the Green Berets. Along with the James Bond pictures, Eastwood's films ushered in a new era of cinematic violence. Some 50 people are killed in *A Fistful of Dollars.* The line between the hero and the heavy was becoming blurred. With the war in Vietnam heating up, there was no time for niceties.

"In *Josey Wales,* my editor said, 'Boy, you shot him in the back,'" recalls Eastwood. "I said, 'Yeah, you do what you have to do to get the job done.' I think the era of standing there going 'You draw first' is over. You don't have much of a chance if you wait for the other guy to draw. You have to try for realism. So, yeah, I used to shoot them in the back all the time."

Eastwood and Leone changed film history together, but they barely knew each other. After *The Good, the Bad, and the Ugly,* Leone wanted Eastwood to do *Once Upon a Time in the West,* but Eastwood had had enough. "I went home, and I didn't see him for a lot of years. I think he was resentful—I had started becoming successful. And he didn't do a lot of movies. Many years later, when I went over to Italy for *Bird,* he called. We went out together one evening and got along better than in all the times we had worked together. I left, and he died. It was almost like he had called up to say good-bye."

Eastwood's first American western, *Hang 'em High,* in 1968, for United Artists, was in the spaghetti mode. His next picture, *Coogan's Bluff,* began a lengthy collaboration and friendship with director Don Siegel. "When we met, it was a very sort of surly relationship," says Eastwood. "'I don't like your suggestion for this.' 'I don't like yours.' Finally, we just zeroed in, started agreeing on a few things, and then we became fast friends."

Eastwood had always wanted to direct, and he picked a small story, *Play Misty for Me,* to start with. The studio, Universal, preferred he stick to his six-guns. This was a sort of proto-*Fatal Attraction,* in which a disk jockey gets involved with a psychotic woman. Eastwood prepared well, perhaps too well. The night before the shoot began, "I was lying in bed, going over the shots in my mind. I had them all planned out. I turned out the light, thought, 'I got this now.' All of a sudden, I went, 'Jesus! I got to be in this thing!' I turned on the light and started approaching the scenes all over again from the actor's point of view. Needless to say, I didn't get much sleep." The critics were not nice, Eastwood recalls. "They said, 'We're not ready for him as an actor, much less a director.' "

*Misty* was a modest hit. And then came *Dirty Harry*. The tenor of the film was evident from a tag line that was never used: "Dirty Harry and the Homicidal Maniac. Harry's the one with the badge." But the critics were not amused. In the highly polarized political climate of 1971, many people felt that *Dirty Harry* said it was okay for cops to trample civil liberties in the pursuit of crooks. Plus, the Scorpio Killer wears a peace sign, as if Siegel and Eastwood were turning a whole generation of kids who fought for social justice and an end to the war in Vietnam into a bunch of Charles Mansons. Kael was particularly vocal. She wrote that Dirty Harry is a man who "stands for vigilante justice" and termed the picture "fascist." Eastwood answered his critics by insisting it was just a defense of victims' rights. "The general public isn't worried about the rights of the killer; they're just saying get him off the streets." So far as the peace sign went, "that was a thing where the actor wanted to do it and everybody just thought, 'Well, that's irony. A lot of people hide behind the guise of being peaceful, and they'll be the first ones out there advocating violence.' "

After *Dirty Harry,* Eastwood was given considerable freedom at Warner's. "The guy had a story sense about his own persona that nobody else had," recalls Wells, who is now president of the Walt Disney Company. "You'd make the deal and not see him again until the preview — of an under-budget movie. We always did what he wanted to do." Except in the case of *Dirty Harry.* Eastwood did not want to do a sequel, but the studio was implacable. Ironically, *Magnum Force* was based on an idea spawned by the febrile brain of wild man John Milius. Eastwood considered it a liberal riposte to *Dirty Harry.* "It showed that just because these guys were killing people who deserved to be killed doesn't mean that's the way society should go about it."

"Eastwood was typed early on as a guy who could do only one thing — Harry — over and over, and he was the only guy in the mix who thought, 'I can do better than that,' " says Dennis Shryack, who cowrote *The Gauntlet* and *Pale Rider.*

In real life, Eastwood was far different from the character he became identified with. He did collect guns, but he didn't care much for hunting. It's said he once stopped his daughter from stepping on a cockroach. "I don't like killing," he says. "It's one thing to fantasize about it in a movie, but I never saw the sport in removing a life from the planet."

In 1976, he directed himself in *The Outlaw Josey Wales*, another tale of revenge and his best western up to that time. Even though critics constantly compared him to John Wayne, Eastwood—and the Duke—knew different. Wayne wrote him a letter after he saw *High Plains Drifter* (1973). "He said, 'That isn't what the West was all about. That isn't the American people who settled this country,'" Eastwood later recalled. Eastwood's westerns were more akin to Elizabethan revenge tragedy than to John Ford. "I was never John Wayne's heir," he once said.

Ford believed deeply in the civilizing impact of society, the transformation of the jungle into the garden. In Ford's dusty towns, there is always a church or a school going up, the frame building standing starkly against the raw landscape. Eastwood's westerns are about darkness and pain, and even when the evil has been avenged, the wounds rarely heal. In *Unforgiven*, there is a house going up, built by Little Bill Daggett, Gene Hackman's sadistic sheriff. At the end, with Munny's weapon aimed at his head, Daggett says: "I don't deserve this . . . to die this way. I was building a house." Munny replies, "Deserve's got nothin' to do with it," and pulls the trigger. Ford westerns are about deserving, and this scene would never have happened.

Until 1976, aside from the Dirty Harry movies, Eastwood for the most part worked for Universal. But he had long been dissatisfied with the way the studio was marketing his movies. The Universal tour was the last straw. "I had a really nice bungalow, a very comfortable place to work," he recalls. "But I'd walk out of my office and the bus would be sitting there with people yelling. So finally I called Frank Wells [at Warner's] and said, 'I'll move over there if you've got a space for me, but if you ever have a tour, I'm leaving.' He said, 'We're not in the tour business.'"

Moreover, Eastwood had an itch. His career has always gone against the grain. He was making genre movies in an era when the most interesting work was devoted to subverting genres, particularly the western, which more or less died under him. He was riding tall in the saddle in an age of antiheroes; he was the laconic star for Nixon's silent majority. If *Dirty Harry* was a decade ahead of itself, when the Reagan-era zeitgeist caught up with him, in 1980, Eastwood had already moved along. While George Lucas and Steven Spielberg were busy reinventing the old formulas that Penn, Scorsese,

Altman, and others had buried, one thought, for good, Eastwood started tinkering with his image, journeying into the shadows of his own persona.

He told writers Shryack and Michael Butler that he regarded their script *The Gauntlet,* in which he plays a feckless cop, as a bridge to a new kind of character. In 1980, the beginning of the Reagan era, he further cut the ground out from under himself in the self-mocking *Bronco Billy,* where cowboy Billy is a purveyor of illusions. While Reagan was using the symbols of the West to promote the illusion of a heroic America that no longer existed, Eastwood was increasingly obsessed by the limitations of the human condition. "Exploring the dark side sort of came about when I started doing things like *Bronco Billy,*" he says. "I've played winners, I've played losers who were winners, guys who are cool, but I like reality, and in reality, it's not all like that. There's sort of that frailty in mankind that's very interesting to explore. Heroics are so few and far between."

When *The Gauntlet* didn't do as well as hoped, Warner's became concerned that Eastwood was making the wrong choices. He always had a streak of Burt Reynolds redneck humor about him, and when he wanted to play opposite an orangutan in *Every Which Way but Loose,* Warner's did some market research that indicated a negative reaction to the title, to the orangutan, and even to the idea of Dirty Harry in a comedy. But Eastwood doesn't have much truck with market research and went ahead anyway. It cost about $8 million and grossed about $85 million (about $150 million in today's dollars), making it his biggest film. Even *Bronco Billy* grossed $33 million.

Finally, the East Coast establishment climbed aboard. In 1980, the Museum of Modern Art in New York gave him a retrospective. Two years later, Robert Mazzocco wrote a widely read appreciation in *The New York Review of Books,* calling Eastwood "the supply-side star." The essay registered his anointment by Upper West Side "neos"—both liberals and conservatives. Then, in 1985, the French, who had always lauded Hollywood directors without honor in their own country, gave Eastwood a retrospective at the Cinémathèque, as well as a Chevalier des Arts et Lettres decoration.

Mazzocco was right. Eastwood had indeed benefited from the Reagan-era cultural shift. But liberals applauded him, too, falling all over themselves to find the bleeding heart behind the "fascist" veneer. His acting, previously "stiff," became "spare and stylized." *Honkytonk Man* was compared with *The Grapes of Wrath.* The *Los Angeles Times,* doubtless with *Sudden*

*Impact* in mind, called him "the most important and influential...feminist filmmaker working in America today."

But just as Eastwood was never a fascist, his new liberal threads did not quite fit him either. In the early years of the Reagan administration, he gave a reported $30,000 to a former lieutenant colonel in the Special Forces named James "Bo" Gritz to launch an "incursion" into Laos, and then agreed to act as Gritz's liaison with Reagan.

"I said, 'If there's a possibility of saving just one person, I would certainly spend any amount of time and effort necessary,'" recalls Eastwood. "But it wasn't *The Dirty Dozen*—I think they ended up spending most of the dough hanging around Bangkok. They brought back a bunch of bones—some of them weren't even human. Remains weren't worth risking lives for." (Gritz denies dribbling the money away in Bangkok and insists that the remains were human.)

A registered Republican for most of his life, Eastwood criticized Reagan for visiting a military cemetery in Bitburg, Germany, where SS troops were buried. He ran for mayor of Carmel in 1986 and won—but spent $25,000 to land a job that paid $2,400 a year. Although Eastwood feels his two-year term was plenty, his editor, Joel Cox, says, "I think it was the best thing that ever happened to Clint. He's always been a loner. It sort of opened his personality a little bit."

Eastwood rejected George Bush's request for help in the last election. "I think what the ultra-right wing conservatives did to the Republicans is really self-destructive, absolutely stupid." He voted for Ross Perot. "Perot was kind of out there, with dirty tricks and all. But in the final analysis, he's the only one I believe. I would have loved to have seen four years of the little guy from Texas rolling his eyes, screaming and yelling, 'Time to bite the bullet.'"

In the last ten years or so, Eastwood has chosen more personal, character-driven projects: *Honkytonk Man; Bird; White Hunter, Black Heart;* and *Unforgiven.* He gets away with it because he is so financially responsible. Asking Warner president Terry Semel about Eastwood is like asking a kid about Santa Claus on Christmas morning: "Clint is the best producer I've ever worked with. He is more careful with our money than he is with his own." Warner's is not going to lose much on an Eastwood picture, no matter what it's about. Says Valdes, "I think if Clint Eastwood wants to make a cooking show, he will call [Warner chairman] Bob Daly or Terry Semel, and we'll be doing a cooking show." *Bird* is a period drama about a black jazz musician—an alcoholic, a smack addict, and a wife beater—who dies at the end. But Eastwood knew he could bring it in under $10 million, including his fee, at a time when an average picture cost $18 million. And he did.

At the same time, Warner's counted on him to deliver commercial product. The problem was that *Heartbreak Ridge, The Dead Pool, Pink Cadillac,* and *The Rookie* were not that commercial. For the first time, Eastwood's career looked as if it might be in trouble. Then came *Unforgiven*—not, on the face of it, much more of a box office draw than *Bird,* a risky project for someone who hadn't had a real hit in nearly ten years. But as with *Bird,* he kept the costs down. He brought it in in 52 days for $14.4 million, excluding his fee. With some exceptions, Eastwood always had trouble getting marquee names for his movies; they were seen as *his* movies. "You'd start talking about Meryl Streep and end up with Patty Clarkson," says Marco Barla, Eastwood's project coordinator. Hackman didn't want to do *Unforgiven.* "The violence of the characters I portrayed had begun to wear on me," he says. But Eastwood convinced him that the film made a statement *about* violence. "He was very explicit about his desire to demythologize violence," adds Hackman. Later, Hackman quipped, "I'm really glad Clint convinced me this was not a Clint Eastwood film."

"When *Unforgiven* came out and started doing business, I was shocked," says Eastwood. "Because I never try and romance the audience. You've got to forget that there's somebody out there eating popcorn and Milk Duds. I figured that if people want to see it, they'll see it. If they don't, screw it." Eastwood, sitting in his trailer between takes on *Line of Fire,* is dressed in a conservative gray Secret Service suit, scuffed and ripped in places from his exertions in the name of national security. He looks tired. There is a half-pint container of milk on the table. "Better get rid of that," he says softly to Frances Fisher, whom he has been seeing for some time and refers to as "Bad Fran." "Else you'll be *Big* Bad Fran."

Eastwood has said he doesn't know if *Unforgiven,* which has now grossed more than $100 million worldwide, will be his last western, but it should be. He's come full circle. *Unforgiven* is *Dirty Harry* turned on its head. After two decades, Harry, still above the law, has become the sadistic sheriff, Hackman's Daggett, while Scorpio has evolved into Munny, the killer now reformed. By killing Daggett, Eastwood purges the identity that has imprisoned him throughout his career.

Richard Schickel once said that Eastwood is a man who works in the American vernacular, an artisan whose art emerges from the craft. As Barla puts it, he is like a body-and-fender man who's been beating out dents for 30 years and then builds his own car. Everybody oohs and aahs, and it goes in a museum. Eastwood, of course, will never make any extravagant claims about his own work. "I sort of just do my thing and make films, and the body of work just sort of adds up year after year," he has said. "Eventually you do something someone thinks is okay."

More than okay, and the beauty of it is, he's still working. *In the Line of Fire* is not *Unforgiven*. But neither is it *Dirty Harry*. Yet the executives at Columbia Pictures just can't get *Dirty Harry* out of their minds.

*Line of Fire*'s killer (played by John Malkovich) has been taunting Eastwood's character, Frank Horrigan, insisting that history is about to repeat itself. There's a scene in which Horrigan stands by Kennedy's grave, staring at the flame, and mutters to himself, "It's not going to happen."

When the execs heard that, a light went on: if he spits out "It's not gonna happen," it could resonate like "Make my day." They could use it in the trailer.

They ask the screenwriter, Jeff Maguire, to add the line during the climactic fight between Eastwood and his doppelgänger. There's no way to do it, unless Maguire makes the killer—a clever fellow, and by no means a cardboard villain given to thundering imprecations—shout something like, "I'm gonna kill you," or "You're a dead man." Maguire doesn't want to do it. But he's only the writer, and, worse, this is his first script. So it's up to Eastwood to draw a line in the sand, tell Columbia, "It's not gonna happen." But it's not his picture.

Under pressure, Maguire rewrites the dialogue. Malkovich looks at the new pages and says, "Why would I say that?" One day, while they're shooting the fight, Eastwood says, "Let's do it." They shoot the scene. Malkovich threatens; Eastwood fixes him with that cold stare and retorts, "It's not gonna happen." But he doesn't pause for effect. He says it quickly, swallows the words. They are nearly inaudible (they ended up reshooting the line so it can be used in the trailer). But no one can say Eastwood is hard to work with, or throws his weight around, or is on a star trip, or acts like Dirty Harry. He doesn't. He's not.

# Clint Eastwood Stepping Out

## JAMES VERNIERE/1993

BASTROP, TEXAS. SITTING IN a custom-built bus during a break in the shooting of his latest film, *A Perfect World,* Clint Eastwood, who can currently be seen in the thriller *In the Line of Fire,* looks relaxed and remarkably fit. But there are signs of heat-induced weariness and work-stiffened joints. As he speaks, for instance, he props his feet on a vibrating pad.

Eastwood, 63, has reason to be footsore. In addition to co-starring with Kevin Costner and Laura Dern in *A Perfect World,* a drama set in 1963 about a charming sociopath (Costner) and the grizzled, relentless Texas Ranger on his trail (Eastwood), Eastwood is also directing the film, his first since his Academy Award-winning 1992 Western, *Unforgiven.*

Costner plays Butch Haynes, a hot-tempered escaped convict who bonds with a seven-year-old boy he saves from a child molester. Eastwood is Red Garnett, a weary Texas ranger who has known Haynes for years and was in fact the first police officer to bust him as a teenager. Laura Dern plays Garnett's fellow police officer. The film is set in the months just before the Kennedy assassination—familiar psychic territory for the man who played Jim Garrison in Oliver Stone's *JFK.*

Outside the trailer, under a blazing Texas sky full of billowing clouds, it's 95 degrees and the humidity is as high. Eastwood, whose instantly recognisable face is a Monument Valley in miniature, seems able to con-

Published in *Sight and Sound* 3 [n.s.], no. 9 (September 1993): 6–9. Reprinted by permission.

serve his energy. He moves and talks with the deliberate ease of a man who's in no hurry. And it's easy to see this personal style as a metaphor for his entire career. To that end, after winning two Academy Awards last spring, Eastwood did just what he's always done, whether his films have been scorned or acclaimed: he went right back to work.

First he finished *In the Line of Fire,* a Wolfgang Petersen (*Das Boot, Shattered*) film that adds yet another memorable Eastwood character to a roster that includes the Man With No Name, Dirty Harry and *Unforgiven's* William Munny. As Frank Horrigan, a secret service agent who was on duty in Dallas when Kennedy was assassinated in 1963 and now has to protect the current president from another assassination threat, Eastwood is more accessible than in any of his previous screen roles. This is no Dirty Harry Goes to Washington. An effortlessly charming wreck, Eastwood's Horrigan is a "borderline burn-out," a jazz piano-playing dinosaur seeking redemption in an age of spin doctors and high-tech politics. When the would-be assassin (John Malkovich) promises to see him "standing over the grave of another dead president," Horrigan's destined to be quoted, though not necessarily inviolable, response is "That's not gonna happen."

JAMES VERNIERE: *Was the film* In the Line of Fire *written for you?*
CLINT EASTWOOD: It sure sounded like Jeff Maguire had me in mind, but I don't know for certain. I've been told he tried to submit the script to me at Warner Bros., but I didn't get it. My agent just called me up one day and said, "Have you ever read this thing at Columbia? It's about a secret service guy who likes jazz and plays a little piano." So I read it and I liked it. It had interesting challenges, and like *Unforgiven* it gave me the chance to play a man who is haunted by a mistake he made in his past. It's tough to find good characters today, characters who have somewhere to go.

*The rapport between you and John Malkovich, even though many of your scenes are telephone conversations, is intense.*
Telephone conversations are hard to make interesting a lot of the time, but John brought a lot of dimension to it. He plays the character as a very intelligent psychotic; it's a pretty formidable combination.

*Did he do anything on set to stay in character? For example, did he avoid you, or give you evil looks, or skulk in the shadows?*

No. We're both of the school of getting in there and doing it, and we were both there when we shot the phone calls, so we didn't have to do them with a script person.

*Like* Unforgiven, In the Line of Fire *represents another revision of your image. In many ways Frank Horrigan is to Dirty Harry what William Munny was to the characters you played in your earlier Westerns. They're both men with guns and badges, and they're both mavericks in a way. But at the same time, they're very different: it's a different time in their lives.*
So your characters have changed as you have changed. I hope I've changed. My father once said, "You either progress or you decay." Sure, as you get older, there are parts you can't play any more. But there are also things you can play that you could never play before. The older you are, the more background the characters can have.

*Is Dirty Harry defunct? Do you have any plans for another film?*
No, no plans at all. Sequels were OK at one time in my life, but now I feel that if I do a film, and it feels right to me, maybe it should then be left alone.

*Then it's not the audiences, but you who have outgrown Dirty Harry.*
I think so. As the years go by I'm attracted to subjects that are a little different from the ones I was attracted to 30 years ago. I don't know where I'd take Harry any more. I could change him philosophically, but that's what Frank Horrigan is.

*Are you still a Ross Perot supporter?*
Well, I voted for him in the last election, and I agree that we need change. I think people have become disenchanted with politics, the constant rhetoric, the lack of substance.

*The reason I ask is that the Dirty Harry films address themselves to the disenfranchised masses who feel at the mercy of corrupt political systems, and like Perot, Dirty Harry has tremendous popular appeal. It must have been edifying when President Reagan quoted your, "Go ahead, make my day!" line.*
I don't know how terrific it was: you get a little tired of people saying, "Make my day!", or asking you to say it.

*Don Siegel, who directed* Dirty Harry *and many of your other films in the 60s and 70s, played an important role in your development as an actor and director. You made two or three films with him before you directed* Play Misty for Me *in 1971, and, of course, in that film you cast him as the bartender.*

I always like to joke that I hired Don in case I got stymied, but he was so nervous about acting that he would have been useless to me. Don's influence will always be with me. He was a unique guy. He didn't have the stature of a Ford or a Hawks and he was often given B-movie projects by the studios, but he made some unique films: *Invasion of the Body Snatchers* and *Riot in Cell Block 11* among them.

Siegel also directed *Coogan's Bluff,* one of the first films I made after working in Italy. We met by accident: Universal had hired a guy named Alex Segal to direct *Coogan's Bluff,* but for some reason he couldn't do it, so the studio said, "We've got this guy named Don Siegel." I said, "Don't you have anybody who's not named Siegel?" I didn't know Don's work at the time. The studio let me see some of his films, including *Madigan* which he had just finished, and he watched my Leone films, and we decided to work together, and I was able to bring a bigger budget to him. It would have been nice for him to have ended his career on a high note, but few do. Not many people are that fortunate.

*There was a time when you played similar types, the mythic, monolithic screen hero. Then there was the middle period during which you did quirky, off-beat films such as* Bronco Billy *and* Tightrope *in between* Dirty Harry *movies.*

Those smaller, different projects are probably what led cumulatively to films like *Unforgiven* and *In the Line of Fire.* I was always too stubborn to believe that straight shoot-em-ups were going to be the end-all for me. Maybe *Bronco Billy* and *Honkytonk Man* didn't do the kind of business that *Sudden Impact* or *Every Which Way But Loose* did, but they gave me the confidence to do something like *Unforgiven.* I feel very much like the John Wilson character in *White Hunter, Black Heart.* When you make a picture, you have to forget that anybody might ever see it.

*What did the smaller films teach you?*

They taught me not to be afraid to step out and do something different. I've seen other actors do some crazy films that they got criticised for, and I've always admired that.

*Do you remember when Burt Lancaster made* The Swimmer?

Exactly. I admired *The Swimmer.* In fact, Lancaster and Kirk Douglas stepped out a lot: Lancaster with *The Swimmer,* Douglas with *Town without Pity* and *Lonely Are the Brave.* I admired those guys then for doing that when they could have played it safe. I've tried to explain that to other film-makers who have made a few successful films. I tell them that they really don't need to make another one. They need to do something different and get themselves satisfied.

*What's different about Clint Eastwood at 63? Some critics have suggested that your films now address moral issues.*

I can't tell you how it happens, but as you get older you tend to get more concerned about the moral values of society. I'm not talking about violence in movies. That's just entertainment. As I said when *Unforgiven* came out, I wasn't doing any penance for the mayhem in my other films. I suppose it's just a time in my life, and maybe a time in history, when violence shouldn't be so lighthearted or glamorous. Maybe there are consequences to violence, for both the perpetrator and the victim, that are important to address.

*So you don't buy the argument that violent films are damaging to society?*

My generation grew up with films like *White Heat* and *Public Enemy,* and they didn't turn us into criminals. It's great to blame it all on the film and television industries, because they always run scared.

*You're a product of the Second World War and Korean War generation, yet you haven't lost touch with today's moviegoing audience. How is that?*

Those were my formative years, but they weren't the end of my life. Music didn't stop in the 40s, although I think they were great years, when swing and bebop came along. Everything moves onwards. You have to live in the world as it is today.

*Although you didn't direct* In the Line of Fire, *you had a say in who would. Why did you choose Wolfgang Petersen?*

I loved *Das Boot.* Some of his later films have been better than others, but I always felt he had a certain size and that he brought a certain scope to his films. I got the feeling that he prefers John Ford movies to television. Too many of our young directors make films that look like television. Although

I don't want to sound superstitious, I also thought that a European might take a different look at American subject matter, in much the way that Sergio Leone did in the 60s. Castle Rock had some other people they might have preferred, but I've been directing for 23 years and I didn't want somebody who was brand new to the field. I wanted somebody with experience.

*It has been reported that you stepped in personally when Columbia studio executives tried to force Petersen to make* In the Line of Fire *more action-oriented once filming had begun.*
A couple of front office people came down and suggested changes. I said, "You know fellas, you liked the story well enough to make it. I like the script. Everybody likes the script. You should let it get made, give us a chance to finish it, and then make your decision." If you let these things get committee-ised, you're through.

*How did you come across the John Lee Hancock script for* A Perfect World? *What did you like about it?*
Warner Bros. had it and showed it to me. It's a crime drama that's also about the family unit and how it has changed.

*You co-star with Kevin Costner:* Dances with Wolves *meets* The Outlaw Josey Wales. *Like you, Costner has played a lot of mythic hero types. But in this film he's an escaped convict and con man. Do you think this role will be good for him?*
I think it's always good to stretch. You can't really hit the ball out of the park unless you step up to the bat. He's been in a few successful films and he's proved he can do that. Now it's his chance to move out to things he really wants to do, to become more versatile.

*Your film sets are notoriously laid back. Did he have any problem getting used to that?*
I think he enjoyed himself, but I can't really speak for him.

*Critics have compared him to Gary Cooper and Steve McQueen. Does he remind you of these actors?*
I think he's got his own appeal—that's why he's successful. Everybody is always trying to make comparisons, but we tend to forget that actors like Gary Cooper played a lot of different roles. Bogart and Cagney did too. They weren't afraid to play villains. Today, actors are more protective of their image, but sometimes you can play it too safe.

*The title and pre-Kennedy assassination setting of* A Perfect World *suggest a* Norman Rockwell *world that's about to go sour. Is there a specific look that you're trying to get to parallel that theme, if that's your theme?*
That's exactly the feeling we're trying to get across—a Rockwell world that's on the verge of fading. Jack Green, who was also the cinematographer of *Unforgiven,* is trying to get some of that Rockwellesque feeling into the film. But it's difficult, and it remains to be seen if we've achieved it. Right now we're down to the last few days of shooting, and I haven't seen all the footage together.

*In the past you've made it almost a point of honour to refuse to get caught up in the awards game. So what was going through your mind at the Academy Awards ceremony?*
Last December the Los Angeles Film Critics Awards and Boston Society of Film Critics gave us the best picture award. We missed at the New York Society of Film Critics by one vote. So you start thinking, "Well, maybe I have a chance," and you get a little irritated because you've gone all your life without this kind of stuff, and you don't really need it. But deep inside, you say it would be nice to get.

I went in feeling good, and I was going to try to be graceful, win or lose. But when we didn't win for cinematography or screenplay, I thought, "So here I am with my 84-year-old mother. I brought her all the way down here, and we're gonna go home empty." Your mind plays tricks on you. But when I saw Barbra Streisand open the envelope and smile, I knew.

*I understand that Emma Thompson wrote you a note after an awards ceremony at which the two of you were winners.*
She wrote me a nice note recalling watching my movies with her late father. He was an advocate of simplicity in acting, and he admired my films, and she liked them too. Now here's a gal who's having a nice successful year, along with me, who watched my films as a child. As you get older you start to run into more and more people who go way back with you, who maybe saw one of your films on their first date. It's as if you've become part of the landscape.

*European critics were among the first to re-assess your films and career and to give you credit for the work you were doing at a time when you were under-appreciated in your own country. What did that mean to you at the time?*

I think European critics were much more interested in the history of cinema. When my first films came out in the early 60s, there were a few American critics who responded—Bosley Crowther was one—but by and large they were in the minority. A lot of them put my films down. European critics were more interested in what Sergio Leone was doing and in what I was trying to do as an actor, and they'd follow me along every step of my career. They were very quick to recognise changes. They jumped on *Bronco Billy* as a major change and when I moved to directing in 1970 they were extremely encouraging, right away, while American critics were saying, "Well, we're not even sure we like him as an actor." There were exceptions to this, of course.

*Do you think that there was a reserve of prejudice against you?*
I think some people are that way. There is a certain snobbery behind it. The French were always laughed at by the Hollywood establishment for taking notice of Jerry Lewis' work. What the hell. The guy was writing and directing films. I always admired that. He was trying things. In the last 20 years a lot of younger American critics who are more knowledgeable and open-minded have arrived. In the 40s and 50s a lot of our reviewers didn't have much knowledge of film or of its history.

*You were born in 1930, the son of a labourer. Do you think that growing up in the Depression made you a firm believer in the work ethic?*
I think that's definitely the case. Every guy I know who grew up in that period feels much the same way. They either give up early, or they work without stop. My mother talks about the past with nostalgia, as if it was a lot of fun. I remember when it wasn't so much fun. But by and large I don't think much about the past. I'm a today and tomorrow kind of guy.

*Have you ever considered retiring? You've had a couple of dry spells over the past ten years.*
Sometimes the films you make don't find an audience. But I never let that bother me. I always think about today and tomorrow. Of course, I've thought about easing back and retiring, but then again I should be doing my best work now, and I think I am. I should be taking advantage of this time. When the day comes that the studios don't want to use me any more, it'll be OK. I've had a long ride.

# America on the Brink of the Void

## HENRI BÉHAR/1993

IN *A PERFECT WORLD* THE chief players are a child
and his kidnapper (Kevin Costner) on the run. If the film
describes an intimate, complex relationship, which allows Clint
Eastwood to reflect on the relations between a father and a son, it
brings to the screen one of the wounds of American society—
and certainly also of ours: the irruption of violence. Furthermore,
the film is the occasion for a confrontation between two morali-
ties, two purely American types of hero, two generations of
actors. All of this is high stakes, as Clint Eastwood explains here.

*After* Unforgiven *and the Oscars, was it difficult to approach a new project?*
Wait, let me think back... That's a long time ago already.

*A long time, barely a year?*
*(He laughs.)* Let's see... *In the Line of Fire* lasted until the Oscars... Yes, *A
Perfect World* was already underway.

*The theme of fatherhood, of the absence of the father...*
... was very clearly developed in the original script, which the film stayed
close to.

Published as "L'Amérique au bord du vide" in *Le Monde*, 16 December 1993. Reprinted by
permission; translated from the French by KC.

*You seem to consider the default of the father, a poor understanding of the notions of "machismo" and virility to be responsible for many social problems...* There's been a lot written about that, it's a major preoccupation of contemporary society, especially in the United States.

*However,* A Perfect World *takes place at the end of 1963, just before the arrival in Dallas of President Kennedy, whose bodyguard you were in* In the Line of Fire. This "Kennedy connection" was already in John Lee Hancock's script. I didn't discuss it with him, but it's always seemed interesting to me to deal with the present day in the context of the past. *Unforgiven* took place in 1880, but it dealt with armed violence, a problem that couldn't be more contemporary. *A Perfect World* takes place at one precise moment of one precise year, just on the brink of a great turning towards the void that will take hold of America.

*This casts a tragic shadow on the whole of the film...*
Yes. You don't really know where this element has its place in the picture, or if there is a place for it directly. But you feel it like an echo of Red's disenchantment and his rebellion with regard to the political system. I though it was good to situate this film at this particular time, which was a bit strange and as though in a state of suspense.

*The action of* A Perfect World *takes place around the time of Halloween also...*
Halloween is a holiday when kids disguise themselves as monsters or witches. That gave me a chance, in the middle of this chase, to play with the Casper the Ghost costume, which the boy is wearing for the first time in his life.

*...thus maintaining a constant presence of death...*
Skeletons, masks, yes...

*...in a film that's sunny for nearly all of its length.*
Exactly.

*The scenes between Kevin Costner and the child, almost always in a moving car, have something very free, nearly anarchic. Your scenes most often immobilize you inside the metallic trailer that serves as your headquarters.*
That was entirely deliberate. Butch is in search of freedom—even though he doesn't have any illusions about his "new frontier," Alaska. He only

knows it from a postcard sent long ago by a father who probably doesn't exist and who, if he exists, doesn't have anything to do with him. Then there's Red in his steel shell, who maybe, at a earlier point in time, could have helped Butch, but he's messed up a number of things in his own life. Among which, specifically, is fatherhood. The two characters have their attractions, but also their limitations.

*There's no winner in the moral fight.*
No. Unless, maybe, it's the child—at least the hope that, in spite of his emotional injuries, he'll profit from the adventure, and will be able to grow up, to mature, to age gracefully.

*Was it you who approached Costner or the other way around?*
We were the ones who approached him.

*He presented a double danger, however: He could play on the sentimental string, as he did in* Field of Dreams, *and he could utilize his incontestable charisma to make Butch a hero.*
I rarely indulge in sentimentality, and Butch couldn't be completely a hero. I tried to preserve a certain toughness in Kevin. I didn't want him to have a "paternal" attitude towards the kid. Butch doesn't know anything about children, he's spent too much time in prison... I wanted him to treat the kid the way he would treat any guy. Kevin isn't used to playing this interior toughness, inasmuch as he's very close to his own children. But he's a determined worker, it was enough to put him back on track from time to time.

*Consequentially, you brought his character closer to those which Bogart, Cagney, Mitchum or Gary Cooper played in the 40s.*
Yes. Actors of that generation weren't afraid to approach this type of role. Those of the present generation have... a certain image of themselves.

*Encouraged by the manner in which Hollywood functions today?*
Yes.

*Pampered by an industry at his feet, would Costner therefore generally play it safe?*
I can't answer for him. But if in certain films he's played it safe like in his first big role, he didn't do it here. Butch isn't a "man who liked children

and dogs," a romantic hero you can take cover behind. Think more of Bogart in *High Sierra* or *The Treasure of the Sierra Madré*; those weren't conventional films or conventional protagonists... But these types of roles let people construct a career that would have duration... In the same way, women in the films of the 40s were much more interesting than those of the 50s, 60s, 70s and 80s. And this is the direction in which we worked on the character of Laura Dern. I wanted her to actively participate in the investigation, I didn't want her to be a jellyfish, or a decorative element, or the gal on the job who adds to the mistakes or gets into situations that only men will be able to get her out of. I wanted her to have a point of view, opinions, a more open conflict with me, and above all not a love story.

*Did you ever consider playing Butch?*
The character could be any age but it seemed that a man of sixty who goes off in search of an eighty-year-old father would be ridiculous. I thought it was better if Butch were about thirty.

*So name five—or even three—Hollywood actresses in your age group...*
*(He laughs.)* I see what you're getting at...

*...who are capable of carrying a film on their own account, or at least of sharing it with you.*
If the script permits it, I'd be the first one to celebrate.

*Speaking of Simone Signoret in* Madame Rosa, *a producer once quipped: "She's lucky to be European. Here, as soon as she got her first wrinkle, she'd have been relegated to playing grandmothers on daytime soaps."*
It's appalling, distressing, idiotic, but unfortunately it's not untrue. In Europe, you keep actresses of the range of Jeanne Moreau or Sophia Loren on top. In the United States, no matter how hard I think, I don't see any. Sometimes an actress of eighty might get a great part, like Jessica Tandy and Miss Daisy, but there aren't any decent parts being written for women of fifty any more. Maybe that's why people like Jane Fonda, if they don't exactly take early retirement, at least stay away from things...

*Or else they have recourse to cosmetic surgery.*
They're almost forced to by the fashion industry, where everyone's got to be eighteen years old, where anyone older than thirty is finished, termi-

nated, the horse kicked out of the barn, if I can put it like that. Moreover, this isn't a question of sex: it applies to men as well, if not as much as to women. The system pushes you to be something you're not and if you give up, you destroy yourself. Unless you completely shut your eyes. For me, a woman who is maturing and aging gracefully is sexier, and more exciting, than one who's determined to want to look twenty years old.

*Both* Unforgiven *and* A Perfect World *strip violence bare of all its allure. Violence is never beautiful.*

*The release of* Unforgiven *in the United States coincided with the controversy surrounding* Cop Killer *and the split-up between Ice-T and Time Warner. Similarly, at the time of* A Perfect World*'s release, we witnessed the staging of a general accusation against the film industry, television and the media, the attack coming from both the Attorney General, Janet Reno, and from President Clinton, scarcely two weeks ago.*

Actually, I'm beginning to be annoyed by politicians who suddenly start blaming television, the movies, and so forth. You can call TV too violent, or movies too violent. You could just simply blame bad television and bad movies. But when a politician gets involved in this kind of diatribe, I never know whether he's doing it to serve his country or to serve himself. When you're looking for scapegoats, the movie and television industry make a choice target: they never fight back. Television puts up its umbrella and Hollywood beats its breast . . . Janet Reno is probably trying to get herself forgiven for the enormous fiasco of Waco, which was the most violent thing I've seen on television lately! And I don't know very many TV programs that display as much violence as the television newscasts.

Recently, a man was arrested in Northern California for kidnapping and afterwards murdering a young girl. As it turned out, he had already been convicted on two occasions for the same offense! The state of Washington is considering passing a law according to which the third conviction for a major crime will condemn you to life imprisonment without possibility of parole. But how many people will have to die before this third conviction? All the values in this country have changed so much.

I was raised with the idea that crime doesn't pay. But the legal system has become unbelievably devious, and the average conviction for murder today is five and a half years in actual fact . . .

*During a recent debate on violence in which the filmmaker Steven Soderbergh took part, some eloquent numbers were advanced: every year, in France, in Italy, in Germany, fewer than about fifty people are killed by automatic or semiautomatic combat weapons. In the United States: more than ten thousand!*
Yes.

*For Soderbergh, the reason was simple: these weapons are forbidden in Europe. The recent adoption of the Brady Bill, the law to which the name of James Brady is attached, Ronald Reagan's bodyguard[1] at the time of the assassination attempt by John Hinckley—does it appears to you to be a first step in the right direction?*
I was always a backer of this bill.

It establishes a Federally mandated waiting period of five days between the application for the purchase of a handgun and its transfer to the purchaser. In California, however, the waiting period is already fifteen days. On the other hand, almost all Swiss families with a family member in the national guard have assault weapons at home. Simply put, Swiss society doesn't encourage people to use them. Could that be because, in our society, the guilty pass through the system so quickly that nothing is taken seriously any more?

*There are several kinds of violence in your film: the brutal kind, to which Costner's character yields during a crucial scene is a reaction to the grandfather...*
...who slaps his grandson almost by routine, as if it were normal that a kid is something to slap, yes.

*There is another, subtler, violence: the one exercised on the small boy by his mother who, as a Jehovah's Witness, forbids him to wear a disguise like the other children...*
It wasn't my intention to attack the Jehovah's Witnesses. It's a fact that they don't celebrate Halloween or Christmas, but you could find plenty of children among them who don't suffer for that. Every religion has its commandments and its constraints—but beyond that, the family group, society, has always played with the punishment that consists of saying: "No, you can't go play with your buddies, you're grounded, you've done something very bad..."

---

1. Brady was Reagan's press secretary, not his bodyguard.—Translator's note.

*Aren't you soon to be directed by Steven Spielberg in* The Bridges of Madison County...?

Spielberg and I have known each other for a long time, I had directed an episode of *Amazing Stories,* with Harvey Keitel, for him. We spoke very briefly about this project but decided to take up the discussion again after the release of our respective films. Mine is out now and his, *Schindler's List,* will be coming out in the United States next week.

*Don't you also have the intention of shooting a film on golf, in which would you direct Sean Connery...?*

After doing *Unforgiven, In the Line of Fire* and *A Perfect World* practically back to back, I intend above all to take a vacation with my family!

# Q & A with a Western Icon

JERRY  ROBERTS/1995

AFTER HELMING NEARLY 20 films and starring in dozens more, Eastwood's work as a director and actor has reaped box office bonanzas and yielded awards all over the world, including an Oscar for his direction of 1992's Best Picture, *Unforgiven*. But he's also got an Oscar on his mantle for producing the esteemed Western pic, and his new Oscar courtesy of receiving the Irving G. Thalberg Memorial Award is for almost 30 years of producing achievements. "The Man With No Name" has been wearing *three* hats since his Malpaso Productions outfit kicked off with *Hang 'em High* in 1968.

This exclusive interview with Eastwood was conducted for *Daily Variety* by film critic Jerry Roberts.

DAILY VARIETY: *The Irving G. Thalberg Award is rarely presented to producers who remain contemporary figures. And it has never been given to someone who is known primarily as an actor. Were you surprised when you were selected?*
CLINT EASTWOOD: Yes, I was surprised. But I formed Malpaso Productions in the mid-1960s, so for 30 years I've been directly involved in the total process of making the movies I've done. If you want to say I'm a contemporary figure, I'm what you would call a longtime contemporary. It's one of those deals where I just outlived everybody. I started in the

---

Published in *Daily Variety*, 27 March 1995, 34, 38, 42, 52. Reprinted by permission.

Italian Westerns in 1963 and '64 and came back here and formed Malpaso for *Hang 'em High*. I didn't take a producing credit then, but started to later on. We worked mostly for Universal first, and after *Dirty Harry*, for Warner Bros. We gradually moved the company over and settled with Warners in 1976.

D V :   *Why did you leave Universal?*
E A S T W O O D :   Universal eventually got more into the tour business than the picture business. You couldn't go outside your office without some tour going by. And Warner Bros. had a bigger lot, more resources and their promotions department was pretty good. The first picture we did at Warner Bros. was *The Outlaw Josey Wales*. With the exception of a film for Paramount (*Escape from Alcatraz*) and one for Columbia (*In the Line of Fire*), we've done everything for a Warner Bros. release. We're not exclusive with them. It's sort of a handshake deal. If somebody else has a great job they want me for — like *In the Line of Fire* for Castle Rock — then I'll go do that.

D V :   *The definition of the title of producer depends on who you talk to. What is your own definition of that job as you perform it?*
E A S T W O O D :   Producers get the least amount of attention and gratification on a film. They're not as hands-on as the director and the actors. But by and large they finance and envision the project. The producer is the person who puts together the elements and then lets the director run with the ball.

D V :   *How has the profession of producing changed over the years?*
E A S T W O O D :   In the old days, producers were knowledgeable on all aspects of filmmaking, plus they were the presidents of the company. In the late '60s and '70s, many producers merely packaged the deal and then walked away from it.

In the old days, the Hal Wallis kind of producers were a little more hands-on. They knew lighting. They knew when the director was b.s.-ing them. They relied on the unit manager to do the auditing, but they had their eyes on the overall project.

How I fit into it — I'm fairly good at watching things. If you're responsible and have figured out your needs, there's no reason to be over budget or have late miscalculations. You hire good people and they're going to make you look good. It's like riding a horse. It can make you look noble and elegant up on it or it can make you look like a bum.

A producer has to be a salesman for the project. He has to raise enthusiasm to finance it. You have to sell it to actors if you want a name cast. You have to sell the different elements to a director. It's a difficult process, but if you have a track record, if the studio has shared in your good luck in the past, it will put its faith in you again. If you have had a hit picture recently, that helps.

DV: *Money management, enthusiasm, persuasiveness and packaging seem, then, to be the major tasks of the job.*
EASTWOOD: Producing is also something that you don't go to school for. You can go to cinema schools and learn cinematography and editing. You can't teach someone how to be a good producer. It's more of an apprenticeship. David Valdes is a good example, a terrific producer. He came up through the ranks with me. He was an assistant director, a unit manager, then after some pictures in those capacities a producer.

DV: *You have said that you learned aspects of directing from Sergio Leone and Don Siegel. Can you recall anyone who influenced your producing style?*
EASTWOOD: I've worked with some really good producers and I've also worked with some who were just deal packagers. But I looked up to Hal Wallis, who was a very intelligent and savvy producer. He seemed to know how to pull together the whole team. He seemed to know every aspect. I never worked with him on a film. I never worked with Billy Wilder, either, but I've admired him from afar.

DV: *Some of the more independent directors have always had aversions to producers.*
EASTWOOD: Don Siegel used to say, "The trouble with producers is that they don't know what they do." He set up an antagonistic scheme between him and the producer, as if the producer was the big, bad tax man in the sky or something. So on a couple of projects I said to him, "This time you be the producer and the director and you'll have nobody to hate."

DV: *It's probably not coincidental that one of the most notorious vilifiers of producers among directors was Sam Peckinpah, who worked for Siegel.*

EASTWOOD:  Those were the last of the cantankerous guys, the guys in the tradition of Ford and Raoul Walsh.

My way of going about things is a little quieter than the way those guys did. I came out of the acting end of the business, which is an odd way to get into producing. Most actors think of producing as headaches. But I was interested in what went on around me, and I found that the more I knew about what other people did on a film, the more understanding I had, the better I liked it.

DV:  *What gives you the biggest joy in the process of producing?*
EASTWOOD:  You read a script you like and say, "OK, I have nothing but a bunch of pages"—but it's the nucleus. It's the most important element. To me the most important thing is the blueprint. Then you organize your team: Who's the director for this? Who do I cast? Who does the production design, the cinematography, the sound? All those components are allied in making the movie and I like matching them to the project.

DV:  *You seem to choose to work with the same people. Jack N. Green, for instance, is your regular cinematographer.*
EASTWOOD:  I've promoted a few people up through the ranks. You're always confident when you have people who are good and who know your shorthand. Because there's understanding there, a shared history. These people understand completely—sometimes without any words at all—what you want.

DV:  *How much did your TV experiences on* Rawhide *aid in your development as a producer?*
EASTWOOD:  *Rawhide* was a good training ground for me. Over seven years I gradually learned how different directors direct, lighting techniques, other aspects. I subconsciously absorbed things and then started paying attention. We had different producers on the show over the years. I tried to emulate the things they did well and discard the methods that didn't work.

DV:  *Several of your associates mentioned that being a child of the Depression in Northern California had something to do with your fiscal responsibility as a producer.*

EASTWOOD: My parents and other people of that particular period had it rough. Some of them were not getting by so well. My father was very conscious of that. It was a struggle and there weren't many jobs. He said, "Nothing ever comes from nothing," and "If you get a buck save it." You finished everything on your plate and we never thought in terms of waste. This gives you respect for financing.

If somebody asks you to be in charge of the funds, you have to have a certain respect for them and for the funds. At Warner Bros. (cochairmen and CEOs) Terry Semel and Bob Daly don't want to look at a film if I haven't finished it. I say to them, "You're financing this thing. You should be able to look at it any time you want."

There's a famous story about Jack Warner. One day he walked onto a big, expensive set on a sound stage and looked up at the ceiling and there are these painters up there painting the ceiling. He said, "What are those guys doing?" Someone told him they were painting the ceiling. "Well," he said, "it better be in the picture."

DV: *There's a running joke about "Malpaso weather"—that your productions have been blessed with getting the shots and getting out in time before a blizzard hits. Also sudden snowfalls necessitated changing locations on a few pictures—* Pink Cadillac *and* Pale Rider *among them. You used an unexpected dusting of snow for effect in* Unforgiven.
EASTWOOD: You occasionally have to think fast on your feet. If a hurricane hits, what do you do? You drop back on fourth down and punt. You do the best you humanly can to bring things in control for the least amount of money. I've been lucky a few times.

DV: *One thing that crops up in conversations with your associates at Malpaso is that your sets are by and large fairly quiet.*
EASTWOOD: You're there to do the job and a good comfort zone is part of that. There was a good comfort zone on *Unforgiven*. It was a pleasure to go to work every day. The same thing was there on *The Bridges of Madison County*. It was very nice and enjoyable. Whether that translates into the final film, we'll have to wait and see.

# Clint Eastwood: The Actor-Director Reflects on His Continuing Career and New Film, *Absolute Power*

## IAIN BLAIR/1997

AS AN ACTOR, CLINT Eastwood remains at 66 one of Hollywood's great film icons. But over the course of four decades and some 40 films, the star has also metamorphosed into an ambitious and accomplished filmmaker. Now Eastwood, whose eclectic credits include the Oscar-winning *Unforgiven*, *The Bridges of Madison County*, *Bird* and the Dirty Harry action series, is back in the director's chair and starring in a new Castle Rock thriller, *Absolute Power*. The actor plays master jewel thief Luther Whitney, a man estranged from his daughter Kate (played by Laura Linney) who finds himself entangled in a murder involving the president (Gene Hackman).

Here, in an exclusive interview, Eastwood talks about the making of the film, his enduring career, and his love of both acting and directing.

*What are the qualities you look for in a directing project?*
Projects come in different forms—sometimes they come to me as a screenplay, sometimes a book. *Unforgiven* was a screenplay that seemed perfect when I read it—I owned it for quite a few years and then decided to make it into a film. And then I started making quite a few changes, realized I was wrecking it by making those changes, and I stopped, went back and just filmed it in its original form.

Published in *Film & Video* 14, no. 3 (March 1997): 70–78. Reprinted by permission.

The last two pictures have come as books—*Absolute Power* was adapted from the best-selling novel by David Baldacci. Before that, someone gave me *The Bridges of Madison County* and I read it and thought, "There's a good idea here but it's written rather flowery. How do we pare it down into a screenplay?" In the case of a book, the big question is, "Can you convert it into a filmable script?" Then you decide if you like the story and if it's one you'd like to see as a film. And then you decide if you also want to act in it.

With *Absolute Power,* I liked the whole setup and I liked the characters, but the problem was that all those great characters were killed in the book, so my question was, "How can we make a screenplay where everyone that the audience likes doesn't get killed off?" So [screenwriter] Bill Goldman came in and wrote it, put in the quest to reconcile between Luther and his daughter and really explored that whole relationship.

*You chose to play* Luther *in* Absolute Power—*what in this character appealed to you?*
He's obviously a thrill criminal who does it for the kick of it, running the numbers down to the end—and then he gets caught in this wild situation with the president. I tend to pick offbeat characters like that because they're fun to play. But yet he has some real concerns in his life, such as his relationship with his daughter. He has his own code and in his own way he's a moral person. He's a thief, yes—but he's not a murderer.

*What were the primary challenges you faced with this film?*
The big problem was finding locations that looked like Washington D.C. because shooting there is so tough. There are a lot of streets you can't use because of all the security. We shot there for *In the Line of Fire,* and it worked pretty well—but we filmed a minimum of scenes. So for *Absolute Power,* we ended up getting our establishing shots in D.C. and then moving to Baltimore. The rest of the logistics were pretty straightforward.

*As both an actor and a director, what is your process with actors?*
It depends on the scene and the actors. Sometimes I like a little rehearsal, sometimes none. I like to try a scene just raw, to see where it goes and what that first impression brings to me. If it's a scene where people are meeting for the first time, I like to try it unrehearsed because it usually captures that newness. If it's a scene where they're supposed to be related

or know each other well, then sometimes I like them to be more familiar with each other and do a few rehearsals.

*Do you storyboard in advance?*
No—I just set up the shot when we get to the location or whatever. I have in mind what I want to do with the overall project, and when I get to the scenes I already have a pretty good idea of how I want to shoot it. But then when I see it played by the actors and what they do—what their instincts are and what their pacing is—it gives me more input. Maybe I don't like it, maybe I love it. It all depends.

As a director I always try to allow everyone to bring something to the party, and not try to be so pre-conceived that I shut down creative ideas from other people. A lot of actors have wonderful suggestions because they've thought very deeply about their characters. The big job for the director is to decide which of those ideas I like and which I don't like.

*How do you and your longtime cinematographer Jack Green, ASC, collaborate?*
[Jack and I] go back to the days when he worked as a camera operator for Bruce Surtees on pictures like *Pale Rider* and *Tightrope*. After so many years, we have a great shorthand way of working to the point where I can now just tell him over the phone how I see something, and he'll immediately understand. He's very fast and efficient, which I really like, and he's a good operator. He had a couple of advantages as an operator that most don't have—he's a really good Steadicam operator and also a good Tyler mount operator in a helicopter. So he can do all the jobs.

*You're renowned for maintaining loyalty to your crew. Do you ever think you want to introduce new elements to the team?*
Sometimes we'll use a lot of new people—the last few crews have had some new faces. But it's good to have staple people we can always depend on, and you hate to pass over someone who's great at the job just to try new blood. There's nothing wrong with the old blood if it's really good. Sometimes when someone's not available we'll try someone new and like them, too, and then it's a dilemma as to who we use the next time.

*Editor Joel Cox, who won an Oscar for his work on* Unforgiven, *has collaborated with you for over 20 years.*

It's a similar relationship to my one with Jack Green. He started working for me as an assistant editor on *The Outlaw Josey Wales* in 1976, and he took over when Ferris Webster, with whom he co-edited films like *Every Which Way but Loose* and *Escape from Alcatraz*, retired. I think we've done 18 films together—again, it's a very collaborative relationship.

*Do you enjoy the editing process?*
Yes, because you can make almost anything happen as long as you have the pieces and have planned for it. And by this point in my career I know exactly what coverage I have. I've always liked editing because it's when we breathe life into [a film].

*What would you say is your favorite aspect of directing?*
I enjoy all of it. The shooting is fun to some degree. In the old days I used to be far more impatient with the shooting—I liked it, but I didn't know how to pace myself as well. At that time my favorite part was editing, because there's no pressure. You're working with one person. But now I like shooting a lot more and I don't kill myself with it so much.

*How do you view the current state of Hollywood?*
I don't think it's healthy. It seems that all of the studio movies are based on some fad or precedent, and that precedent may just be a week old. Before, I think [producers] were more interested in making stories, not in just copying ideas.

*Between acting and directing, which do you enjoy more?*
Probably directing. If I was forced to drop one, I'd probably drop the acting. It's still a lot of fun to act, but I'm not so obsessed with it now. I could hang it up. But I like it and I still have the energy for it, so I just pace it out.
     I guess I'm schizophrenic. My career in directing started strictly by accident. The only way I could get to direct was to act in the picture and the only way I could get the picture made was to act in it. So in 1970 I got the job to do both in *Play Misty for Me,* and back then very few actors also directed. Then I'd find a story like *High Plains Drifter,* where I liked the story and also liked the character, so I interspersed them with other films where someone else would direct.

*What do you find most rewarding about directing?*
It's more rewarding if I can reach out for new ground and bring out scenes I haven't explored before. If I had to just repeat movies I'd already made, I don't think I'd do it at this point in my life.

*So there won't be another "Dirty Harry" movie?*
Right.

*You've taken a lot of risks in your career.*
Yeah, and I've experimented with a lot of risky projects in the last few years. In my early years I acted in a lot of cop dramas and Westerns, and once in a while there'd be a movie like *Every Which Way but Loose* that would capture the public's imagination and do real well. You just never know what's going to work.

I think it's just part of my nature [to take risks]. Maybe I'm an excitement freak or something, but there's really no reason to have a career if you're just going to sit there and do the same old thing. So that's why I did a jazz film like *Bird* [Eastwood's film biography of jazz musician Charlie Parker]. Americans are notorious for not supporting their own art forms like jazz, while people in England or France are much more aware of these arts.

*Of your films, what are your personal favorites?*
I like *Outlaw Josey Wales* a lot, *Bronco Billy*, *Unforgiven* and *Play Misty for Me* because it was my first directorial job. I remember that after I'd finished [*Play Misty for Me*], I was a wreck. I disguised myself and went and sat in a theater and there were these teenage girls right in front of me. I was sweating bullets and I thought, "What happens if they boo?" and then [actress] Jessica Walter came flying out from behind a screen and everyone screamed and I thought, "Hey, this isn't so bad. It's working."

*What motivated you to try acting in the first place?*
I knew a lot of actors while I was in the army and I thought I'd try it. It's one of those things you can't try for just five minutes. It gets in your blood and then the more people tell you you're no good and to get out of their office the more determined you become.

*How do you look back on your experiences acting with director Sergio Leone in such seminal "spaghetti" Westerns as* A Fistful of Dollars *and* The Good, the Bad and the Ugly?
It was great because it was a new experience in my life. I'd never done a Western as the lead and that character was developed from years of playing on *Rawhide* where I was the dumb sidekick.

*Is it true you were advised against these Westerns?*
I've been advised against nearly everything I've ever done (laughs).

*So how do you know when a film is right?*
By feel. I've always said I'm whimsical about choosing things, but it's instinct—and you have to trust it.

# Eastwood in His Carmel

## PASCAL MÉRIGEAU/1998

SOME FILMMAKERS MAKE MOVIES the way they think, others the way they dream (Fellini), and still others the way they talk (Scorsese). Clint Eastwood makes movies the way he walks. Naturally, with strides that are measured but not calculated, seeming barely to skim the ground as he glances around with a warm and tranquil look, which goes with a slight smile that hasn't a trace of either irony or distance, but clearly indicates that this fellow will always be thinking more than he will say. When you see him arrive, in tennis shoes, khakis and jacket, in this restaurant where everyone calls him Clint, where he inquires naturally about everybody, tosses a sign to the pianist, then heads at his own pace towards his table, over there, way at the back, in front of the fireplace, you say to yourself that for him everything is simple.

He is at home. On the property he bought in 1986, back when it was threatened by a real estate project, which he has turned into the Mission Ranch, with tennis courts, a restaurant and an icebox for everyone's use, off behind the tall eucalyptus trees, among the mimosas and the cypresses. One of the houses is a replica of a pioneer dwelling, another lays claim to a half-century less; all have been constructed with respect for tradition. The sea is very close; during the last war, the occupants of the place camouflaged their windows for fear of a possible landing by Japanese troops.

Published as "Eastwood en son Carmel" in *Le Nouvel Observateur*, 5 March 1998, 50–52. Copyright © *Le Nouvel Observateur*. Reprinted by permission; translated from the French by KC.

There was no Japanese invasion in Carmel-by-the-Sea, California, the town where Clint Eastwood was mayor (from 1986 to 1988), about ten minutes from Monterey by road, about a half-hour from San Francisco by air. He chose the town and loves it because, he says, *"The population is made up of extremely diverse people, artists and dropouts, who've turned it into a sort of rural Greenwich Village."* Jack London lived nearby, and Big Sur, Henry Miller's retreat, isn't far off. The same diversity of origins, of social status, of behavior is what he went looking for in Savannah, Georgia, the location of his new film, *Midnight in the Garden of Good and Evil,* adapted from the novel by John Berendt. He read the novel after having discovered the screenplay drawn from it by John Lee Hancock, who had already written *A Perfect World* for him.

At the beginning of the film, the third directed by Eastwood in which he does not also act (after *Breezy* and *Bird*), a journalist arrives in Savannah to sketch a word portrait of Jim Williams (Kevin Spacey), cynosure of the local bon ton. Interpreted by John Cusack, the journalist existed in the novel only in the voice of the narrator; it was necessary to make him a true character, the principal difficulty Hancock met with after Eastwood announced he was attracted by the project. Why this attraction? *"The characters, who are interesting just because they're so diverse, and then Savannah, a very unusual city, which we wanted to make into a character in its own right. This isn't the South the way it's portrayed most of the time, with an overabundance of clichés."* In Savannah, you can encounter elderly black homeless women who perform voodoo rites at night in the cemeteries, on behalf of people who are *"sophisticated, cultured, intelligent, very much in the public view, people no one would ever think could be interested in sorcery."* You meet trained manservants walking dogs on invisible leashes, or an oddball who strolls around with insects buzzing around him, connected to his clothes by wires (Geoffrey Lewis, one of Eastwood's favorite actors). You also discover the Lady Chablis, an exuberant transvestite Eastwood engaged to play herself. A strange film, in the course of which the journalist passes from surprise to astonishment and gradually becomes aware of the constant presence of the dead in the existence of the living, at the same time as he grasps that not everything is explicable, that the majority of mysteries are destined never to be resolved.

How could Eastwood have passed up this story, Eastwood who has often appeared as a ghost, in his westerns (*Pale Rider*) as well as in his cop pictures (*Sudden Impact*), who, above all, zealously refuses to provide any sort of explanation whatsoever for his films. *"When people ask me to explain something or other, I always answer that the films are open, that everyone will find in them whatever he brings to them. I don't know who is guilty, I don't know who is innocent. And without a doubt it's infinitely better not to know."*

Thus *Midnight in the Garden of Good and Evil* retraces the history of a murder, of a scandal, of a trial, and yet it appears as a strangely peaceful film, whose very serenity at times becomes almost ominous. In the mode of the songs of Johnny Mercer, Savannah's most famous son. A shot of his tomb opens the film; the mansion built by his great-grandfather, Mercer House, became the residence of Jim Williams. Johnny Mercer, who wrote, notably, the lyrics of "Laura," for the film by Otto Preminger in which Gene Tierney returned from among the dead. A disturbing relationship, a singular osmosis of a theme, in the musical sense, and of a style of filmmaking and a way of conceiving the cinema. The "Eastwood touch," no doubt, which causes his films, when they are successful, to resemble nobody else's.

He is not only, in effect, the only filmmaker who regularly completes his shoots several days in advance of schedule. He is also one of the last to reject the technique of the storyboard, which consists of making precise drawings of every shot in the film before shooting begins, and he even dispenses with establishing a list of shots to be completed every day. Jack N. Green, his regular cinematographer, lights the set entirely, so that Eastwood and he can modify the camera's position at any time and shoot from different angles without any supplementary preparation. *"Thanks to this technique, the cast never gets tired of playing the scene. If I didn't always work with the same crew, I'd probably have to change my method, but this way, everyone is ready to shoot very quickly, there's never a problem. You don't stop, you shoot everything that has to be shot. I'm not capable of spending hours thinking about storyboards, anticipating this or that. I believe that when you're making a film, you've got everything in mind, in an almost subliminal way, and that all you have to do is make all that become reality on screen. I want to believe that even when you don't know how to solve a filmmaking problem, how to film a shot, something in you tells you clearly what you ought to do. This must be something that goes beyond consciousness. I'm sure a painter will paint something thousands of times in his head before attacking the canvas. It's the same thing for the filmmaker, except that movies take time and so he's got to keep his energy intact, his enthusiasm. I wonder how directors who are reputed to be slow, like George Stevens used to be (A* Place in the Sun, Giant*), managed to keep up the necessary tension, when they were always having to re-shoot the same scene, from different angles, day after day, week after week."*

He is no different with the cast, to whom he listens attentively when they talk about their characters before telling them that they shouldn't worry too much, that they will know what to do when the time comes. The results sometimes prove to be spectacular. So it was with Meryl Streep, an actress who is reputed to be an intellectual, who delivered probably her most astonishing portrayal in the role of the farmer's wife in *The Bridges of Madison County. "Meryl's used to working with directors who do a lot of rehearsals, take a lot of preparation time. In this case, she didn't have time to think, she couldn't do anything but concentrate on her character and play it, nothing else. She couldn't think about the scene beforehand. After a very short time, she was asking to shoot with no rehearsal herself. Sometimes I'm content with talking a little with the cast, then, in front of the camera, I ask them to say something other than what had been planned, to change the lines. In* The Bridges of Madison County, *for the scene with me telling the yarn in the kitchen, we shot with no rehearsal. But since I had to film the scene from different angles, every time I told the yarn differently."*

He hates to expound on finished films, but he is happy to talk about the work itself, about the process of filmmaking. He admits he has changed: *"I think in the beginning, the stage of filmmaking I liked best was the editing. To work with just one or two people, in the editing room, I loved that. I still do, but now I take more pleasure in the shooting itself. On every film, I discover some-thing new, I want to try things out. That's also why I loved making* Midnight in the Garden of Good and Evil: *this kind of story was something new for me. In fact, I'd like to try out all the genres, I'd like to attempt every time to do some-thing new. If I had the time . . ."*

He will be 68 years old on May 31 and over the last twenty years he has been the most active American filmmaker. Only Woody Allen can vie with him in this regard. His desire to make movies, his energy are intact (*"With regard to that, you have to know how to stop from time to time, to catch your breath a little, think about what you've done . . . or don't think about it"*), and this evidence squelches the rumors that have circulated in Hollywood according to which he was ready to retire and live peaceably with Dina Ruiz, a 32-year-old journalist he met on the occasion of an interview, who became his second wife in 1996, and Morgan, their daughter of 13 months, of whom he asserts with a huge smile that *"she is fabulous"* and that she gives him the chance *"to stay young... and tired."* The American commercial failure of *Midnight in the Garden...*, therefore, hasn't unduly affected him. *"Some spectators got it, others didn't get it at all. Sometimes I think Americans don't have much of a sense of subtlety and that they just overlooked this story of tolerance, of very different sorts of people who know how to live together. They like it more and more when you hit them over the head with a hammer... You don't have any control in the matter. Certain films work, others don't, that's all. For example,* A Perfect World *wasn't appreciated here very much, in my opinion because people were expecting Kevin Costner and me to do more fighting, make it more of a Western, but it worked very well in Europe. What matters is to have done what you wanted to do, to be happy with the film, to know you didn't cheat."*

Next May he will begin shooting a new film in which he will play a journalist *"who has all the faults a man can have, he smokes, drinks and womanizes, he's known better days, he's worked for the* New York Times, *now he's writing for a small paper and he finds himself in a spot where he has to try to save a condemned man he knows is innocent."* A film that *"will go very quick, the opposite of this one."* The location for the shoot is Oakland, California, where he lived as a young man. At the age of sixteen, he practiced the cornet or the trumpet in the city parks after discovering, on the stage of "Jazz at the Philharmonic," an unknown by the name of Charlie Parker, one evening when he had gone to hear Lester Young and Coleman Hawkins. Loyalty to the places, the people, the films and the music he loves, loyalty to himself. One of the keys, no doubt, to this nature that seizes you as soon as you approach him, anywhere, but even more here, where he lives, plays golf and goes to the movies. Recently he was enthusiastic about *The Full Monty,* which he thinks infinitely superior to all the American films nominated for the Oscar (*"even if I haven't seen them, with the exception of* L.A. Confidential, *which is a very good film noir"*), and he is asking himself how he will be able to designate, as he has been requested to do, the hundred best films in the history of the movies: *"They've given me an impressive list, but I'm sure some very important films aren't on it, because they're marginal to the big trends. For instance* Out of the Past, *by Jacques Tourneur, which is a masterpiece."* He talks of cinema, of Spencer Tracy, whom he defines as *"the American Jean Gabin"* (what other American would say that?), of John Huston, to whom he paid homage with *White Hunter, Black Heart,* and who, just like himself, made movies naturally, *"on a human scale"*: *"It's my impression that the more distractions he had outside the film, the better the film was.* The Man Who Would Be King *is a tremendous film and* The Dead, *which he made at the end of his life, when he was greatly worn down by age and illness, is a masterpiece."* Eastwood is never happier than when he is talking about others.

Voilà, the swordfish was excellent, the accompanying merlot was Californian. *"In America,"* he is amused to note, *"people eat to fill up. In Europe, every meal is an event, every dish is treated like a work of art. Which is undoubtedly better for your stomach!"* Towards the middle of the dinner, a woman approached, a photo in her hand. A photo of her daughter, for whom she wanted an autograph, proof that she had really approached Clint Eastwood. He took a pair of tiny rectangular glasses out of his pocket, accepted the pen she held out to him and complied. He didn't scribble distractedly on the photo, he signed his name at length, carefully, with application. As if this autograph that he was being asked for were the first.

# INDEX